Collaboration

Collaboration

How Leaders Avoid the Traps,

Create Unity, and

Reap Big Results

Morten T. Hansen

Harvard Business Press
Boston, Massachusetts

Printed in the United States of America
12 11 10   6

Library of Congress Cataloging-in-Publication Data

Hansen, Morten T.
    Collaboration : how leaders avoid the traps, create unity, and reap big results / Morten T. Hansen.
        p. cm.
    Includes bibliographical references and index.
    ISBN 978-1-4221-1515-2 (hardcover : alk. paper)   1. Industrial management.
2. Leadership.   I. Title.
    HD31.H317 2009
    658.4'092—dc22

                                                                        2008046132

The paper used in this publication meets the requirements of the American National Standard for Permanence of Paper for Publications and Documents in Libraries and Archives Z39.48-1992.

To my family:

My daughters, Alexandra and Julia

My wife, Hélène

And my father and mother

CONTENTS

FOREWORD

A number of years ago, I asked Morten Hansen why he chose the topic of collaboration as a research focus. "Because if people knew how to collaborate well, the world would simply work better," he replied. This book represents the culmination of fifteen years of some of the best research on the topic of effective collaboration. And it comes with a vitally important, counterintuitive message: *good collaboration amplifies strength, but poor collaboration is worse than no collaboration at all*. In reading these pages you will come to understand the power of effective collaboration and the great dangers of incompetent collaboration. You will also learn sound principles for *how* to collaborate.

I first met Morten in 1991 when he set aside his lucrative consulting job at the Boston Consulting Group to accept a Fulbright fellowship and join our research team at the Stanford Graduate School of Business. I quickly came to see that Morten has unusual intensity about his work when he volunteered for the task of selecting a comparison company to Motorola in our study of what makes visionary companies. We needed to determine the closest "twin" to Motorola during its founding era (the company most similar to Motorola when it was a small enterprise.) Motorola made car radios in the 1930s, and we faced a problem: how on Earth to construct a list of small companies that made car radios all the way back to the 1930s?

Morten came up with an ingenious solution. He drove fifty miles to a remote library warehouse located in Richmond, California, a crime-infested city ranked in the top twenty-five "most dangerous cities" in America. He ambled up to the antiquated reference desk—no fancy electronic search, no Internet—and filled out a card asking for phone books from the late 1920s and early 1930s. The librarian disappeared for nearly an hour, and finally returned with a stack of dusty phone books. Using the Yellow Pages from the 1920s, Morten constructed a list of car radio companies, from which we discovered Zenith as a near-perfect comparison control case to Motorola for the middle part of the twentieth century.

I knew then that Morten would have the tenacity and creativity to do great research. After his stint as an invaluable team member with Jerry Porras and me, on what later became the book *Built to Last*, he completed a PhD at Stanford and began his research on collaboration. He went on to join the Harvard Business School faculty, where he continued his research and taught in the MBA and executive education classroom. He now holds a prestigious professorship at the University of California, Berkeley.

Morten has continually impressed me with three characteristics of his approach:

1. *Rigor.* One of the most intellectually honest people I have ever known, Morten brings a meticulous analytic approach to his research. As we've worked together over the years, I've been impressed by his discipline and thoroughness. In one piece of research we jointly conducted, Morten constructed a ten-layer selection process, starting with more than twenty thousand data points and applying a systematic series of tests and screens to find a bulletproof study set. Every time I thought we were about done, Morten would offer, "There is another step I think we should take to ensure the quality of our underlying research." In *Collaboration*, you will see an edifice of ideas that Morten developed over the years, supported by a solid foundation of quantitative data, rigorous method, and painstaking analysis.

2. *Relevance.* John Gardner, the former Secretary of Health, Education and Welfare and founder of Common Cause, once commented that the academic enterprise has moved increasingly toward answering "questions of increasing irrelevance with increasing precision." Morten has vigorously resisted that trap, choosing to answer questions of increasing significance with increasing rigor, making his work relevant to those who must

lead and manage. Morten has translated his scientific inquiry into practical levers for application: *how* to unify people, *how* to cultivate collaborative leaders who deliver on their personal commitments, *how* to harness the power of networks. Very few practical books have a basis of punctilious research, and equally few academic books offer useful, practical guidance. *Collaboration* has both—it offers the why and the how, the science and the practice, of working together.

3. *Aspiration*. Morten has a passion for questions of larger human significance, not just how businesses can make more money. Yes, the ideas in this book will help business leaders make more money. But the concepts herein extend beyond business to the question: how can people work more effectively together in ways that make organizations more productive and society more civilized? The best management thinkers look for the *and*: how to achieve purpose *and* profits, how to be responsible to shareholders *and* the environment, how to reduce costs *and* build people, how to deliver results for the long term *and* short term, how to be noble *and* practical. Morten exemplifies this quest for the *and* here in this work: how to achieve a culture of individual accountability *and* shared responsibility.

Morten Hansen has done a great service in assembling his fifteen years of research into this insightful and practical book. It does not matter whether you lead a business, conduct an orchestra, guide a school, operate a hospital, command a brigade, run for public office, direct a government agency, coach a sports team—every complex enterprise requires collaboration. If poor collaboration is dangerous, then you have no choice but to collaborate well.

Jim Collins
Author, *Good to Great*
Coauthor, *Built to Last*
Boulder, Colorado
November 21, 2008

The Perils of Collaboration—In Good Times and Bad

BAD COLLABORATION is worse than no collaboration. People scuttle from meeting to meeting to coordinate work and share ideas, but far too little gets done. Employees from different units in a company squabble over who should do what on a common project and infighting consumes their work.

This is a terrible way of working in the best of times: resources are wasted while better players pull away. It's downright reckless in tough times, such as in a crisis, where the ability to pull together can make the difference between making it or not.

Poor collaboration is a disease afflicting even the best companies. I learned this sobering lesson in the 1990s when I studied Hewlett-Packard as part of my PhD at Stanford University. Something odd struck me about the legendary company back then: many innovation teams collaborated across divisions, and yet they found it awfully difficult. How could this be? I found this question so fascinating that I decided to throw everything I had at it and do my dissertation on the topic.

I went to work, visiting HP facilities all over and collecting lots of data on 120 projects and 41 business units. It took a painstaking two years. The picture that emerged mesmerized me. For some teams, collaboration across divisions in HP worked out spectacularly well. They got hold of some great software, hardware, and talent, and they did their projects better and faster. For other teams, it was a dismal failure. They fell into collaboration traps, spending time fighting across divisions rather than working on the product. Some teams were worse off collaborating than not doing it all.

The HP study brought home to me the essential question about collaboration. It is not, How do leaders get people to collaborate more? That question presumes that more collaboration is necessarily a good thing, but it isn't. Rather, the essential question is, What is the difference between good and bad collaboration?

For the past fifteen years, I have searched for answers to this question, concentrating on collaboration within companies. The HP study provided some pieces to the puzzle, especially on how to build company-wide networks that make collaboration work. After I earned my PhD at Stanford, I joined Harvard Business School as an assistant professor and continued my quest there. When I got a chance to study one of the largest information technology consulting companies in the world, I jumped at it, for here was a very different setting from HP. Along with colleague Martine Haas, I ploughed through data on 180 sales teams, hunting for clues about why some teams performed better when they collaborated but others did worse. This study gave us another piece of the puzzle: rules that managers can use in deciding whether or not to collaborate.

The search went on. One day while I was sitting in my office at Harvard I got a phone call from Bolko von Oetinger, a senior partner at Boston Consulting Group (BCG) and head of the BCG Strategy Institute. "Anything interesting we could do together?" he asked. Because I yearned to study collaboration in more firms, we decided to interview senior executives in large multinationals in the United States, Europe, and Asia. Hopping from place to place and racking up air miles, we probed fifty executives about the difference between good and bad collaboration. We gained invaluable insights, especially about the kind of management it takes to do well in collaborative companies (what we refer to as T-shaped management).

Then, when I took a leave from Harvard to go to work at BCG, I got a chance to work with clients on putting collaboration in place. That proved a valuable learning experience, because I could apply some of these concepts in practice and in turn learn from the companies. Later, back at Harvard, I launched new research surveying more than one hundred firms; here I learned that companies experience four kinds of barriers to collaboration and that there is no "one size fits all" solution (see the appendix for an overview of all the research).

Crunching hard data to figure out when collaboration works, and when it doesn't, is a helpful exercise, but not in isolation. Fortunately, I was lucky to be a professor at two places that excel at blending academic research and practice: Harvard Business School and INSEAD, a leading business school in Europe. I could run a statistical analysis on collaboration in the morning and talk about it in the afternoon with a talented group of MBA students or executive education participants. I also wrote and taught several in-depth case studies and gave speeches on collaboration, and I learned a great deal through these interactions.

I have had a long and immensely rewarding journey figuring out the difference between good and bad collaboration. I have worked with great people, have been mentored by some of the best in the world, and have learned from extraordinary students and executives. But now it's time to stop searching and put down on paper all I have learned.

This book is my completed puzzle. The answer I provide to the question of what's the difference between good and bad collaboration is a set of principles I refer to as *disciplined collaboration*. It is an answer to a simple question that confronts us all, whether we are business executives, nonprofit leaders, government officials, politicians, mayors, school principals, doctors, lawyers, or church leaders: how do we cultivate collaboration in the right way so that we achieve the great things that are not possible when we are divided?

CHAPTER ONE

Getting Collaboration Wrong ... or Getting It Right

I N EARLY 2003, Howard Stringer, head of U.S. operations for Japanese electronics giant Sony, was plotting to respond to Apple's amazing success with the iPod, a recently introduced small portable music player. Sony did not want to let Apple take over the market. It was, after all, a market Sony should own. It had invented the idea of carrying music around on people's heads with the iconoclastic Walkman, which was introduced in 1979 and had sold nearly 200 million units by the time the iPod became the new kid on the block.[1] Stringer was the right man to lead the charge. A jovial, Oxford-educated Englishman in a six-foot-three-inch frame, he had been brought into Sony in 1997 to help forge unity among its headstrong and independent music, film, and electronics divisions in the United States. Stringer had had a long career in media—as a journalist, head of CBS News, and president of CBS—and was an experienced executive who understood media and could cultivate collaboration in Sony.[2]

By 2003 Sony was a formidable company. With annual sales of $62 billion, it was ten times as large as Apple, which had $6.2 billion in sales.[3] And Sony was much better placed than Apple to launch portable music players and an online music store. Sony had the Walkman division (and so could develop its own hard-disk music player), the VAIO personal computer line (and so it knew computers), Sony Music (and so it knew a thing or two about music[4]), and Sony Electronics (and so it had a range of devices and batteries). Ironically, it supplied the batteries for the iPod. Sony was also well known for sleek design. From the vantage point of his Manhattan office, Stringer could see that he had all the pieces to mount a counterattack against the iPod. Philip Wiser, chief technology officer of Sony U.S., told him, "We can do this in nine months. We got the product, hardware, software."[5] By this time, Apple had offered the iPod device and the iTunes software only for computers, and not the online music store. There was still time to catch up.

Stringer and Wiser set it all in motion. They aptly named the venture Connect, reflecting the vision of linking the various pieces of Sony to connect portable music players with an online music store.

Sony's headaches had come to light some eighteen months earlier, on October 23, 2001. That day Steve Jobs, the magnetic leader of Apple, introduced the iPod to the world: "This amazing little device holds a thousand songs, and it goes right in my pocket."[6] Wearing his classic business attire of jeans and a black mock turtleneck, Jobs stood on a small stage in an unassuming auditorium at Apple's headquarters in Cupertino, in the heart of California's Silicon Valley. The two hundred invited guests, many of them journalists, had no idea that Apple was introducing a portable music player that day. (The coy invitation letter read, "Hint: It's not a Mac.")

Jobs, ever the showman, teased his audience, spending about ten minutes going through slides and then coming to the climax: "Let me show you." First he displayed a skinny side view of the iPod. Then he showed the back. Finally, with, "This is what the front looks like, Boom!" he capped the reveal: "I have one here right in my pocket." He pulled it out for the world to see, and the audience burst into applause.

It was a great comeback moment for Jobs, who had cofounded Apple in 1976 at age twenty-one, was fired by CEO John Sculley in 1985, and then resurfaced as interim chief executive in 1997 when Apple had sunk close to bankruptcy.[7] The iPod was not the first portable music player using a hard drive to hit the market (the Rio, a portable music player holding about one hundred songs, appeared in 1998).[8] But the iPod was easy to use, looked cool, and worked with Apple's iTunes software to allow users to manage music on their computers.

As people started looking under the hood, they soon realized that the iPod wasn't a marvelous technological revolution but rather a shrewd combination of many existing pieces. "This was a highly leveraged product from the technologies we already had in place," explained Jon Rubinstein, Apple's senior vice president of hardware.[9] The hard disk holding all those songs was a tiny 1.8-inch drive from Toshiba; the minute battery was from Sony; the hardware blueprint was provided by a small Silicon Valley company called PortalPlayer; the digital-to-analog converter came from Wolfson Microelectronics; the FireWire interface controller was shipped by Texas Instruments; and some of the software came from Pixo.[10]

Inside Apple, a hardware team led by Tony Fadell and reporting to Rubinstein had crafted the architecture of the dwelling that housed these technologies. According to *The Perfect Thing*, Steven Levy's book on the iPod, the team had had to integrate all the pieces from outside Apple *and* work across several units inside the company. This included Rubinstein's hardware division, Jeff Robbin's iTunes division, and Apple's vaunted industrial design unit, headed by design wizard Jonathan Ive (dubbed the "Armani of Apple").[11] Resolving complicated issues required many interactions between the hardware and software teams. Robbin described this complexity: "We had to figure out how iTunes was going to sync the content onto the 'pod, how the 'pod was going to access that information, how we could do a database on the device that was just incredibly simple to use."[12]

It was no small task. Apple had had a troubling past as a company with lots of infighting between managers. Jobs himself was no exception: in the early 1980s, when he led the team that developed the first Macintosh computer, he put the team in a separate building and launched the theme "Let's be pirates." Soon a pirate flag flew from the roof of the building: for the renegades, the "other side" was the rest of Apple.[13]

But the Jobs who had returned to Apple was not the pirate of earlier years. Instead, people were racing to get the iPod out the door. "We were all working together late at night, and it was highly energized," recalled Robbin. "It was just an incredible team project. There were no boundaries. The software guys, the hardware guys, the firmware guys, everybody worked together. It was a pretty amazing experience."[14] And all the collaborations paid off. Tony Fadell had started the project in February 2001, and the product was ready by October 2001, just before the Christmas season. The spectacular eight-month sprint was worthy of an Olympic gold medal.

———————

Meanwhile, at Sony, Stringer and Wiser were busy connecting the parts of the company. Or at least trying to. The problem was that a critical piece was missing from Stringer's plan: a culture of collaboration among Sony's various divisions. "Sony has long thrived on a hyper-competitive culture, where engineers were encouraged to outdo each other, not work together," observed *Wall Street Journal* reporter Phred Dvorak.[15] In the past, Sony's competitive culture had worked wonderfully, allowing entrepreneurial groups to work largely by themselves to develop hit products like the Walkman and the PlayStation video game player. But Connect was not a stand-alone product. It required collaboration among five Sony divisions: the personal computer group based in Tokyo; the portable audio team responsible for the Walkman; another team responsible for flash memory players; Sony Music in the United States; and Sony Music in Japan. It was a new ball game, and Sony's organization was not up to it.

For starters, each division had its own idea about what to do. The PC and the Walkman groups introduced their own competing music players, and three other groups—Sony Music in Japan, Sony Music in the United States, and Sony Electronics in the United States—had their own music portals or download services. Stringer, who had no authority over Japanese operations, complained, to no avail, that the Connect software being developed in Japan was hard to use. Whereas the U.S. team wanted a hard disk for the music player (as in the iPod), the Japanese team went with the arcane MiniDisc. And whereas the U.S. group pushed for using the MP3 format—the de facto U.S. standard—the Japanese PC division chose a proprietary standard called ATRAC. Complained Stringer, "It's impossible to communicate with everybody when you have that many silos."[16]

It was a mess.

When Connect finally debuted in May 2004, the mess turned into a market disaster. The influential Walt Mossberg of the *Wall Street Journal* panned the product in a review: "The Walkman's biggest weakness is its lousy user interface, which is dense and confusing. The SonicStage 2 software and the Connect music store are also badly designed. This is because, for all its historic brilliance in designing hardware, Sony stinks at software. . . Until Sony fixes the multitude of sins in this product, steer clear of it."[17]

After sending this review to Tokyo, Stringer finally got Sony's chief executive, Nobuyuki Idei, to take action. In November 2004, Idei moved all the pieces required into one group, also called Connect, and as copresidents of the group appointed Philip Wiser and Koichiro Tsujino, a Sony veteran and skilled collaborator.

But the problems didn't go away. A team that made flash memory players was not transferred to the new group, as promised, because of internal politics.[18] And when Wiser and Tsujino moved software development to a digital media start-up called Kinoma in Silicon Valley, the Sony people could not collaborate with the Kinoma engineers. CNET reported that "relations between the core Sony programmers and Kinoma declined so far that a team in Japan was asked to serve as a buffer between the two camps."[19] The improved Connect software that came out at the end of 2005 hadn't improved much at all. Executives in Sony U.S. refused to release it—it was that bad. By January 2006, Sony had to issue an apology to customers in Europe and Japan.[20] Connect limped on for a while, but in August 2007 Stringer killed it.

With this kind of blow—the proud Sony had been trounced by Apple in a way that recalled a great Muhammad Ali knockout—someone had to pay. Would Stringer be fired? Far from it. As Connect went down, Stringer went up. On March 7, 2005, Sony announced that Nobuyuki Idei would step down as chief executive officer and be succeeded by none other than Howard Stringer. Even though he had failed to compete against Jobs and the iPod, Stringer climbed to the top job. It wasn't Stringer's fault after all: he had tried to cultivate collaboration across Sony but had controlled only the U.S. part of the venture. He had been a helpless line executive struggling to collaborate in a culture celebrating internal rivalry. The responsibility rested with Idei, who as Sony's top boss was the leader who could have stitched together the company's many pieces.

Without serious competition from players like Sony Connect, and with a red-hot iPod–iTunes combo, Apple's sales exploded. The iPod juggernaut went from sales of 125,000 units in first quarter of 2002 to the sale of the 100 millionth iPod on April 9, 2007.[21] Apple's annual sales of the iTunes and iPod went from zero in October 2001 to $10.8 billion in 2007. Meanwhile, Sony's portable music players took a dive in the United States, leading to declining sales in its audio division (Sony does not provide separate financials for Connect and the Walkman line). In part because of this, Sony's stock price declined 20 percent from 2002 to 2006 (see figure 1-1).[22] In contrast, Apple's share price

FIGURE 1-1

A tale of two products

The iPod was a grand collaboration and a great success. . .

Surging sales for iPod and iTunes

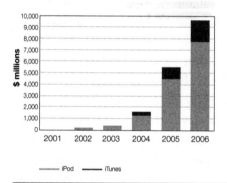

. . .Lifting Apple's share price

Apple share price versus index (Jan 2002 = 100)

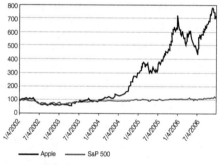

Connect was a poor collaboration, sending sales down. . .

Falling sales in Sony's audio group

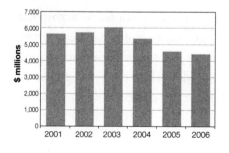

. . .Hurting Sony's share price

Sony share price versus index (Jan 2002 = 100)

exploded from a miserable \$11 at the beginning of 2002 to \$84 at the end of 2006—a sevenfold increase.[23] Steve Jobs could hardly have imagined the success he pulled out of his pocket that day in Cupertino.

Clearly, the battle between Sony Connect and Apple iPod is about much more than collaboration. Apple had great software skills. It had superb design. It developed magnificent user interfaces. The team was talented and experienced. Steve Jobs gave it his full support.[24] Collaboration was only one factor in iPod's success. But consider this: what if Apple had failed dismally at collaboration? What if people in the software and hardware divisions had worked against each other, preventing the iPod from working well with the iTunes software? What if the project had been marred by constant cross-unit fighting and delayed by years?

More importantly, consider also the possibility of a flawless collaboration inside Sony—a great team effort in which the various divisions had put together their expertise in portable music, computers, electronics, batteries, and music to produce a great Sony Connect. What if Sony had excelled at collaboration? Then the fight between Sony and Apple would have been much closer, with an uncertain outcome. The upshot: In complex organizational activities, effective collaboration is often a *necessary requirement* for success.

Collaboration Traps: How Smart People Get It Wrong

As Sony Connect illustrates, smart managers can easily get collaboration wrong. In fact, many companies fall into a number of collaboration traps.

Collaborating in Hostile Territory

Sony fell into the trap of collaborating in hostile territory. Some organizations are not set up to collaborate, and collaboration projects soon hit a wall. Sony was a decentralized company whose divisions took pride in competing against each other. It was a toxic environment for any collaboration effort. It doomed Connect from the get-go. Should we be surprised that collaboration fails in environments that are designed for the opposite practice—competition and independence? Of course not.

The trap is to believe that competing units can collaborate and then launch ambitious projects in such unreceptive environments.

Overcollaborating

Another trap, surprisingly, is the tendency to overcollaborate. When oil giant British Petroleum (BP) started to promote cross-unit collaboration, leaders encouraged the formation of cross-unit networks focused on areas of shared interest. Over time, this idea flowered into an unforeseen number of networks and subnetworks (the "helicopter utilization network" was one), which consumed increasing amounts of managers' time. An audit within the exploration business alone identified several hundreds of these networks. As executive John Leggate said, "People always had a good reason for meeting. You're sharing best practices. You're having good conversations with like-minded people. But increasingly, we found that people were flying around the world and simply sharing ideas without always having a strong focus on the bottom line."[25] The trap is that when leaders promote collaboration in their companies, they get more than they bargain for; people often overdo it.

Overshooting the Potential Value

Then there is the trap of overshooting the potential value of collaboration. It's easy to get carried away, believing that there are huge synergy benefits to be gained by collaborating across business units in a company. When Sony bought Columbia Pictures in 1989, the idea was that people in the electronics-device business could collaborate with filmmakers on cross promotions and the use of novel technology in film distribution. But these benefits were actually quite small, according to University of Virginia Professor Robert Bruner, an expert in finance who studied the deal and wrote about it in his book *Deals from Hell*.[26] For example, the Columbia Pictures movie *Last Action Hero*, starring Arnold Schwarzenegger, was linked to a soundtrack produced by Sony Music, and executives from various divisions had also collaborated on joint marketing of television sets, video recorders, and the film. The problem was, the film bombed, losing $124 million, so no synergies materialized. One analyst quipped, "Synergy: big wind, loud thunder, no rain. It's great to talk about conceptually . . . but at the end of the day it's minimal."[27] Sony executives had overestimated the potential value of collaboration.

Underestimating the Costs

"I'll get my head cut off if I help the other side," a manager confessed to me in confidence. He was talking about his deep distrust of the division he was collaborating with. The two divisions were supposed to share their customer contacts so that they could sell more products. But soon the project was marred by problems. People in the two divisions distrusted each other and thought that the others were out only to maximize their own gain. The project devolved into infighting over who should be doing what, consuming management time and resulting in large costs: very few extra sales were realized, and time was wasted trying to resolve the conflict. The project's managers had not anticipated this downside but instead had made financial projections based on the assumption that everything would be rosy. When it comes to collaboration, sometimes managers *hope* things will go well but do not fully appreciate the costs of working across the organization and resolving conflict.

Misdiagnosing the Problem

Many leaders fall into the trap of misdiagnosing the reasons people don't collaborate. A manager of a large U.S. financial services company told me, "We thought the key problem was the difficulty in finding knowledge and people in our company, when in reality the key problem is people's unwillingness to collaborate." Well, those are two entirely different problems; the first has to do with the inability to find stuff, and the other has to do with the fact that people don't give a hoot about working across units. Leaders must understand which barriers to collaboration are at play in their company and which are not.

Implementing the Wrong Solution

The misdiagnosis trap is often followed by the wrong-solution trap. "We invested in an elaborate knowledge-management system to help people find information in the company," the same manager explained. But it didn't help much, because the problem wasn't that people couldn't find what they were looking for. The problem was that they didn't want to look in the first place. This trap often fells managers when they assume that a solution—an IT system, an incentive system, a common goal—will promote collaboration in any circumstance. But different barriers to collaboration require different solutions.

All these traps lead to *bad collaboration—collaboration characterized by high friction and a poor focus on results*. As I have seen repeatedly in my research, smart executives fall into these traps. That's because the traps are not obvious. They are subtle, often lurking under the surface. Important projects are launched in the hope that they will survive an anticollaborative environment. Well-intentioned efforts to promote collaboration in a company can easily lead to too much collaboration. True synergies from cross-business collaboration are hard to assess. The costs of working across the organization are difficult to pin down. The existence of different barriers makes it difficult to spot them. And it's very hard to design solutions to promote collaboration.

Leaders don't fall into these traps because they are not smart. Smart leaders fall into them because they don't have a framework that helps them clearly see the difference between good and bad collaboration.

The Solution: Disciplined Collaboration

How do leaders avoid these traps and instill the kind of collaboration that produces great performance? The answer, I have found, is a set of principles I call disciplined collaboration. Before I discuss these principles, let's define what collaboration means in this book.

Collaboration Defined

Cross-unit collaboration takes place when people from different units work together in cross-unit teams on a common task or provide significant help to each other. It can be joint work between units or a one-way collaboration, as when one unit provides advice to another. In all cases, collaboration needs to involve people: if all that is going on is shipping data back and forth between units, that's not collaboration.

In this book I focus squarely on collaboration *within* a company, not outside it (the ideas can easily be extended to outside collaboration, but that's not the focus here). The focus of this book is on collaboration *across* organization units, including across divisions, business units, product lines, country subsidiaries, departments, functions, factories, and sales offices in a company. That's *companywide collaboration*. For governments, the equivalent is collaboration across governmental departments, agencies, and branches of government; for nonprofits, it's collaboration across geographical offices and departments.

Companywide collaboration differs from traditional teamwork, which often refers to local teams of five to ten people *within* a business unit, division, or department. Most books and research on teams look at how a manager can best manage small teams in a local setting.[28] Companywide collaboration instead focuses on how to get people residing in different units throughout the company to work together. Most important, this book focuses not on how to manage a team but rather on how to lead a company so that its people will carry out the right kind of collaboration. It's an organizationwide lens and not a small-team lens.

Disciplined Collaboration: Three Steps

The idea of *disciplined collaboration* can be summed up in one phrase: *the leadership practice of properly assessing when to collaborate (and when not to) and instilling in people both the willingness and the ability to collaborate when required.* To accomplish disciplined collaboration, leaders follow three steps (see figure 1-2).

Step 1: **Evaluate opportunities for collaboration.** The first question is, "Will we gain a great upside by collaborating?" Executives can easily set in motion a movement in which people collaborate for the sake of collaborating. Yet the goal of collaboration is not collaboration, but better results. In business, the goal of collaboration might be outstanding

The three steps of disciplined collaboration

Disciplined collaboration framework

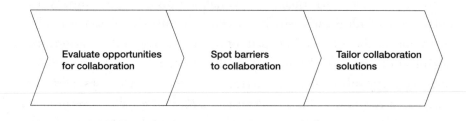

innovation (think Apple), remarkable revenue growth (as at U.S. bank Wells Fargo), or great cost savings (as at BP). For governments and non-profit agencies, the goals are great project performance, better decisions, and lower costs. For legislatures and governmental administrations, the goals are solving problems that citizens care about.

Leaders who pursue disciplined collaboration never lose sight of this dictum: collaboration is a means to an end, and that end is great performance. This means that often it may be better *not* to collaborate, because there is simply no compelling reason to do so. To be disciplined about collaboration is to know when not to collaborate. As detailed in chapter 2, leaders need to be rigorous in deciding whether to prioritize collaboration in their companies, in which areas to collaborate (innovation, customers, costs), and which specific projects to pursue (and which not to pursue) as collaboration activities. If the upside looks small, leaders are better off not trying to cultivate collaboration in their companies.

Step 2: Spot barriers to collaboration. Once you have answered yes to the question of whether there is an upside, the next question is, "What are the barriers blocking people from collaborating well?" People don't collaborate well for various reasons. Some reasons have to do with lack of motivation—people are not willing. Others have to do with ability—people can't do it easily. As chapter 3 outlines, the disciplined collaboration framework targets four barriers:

- The not-invented-here barrier (people are unwilling to reach out to others)

- The hoarding barrier (people are unwilling to provide help)

- The search barrier (people are not able to find what they are looking for)

- The transfer barrier (people are not able to work with people they don't know well)

All four barriers need to be low before effective collaboration can really take place. Each one is enough to stop people from collaborating well.

The problem is that it's not always apparent which barriers have sprung up in a company. Not all situations are the same. Many managers start at the wrong end, first assuming what the problem is and then devising a solution for it. To avoid this, leaders first need to analyze which barriers are present and then devise an appropriate solution.

Step 3: Tailor solutions to tear down the barriers. Armed with an understanding of which barriers are operating, a leader can now tailor solutions. Different barriers require different solutions. Motivational barriers require leaders to pull levers that make people willing to collaborate. Ability barriers mean that leaders need to pull levers that enable motivated people to collaborate throughout the company.

In tailoring their solutions, leaders can choose a mix of three levers. When leaders want to motivate people to collaborate, they can use what I call the *unification lever* (discussed in chapter 4): they can craft compelling common goals, articulate a strong value of cross-company teamwork, and talk the talk of collaboration to send strong signals that lift people's sights beyond narrow interests and toward a common goal.

With the *people lever*, leaders can seek to cultivate a certain type of management. The solution is not to get people to collaborate more, but to get the right people to collaborate on the right projects. As I discuss in chapter 5, that means cultivating what I call *T-shaped management:* people who simultaneously focus on the performance of their unit (the vertical part of the *T*) and across boundaries (the horizontal part of the T). They are willing as well as able to collaborate when needed but disciplined enough to say no when it is wrong.

By using the *network lever*, leaders can build nimble interpersonal networks across the company so that employees are more able to collaborate. Collaboration runs more on interpersonal networks and less through formal hierarchies. However, there is a dark side to networks—they can run amok. When people spend more time networking than getting work done, collaboration destroys results. Chapter 6 outlines network rules that put discipline into networks.

––––––––––

Disciplined collaboration is not complete without a focus on the individual leader. While chapters 2 through 6 focus on how leaders can cultivate collaboration *in others*, chapter 7 shifts the spotlight to *the individual leader*. To practice collaboration well, leaders, too, must change. Chapter 7 lays out what it means to take on a collaborative leadership style and describes the personal barriers that can block leaders from doing so.

The Best of Two Worlds: Decentralized *and* Collaborative

Disciplined collaboration helps you avoid one of the greatest sins of collaboration: in the quest for collaboration across the enterprise, leaders sometimes centralize decision making, and information flows to the top of an organization pyramid, where a few managers rule. In the name of collaboration, decentralization goes down. This approach implies a trade-off—that you must choose between the benefits of decentralization and the benefits of collaboration.

Disciplined collaboration rejects this compromise. Organizations can have it both ways—performance from decentralized work *and* performance from collaborative work. Indra Nooyi, CEO of PepsiCo, and her team call this "connected autonomy."[29]

The idea of disciplined collaboration is to let organization units work independently when that approach produces the best results. This practice maintains the benefits of decentralization—giving people the freedom to "own" a chunk of work, to be responsible, to be entrepreneurs building something great, to be close to customers, and to be rewarded for the results.

This approach, however, needs to be complemented—not replaced—with a "behavioral overlay" of collaborative behaviors, which occur when people throughout the organization appropriately select collaboration projects. They don't need orders from the top on where and how to collaborate. Rather, they themselves see opportunities, know when to (and when not to) collaborate, and are willing and able to execute the selected projects. They act as disciplined collaborators.

Leaders who seek the best performance need to move their organizations to the top-right corner in figure 1-3. The challenge varies depending on where a company currently falls in this chart. For a company where managers have a great deal of autonomy but do not collaborate well (as in the bottom-right part of the chart), the trick is to carefully roll out disciplined collaboration while preserving the benefits of decentralization. For leaders who think their organizations are pursuing undisciplined collaboration (as in the upper-left part of the chart), the challenge is to force more discipline into collaboration and regain some of the autonomy that might have been lost. For leaders of highly centralized organizations (as in the bottom-left part), the challenge is to

FIGURE 1-3

Disciplined collaboration: High performance from decentralization and collaboration

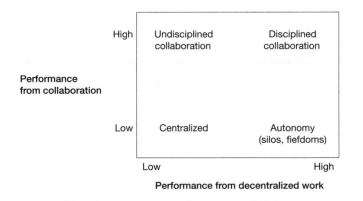

simultaneously move to autonomous units and overlay that with disciplined collaboration.

Companies, nonprofits, and governmental agencies that embrace disciplined collaboration perform better than those with an exclusively decentralized approach, because disciplined collaboration combines the results of all the independent units and results based on collaboration. As this book shows, that kind of performance is hard to beat.

PART ONE

Opportunities
and Barriers

CHAPTER TWO

Know When to Collaborate, and When Not To

O N JUNE 8, 2000, A. G. Lafley stepped into one of the most difficult jobs in corporate America. In San Francisco two days earlier,
Lafley had received a phone call from John Pepper, former CEO
of Procter & Gamble and then a board member. Would Lafley become
CEO? A boardroom coup unprecedented in the 163-year-old company's
history had just taken place back at headquarters in Cincinnati.[1]

Only eighteen months earlier, P&G CEO Durk Jager had launched a
torrent of initiatives, determined "to rip apart P&G's insular culture and
remake it from the bottom up," as *Business Week* put it.[2] But the changes
had provoked untold turmoil.[3] Rather than giving employees clarity,
the change overwhelmed them. Instead of speeding things up, it slowed
them down. In focusing on new, breakthrough products, it neglected
existing brands. On March 7, 2000, P&G said its earnings would be
down 10 percent instead of the expected 8 percent increase. The stock
price plummeted by 30 percent. Some seven weeks later, when net earnings sank 18 percent, the stock dropped another 10 percent. In June, the
company said that profits had not grown at all, even though analysts
were expecting a 15 percent increase. The stock fell another 7 percent.
Jager, too, fell that month.

A fit-looking man with short silver hair and glasses, the soft-spoken
Lafley looked like a steady hand—someone to count on in a time of crisis.
Lafley had grown up in P&G. After serving in the U.S. Navy in Japan for

five years, he went on to Harvard Business School, class of 1977, and then signed on at P&G. His first job was marketing Joy dishwashing detergent. After swiftly rising through the organization, he eventually was promoted to run the company's operations in North America. By June 2000, he had spent twenty-three years with Procter & Gamble and knew the organization better than most.[4]

"We'd made a mess, and everybody knew it," Lafley acknowledged.[5] In what amounted to a stoic move when the army in the battlefield was about to collapse, Lafley did not respond to turbulence with more turbulence. Instead he refocused the company on what P&G has always done best—growing existing brands bit by bit through innovation and collaboration across the company. He realized that the Jager reorganization had been fundamentally right but that the moves had created chaos, undermined the big brands, and overemphasized radical innovations. A *Fortune* article commented, "If the plan was shocking in anything, it was its simplicity. Everyone down the chain of command could understand it: Selling more Tide is less complicated than trying to invent the new Tide."[6]

Collaboration was an important ingredient in Lafley's recovery plan. He articulated a new goal: "We want P&G to be known as the company that collaborates—inside and out—better than any other company in the world." To do this, Lafley had to unite the company: "In June 2000, we weren't a team. We were all fighting fires and trying to fix problems in our individual businesses."[7]

Lafley is not a flamboyant man. He collects basketball cards and comic books and keeps two Vespa motor scooters—not a fancy Ferrari—in his garage. He retains a dose of humility. Whereas Jager was gruff, Lafley persuaded people to unite. "I am not a screamer, not a yeller," he says. "But don't get confused by my style. I am very decisive."[8]

To create more innovations, Lafley encouraged product developers to work with external parties.[9] He also emphasized P&G's traditional approach to product innovation: collaboration across units to combine technical expertise in different ways to create new products. Given its breadth of products—soap, diapers, toothpaste, potato chips, lotions, detergent—the company had an enormous potential to put things together in various ways to launch exciting new products. Take Crest Whitestrips, which P&G introduced in the United States in 2001. What do you do if you want to whiten your teeth? You can go to your dentist and pay $500 to sit in a chair for an hour to get a whitening treatment. Or you can ask the dentist to make an imprint of your teeth for $200 and then stick it in your mouth with some liquid for the night. Or you can to Walgreens and buy Crest Whitestrips for $24.99.

Product developers from three different units in P&G got together to create Whitestrips. People at the oral-care division provided teeth-whitening expertise; experts from the fabric and home-care division supplied bleach expertise (originally developed for washing clothes); and scientists at corporate research and development provided novel film technology.[10] Three separate units, by collaborating and combining their technologies, succeeded in developing an affordable product to brighten smiles and, according to the Web site, bring "greater success in work and love."[11]

Such collaborations don't happen by chance; they are the outcome of well-established organizational mechanisms. P&G, for instance, has created more than twenty communities of practice with eight thousand participants; each group comprises volunteers from different parts of the company and focuses on an area of expertise (fragrance, packaging, polymer chemistry, skin science, and so on). The groups solve specific problems that are brought to them, and they meet to share best practice. The company also has posted an "ask me" feature on its intranet, where employees can describe a business problem, which is funneled to those people with relevant expertise. At a more fundamental level, P&G promotes from within and rotates people across countries and business units. As a result, its employees build powerful cross-unit networks.[12]

Lafley's approach has yielded remarkable results. From a company whose managers were fighting fires in their businesses, Lafley created unity at the top. In 2003, he remarked about the company's global leadership team: "What most distinguishes this group of men and women is their ability to work together collaboratively."[13] Procter & Gamble's organic growth has averaged about 5 percent per year since Lafley took over in 2000, a hefty number considering the size of the company. Sales shot up from $39 billion to $83 billion from 2000 to 2008, with $10.5 billion coming from the acquisition of Gillette. At the same time, operating margins increased from 14.2 percent to a robust 20.5 percent.[14] Collaboration was only one factor in this success—but a critical one.

The Procter & Gamble story shows that collaboration can produce amazing results, provided it is done intelligently. As A. G. Lafley understood, the goal of collaboration is not collaboration itself, but better results. Leaders of any large-scale organization need to know when to collaborate, and in which areas, and when not to collaborate. This chapter offers guidelines for being disciplined about when to collaborate:

- The first task is to understand the case for collaboration—to appreciate how collaboration can increase performance.

- The second task is to evaluate the upside for the company—to consider the potential for the organization overall.

- The final task is to understand when to say no to a collaboration project—to articulate a decision rule for when to go ahead, and when not to, at the project level.

The Case for Collaboration

There are three areas of potential upside in business: better innovation, better sales, and better operations. In a nonbusiness context, these can be thought of as new services, greater client satisfaction, and better-run organizations. Let's examine each case.

Better Innovation

Better innovation happens because people from different areas—business units, divisions, country operations, technology centers, sales offices, marketing, labs—come together, create new ideas through these inter-actions, and go on to develop exciting products. The economic logic here is to *recombine existing resources*—products, expertise, technologies, brands, ideas—in order to create something new from something old.[15] This practice leads to more innovations, done more cheaply.

P&G's entire history is replete with innovations based on recombinations of existing technologies. It's in the corporate blood. When William Procter and James Gamble started collaborating back in 1837 on the banks of the Ohio River, they made candles and soap. This formed the basis of many subsequent product combinations.[16] Soap brought fundamental expertise in fats and oils, explains P&G's chief technology officer Gordon Brunner, "and that led to the creation of vegetable oil products like Crisco."[17] From that the company expanded into producing peanut butter and potato chips. Crushing seeds to produce oil led to an expertise in plant fibers, and that led to creating paper and absorbent products like paper towels (Bounty, introduced in 1965), feminine protection, and disposable diapers, such as Pampers, first introduced in 1961 and now a $8 billion brand.[18]

The science of fat and oils is a base for surfactants, the technology used for detergents like Tide, introduced in 1946, the year Harry Truman was president. And from there P&G went into shampoos, such as Head & Shoulders (1961) and Pantene Pro-V, introduced in 1992, the year Bill Clinton became president. Making detergents yielded experience with hard water and calcium. Expertise in calcium led to knowledge of how to strengthen teeth, providing an opportunity to offer toothpaste. This led to knowledge about strengthening bone, and that brought P&G to create drugs for osteoporosis.

When the new products became successful, they often expanded into their own product lines and organization units. To continue to mix and match technologies to create new products, people at P&G had to learn to collaborate across these many units.

What has collaboration done for Procter & Gamble? Well, let's check. According to its 2008 annual report, P&G has twenty-four brands, each racking up $1 billion or more in annual sales. Of these, thirteen come right from the collaborative lineage: Crest, Head & Shoulders, Always, Pampers, Tide, Downy, Bounty, Ariel, Pringles, Gain, Dawn, Pantene Pro-V, and Actonel, the osteoporosis medication.[19] That's a bunch of $1 billion-plus brands, thanks to collaboration.

Better Sales

Another advantage of collaboration is *cross-selling,* which means selling different products to existing customers. It often involves crossing organizational units so that one unit can sell its products to another unit's customers. The economic logic is that it is cheaper to sell more to current customers than to acquire new customers.

Richard Kovacevich is a cross-seller supreme in the banking world. A baseball star at his high school in a small town in Washington state, Kovacevich injured his pitching arm and blew his chances of accepting a contract with a major league club.[20] But that didn't put a stop to his ambitions. After he graduated from Stanford University, he embarked on a career in banking that saw him become CEO of Norwest, a regional bank based in Minneapolis, in 1993. In 1998, he triumphed when Norwest and Wells Fargo merged to form the seventh largest bank in the United States, with Kovacevich as CEO.[21] The merger was greeted with a good dose of skepticism, however, because it was announced that it would entail only minimal layoffs and no short-term gains. "The investment community threw up when we announced that," Kovacevich told a reporter with a laugh.[22] But he knew what he was doing, because he had powerful armor in his arsenal: cross-selling. More than any other bank in the United States, Wells Fargo has excelled at selling many products to its customers, including checking accounts, savings accounts, mortgages, investment accounts, debit cards, credit cards, home equity loans, you name it.

I am a Wells Fargo customer and can describe how it works. You open a regular checking account, and before you know it, the teller will suggest that you might want a savings account, and then perhaps a CD with better interest rates. On your next visit, the teller will suggest that you may want to have an interview with a financial planner (who sells Wells Fargo products). You say OK and forget it, but later that week a Wells Fargo planner calls you and suggests a face-to-face meeting in the branch closest to your home. If you don't commit to a date, soon the planner calls you back and gently reminds you of this possibility. Eventually you go to a meeting, where you get advice and end up buying more Wells Fargo products.

You may say, "Well, all banks try to do this. No big deal." But Wells Fargo has done it for longer and does it better (see figure 2-1[23]). When Kovacevich became CEO in 1998, banking households on average had 3.2 products with the bank. Through a relentless focus on cross-selling, Kovacevich and his team improved this number to 5.6 within a decade. Their goal is to reach 8 products per customer (the average U.S. household has 16 financial products).[24] This is a big deal. "The cost of us selling a product to an existing customer is only about 10 percent of selling the same product to a new customer," notes Kovacevich.[25]

Wells Fargo is able to collaborate internally across its eighty-four businesses to present "one Wells Fargo" to customers, who in turn buy more products. This collaboration contributes to profitable growth.[26] In 1999, Wells Fargo garnered about $800 in sales-per-customer.[27] That number doubled to $1,634 in 2007. By comparison, Bank of America's number in 2007 was $808, about what it was for Wells Fargo eight years earlier! And profit-per-customer at Wells Fargo was a whopping $304 in 2007 compared with $160 for Bank of America.[28]

Leaders can also grow revenues by bundling existing products from different units into a solution and charging extra for it. Consider Jardine Pacific, a large conglomerate based in Hong Kong. If you once hopped

FIGURE 2-1

Number of Wells Fargo products per household

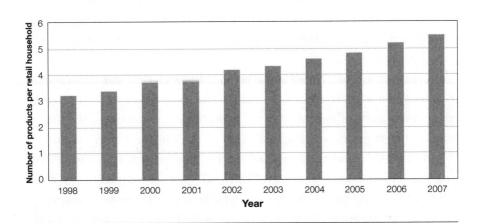

onto one of the Star ferries that departed from the island of Kowloon at night and took the ten-minute ride across the strait, you would have stared in wonder at Hong Kong's skyline, filled with millions of lights. It's no ordinary skyline: Hong Kong is home to the greatest number of skyscrapers in the world, more than seven thousand.[29] Of course, all these buildings need to be serviced. Jardine Pacific, a highly decentralized company, had several businesses servicing them: the elevator folks dealt with elevators, the air conditioning workers handled air conditioning, the cleaning unit cleaned, and the real-estate business worked on property issues. But as the business unit heads looked into this, they saw an opportunity for collaborating across their businesses.

The outcome was a business that provided total facility management to property owners. Together, elevators, air conditioning, cleaning, and real estate became a booming service business, thanks to collaboration. What the Hong Kong real estate barons saw was one solution, one service provided by Jardine Pacific, and behind that front was a close collaboration among four otherwise independent business units. Bundling products into a solution can be a potent way of selling more through collaboration.

Better Operations

The third case for collaboration centers on making operations more efficient, either by cutting costs or by passing on advice that improves the quality of decisions. The economic logic is based on *reuse of existing resources:* good solutions and expertise that are created, proven, and used in one part of the organization can be transferred to other units, lowering the costs of operations.

A few years back, Deborah Copeland, head of BP's gas station business in the southeastern United States, was looking for ways to improve the performance of her stations.[30] Through her connections, she discovered pilot programs at BP gas stations in the United Kingdom and the Netherlands that were testing innovative ways of ordering and delivering convenience-store supplies. Copeland enlisted help from her counterparts in those two countries, as well as from BP retail managers in seven other countries. They met and provided best practices in supplier management and store layouts. Copeland then launched three pilot programs in the Atlanta area. The results were dramatic. The pilot stores stocked 26 percent fewer stockkeeping units than similar control sites. This inventory reduction in turn led to a 20 percent decrease in working capital even while sales increased 10 percent.

Collaboration can also improve the quality of decisions. Professor Martine Haas of the Wharton School has chronicled a team in a large, multinational relief organization that succeeded in doing this.[31] This team was working on a $50 million project to improve the slum conditions in an overcrowded city in a desperately poor West African country. Urban poverty is a gigantic problem worldwide: about 1 billion people live in city slums, where children as young as five years old roam the garbage dumps for food, beg on the street, and die of disease.[32]

The team focused on improving living conditions for more than a million destitute people by helping with access to housing and clean water. Because this organization had worked in many poverty-stricken cities, it had great expertise in urban planning, sanitation, engineering, housing, and public finance. Rather than work alone, the team decided to tap in to this vast pool of expertise. It sought input from managers of similar projects in Asia and Latin America and from experts on urban poverty. By incorporating this advice, the team developed a high-quality proposal for improving access to housing and basic utilities. The team succeeded because it made better decisions by incorporating advice from colleagues.

What can all this disciplined collaboration add up to? What's the total impact of better innovation, sales, and operations based on collaboration? Collaboration in companies can have a significant impact on financial returns through three mechanisms: increased sales, cost savings, and improved asset efficiency. Figure 2-2 shows the various ways collaboration affects these metrics.

Because collaboration affects sales, costs, and asset efficiency, the combined effect on a company's return on equity can be substantial. Consider a hypothetical example of a company with $1 billion in sales. If this company can deploy disciplined collaboration to grow revenues by

FIGURE 2-2

How collaboration can add up to substantial financial performance

The three areas of collaboration—innovation, sales, operations—improve sales growth, cost savings, and asset efficiency, leading to better return on equity.

Collaboration area	Sales growth	Cost savings	Asset efficiency
Innovation •Product innovation through recombination •New business creation	New products, developed more quickly	Higher research productivity	
Better sales •Cross-selling, bundling •Coordinated customer service	More products sold to each customer; better service through "one face to customer"	Lower cost of sales	
Better operations •Cost cutting through best-practice transfers •Better decisions through consultation	Better sales by transferring best practices on selling	Lower costs by transferring best practices and making better decisions	Lower working capital and capital investment through best-practice transfers and better decisions

Possible impact over three years (hypothetical scenario for a $1 billion company)

Collaboration impact on ROE

Sales Growth 3% per year

Cost Reduction 3%

Asset Efficiency 2%

Profit Growth +29%

Equity Requirement – 2%

Return on equity (ROE) +25%

9 percent (3 percent per year), cut costs by 2 percent, and improve asset efficiency by 2 percent over three years, its return on equity goes up 25 percent.[33] That's substantial.

Does it sound implausible? Well, let's take a quick look at Procter & Gamble's performance from 2002 to 2005. During this time, P&G's

revenues increased by 41 percent, operating costs went down 2.7 percent, equity for a given amount of sales went down 3.3 percent, and return on equity grew 30.8 percent. A realistic assessment is that one-fourth to one-third of this increase in return on equity can be attributed to collaboration (I have estimated the effect of collaboration for P&G in the footnote).[34] That's a hefty contribution.

What's the Upside for Your Company?

Companies differ in how much value they can create from innovating, selling, and improving operations based on collaboration. For some, like Steve Jobs and Apple, it's mostly in innovation. For others, like Richard Kovacevich at Wells Fargo, the key is cross-selling. For still others, companies like BP that do similar things worldwide, the main value lies in transferring best practices.

A leader needs to be disciplined in evaluating the potential upside from collaboration. I have found it useful to approach this evaluation in two ways.

Overall Calibration

One way is to look across your entire company and ask, "What is the potential for innovation, sales, and operations based on collaboration in our company, assuming we could do it well?" This quick assessment can produce a shared understanding of the upside.

Consider how a large European media company did this. The company runs newspapers, magazines, TV stations, and online classified businesses in eight countries in Europe, including Italy, the United Kingdom, Spain, France, and Sweden.[35] Even though media markets are somewhat local (the French don't want to watch German television), the managers thought that they could take a successful product from one country into the others, team up to sell advertising, and jointly develop new online media products. When the top two hundred managers took a brief survey, they determined that there was a large upside in all three areas: innovation, sales, and operations. Their average responses were high, and they were similar to the average responses from a benchmark sample of 107 European and U.S. companies from a variety of industries (see figure 2-3).

When the managers also assessed their current level of activities in the three areas, they realized that the potential was far higher than what

FIGURE 2-3

Upside for a media company (compared with a benchmark sample)

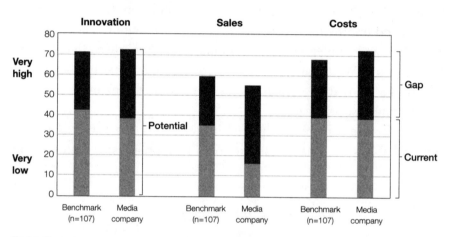

The questions were:

- What is the *potential* for *cross-unit product innovation* by combining people, technologies, resources, and ideas from different units in your company? (enter from 0 to 100 points)
- What is the *current* degree of *cross-unit product innovation* by combining people, technologies, resources and ideas from different units in your company? (enter from 0 to 100 points)
- What is the potential for realizing *revenue gains* by working together across units to cross-sell, customize products, and package solutions for customers? (enter from 0 to 100 points)
- What is the *current* realization of *revenue gains* by working together across units to cross-sell, customize products, and package solutions for customers? (enter from 0 to 100 points)
- What is the *potential* for realizing *cost savings* by transferring best practices across units in your company? (enter from 0 to 100 points)
- What is the *current* level of *cost savings* by transferring best practices across units in your company? (enter from 0 to 100 points)

Potential = Maximum upside. Current = What currently doing. Gap = Potential – Current.
Benchmark data show the *average* for 107 firms. This benchmark sample is based on a survey that I conducted among European and U.S. companies from a variety of industries. Number of employees varied from 50 to 50,000 (mean = 11,076). Industries included manufacturing, financial services, high-tech, consumer goods/retail, healthcare, professional services, energy. It is a fairly representative sample, but it is not a random sample, so caution must be exercised in drawing conclusions.
Innovation refers to cross-unit product innovation; sales refers to cross-selling; costs refers to cost reductions due to best practice transfers.

they were currently doing; a large gap existed between the potential and current levels. The gap—which represented roughly 50 percent of the potential (and even more so in cross-selling) for this company—is really the measure of the upside of collaboration. It represents the additional value that can be created from collaboration if an effort is made.

Even though it was a brief assessment, it quickly became clear to everyone in the media company that collaboration was a business opportunity worth pursuing.

However, taking such a broad sweep overlooks differences within a company. In many companies, different types of opportunities exist in different areas. Two divisions may have a great potential for cross-selling, whereas two other ones may find that cross-unit innovation is their strength. And others might discover that they have nothing in common. This reality means that you need a nuanced approach to evaluating the upside, as discussed next.

The Collaboration Matrix

One way you can gain a nuanced evaluation of your company's upside is to use a collaboration matrix. The idea here is to divide the evaluation into pairs of businesses; for example, two divisions form a pair. It's a systematic way of evaluating—pair by pair—where the opportunities for collaboration exist.

Let's take a closer look at a company where this tool proved useful. With headquarters on the bank of the beautiful Oslo fjord in Norway, Det Norske Veritas (DNV) specializes in classifying ships and in providing other risk-management services. Like its competitors, such as Lloyds Register in England, DNV not only verifies ships but also undertakes highly technical research to advance safety standards at sea.

This industry is no stranger to disasters. The sinking of the *Titanic* in 1912, when 1,517 people died, led to better safety standards, but accidents at sea continue, such as the 1994 sinking of *MS Estonia*.[36] During an overnight voyage, the front "door" of the cruise ferry, used for cars, separated from the ship and caused the ship to tilt 30 to 40 degrees to the right, making it almost impossible to move around safely. Those who ultimately survived that night were already on deck by the time the ship tilted, but most weren't. All told, 852 people were buried with the ship in the Baltic Sea. In the aftermath, investigators discovered that the locks on the door had failed, flooding the car deck and causing the ship to tilt.

Working to ensure that ships would not meet such tragic ends turned DNV into a large operation, spanning three hundred offices in one hundred countries.[37] DNV's expertise in safety standards for ships provided a good stepping-stone for entering other industries. Over the years the company created new businesses in the oil industry and also moved into new lines of services, such as consulting. But this proliferation of businesses also meant that the company had become decentralized, with four business units running their own shows: maritime (ships), energy (oil rigs), industries (food safety, health care, etc.), and information technology.

In 2006, new CEO Henrik Madsen, an affable Dane who had spent many years living in Norway, saw an interesting opportunity in cross-selling. Each business unit had established customer relations, and services from the other businesses could be sold to these customers. Opportunity knocked. Madsen's top team of seven executives went to work. They first saw each business unit as a provider of a service and asked, "What do you have that the other units can sell to their customers?" They then asked the mirror question: "What valuable customer relations do you have that the other units can use to sell their services?"

Plowing through this method, the team hunted down nine pairwise opportunities for cross-selling (see figure 2-4). Take the opportunity between the maritime and the IT businesses (number 3 in DNV's matrix). Since ships nowadays have a large number of sophisticated computer systems, someone needs to verify that those systems will not break down and wreak havoc. This opportunity was not lost on Annie Combelles, a French woman heading up the information technology business: her business could sell its services to maritime's customers. Maritime had the customer relations, and IT had the services—a good match.

FIGURE 2-4

The collaboration matrix at DNV

This example shows how DNV (a professional services firm in risk management) deter-mined opportunities for cross-selling among its four business units. Managers identified nine opportunities where one business unit could provide a service or competence to another's customers.

Provider of competencies/services

Business unit	Maritime	Energy	Industry	Information technology
Maritime		1. Sell Energy's competencies in material and testing, fire and explosion, and asset risk to Maritime customers (20 million).	2. Sell Industry's leadership systems to Maritime's customers (10 m).	3. Sell IT risk management services to Maritime customers (100 m).
Energy	4. Sell Maritime's Mobile offshore platform classifica-tions to Energy customers (200 m).		5. Sell Industry's integrated leader-ship systems to Energy's customers (10 m).	6. Sell IT risk management services to Energy's customers (100 m).
Industry		7. Sell Energy's competencies in material and testing, fire and explosion, and asset risk to Industry customers (50 m).		8. Sell IT risk management services to Industry's customers (300 m).
Information technology		9. Sell Energy's technology in risk and reliability to IT customers (10 m).		

Holder of customer relations

Source: Morten T. Hansen, "Transforming DNV: From Silos to Disciplined Collaboration Across Business Units—Changes at the Top (B)," Case 08/2007-5458 (Fontainebleau, France: INSEAD, 2007).

Revenue opportunity estimates represent five-year targets, as estimated by executive board members. Million Norwegian Kroner (NOK) in parentheses. Total revenue opportunities are about 8–10 percent of company revenues.

The DNV matrix reveals something equally important: empty boxes. These are business-to-business areas where there are no real opportunities for collaboration. For example, there are no real opportunities for selling maritime's services to industry's customers, leaving that box empty.

As the DNV story shows, the collaboration matrix allows executives to pinpoint with some precision whether there are any opportunities between the businesses—pair by pair—and, if so, how large they are. When leaders use this approach, they engage in a disciplined and fine-grained evaluation of where the upsides really exist and where they don't.

Don't Overshoot

It's easy to get carried away with collaboration, believing that you will gain many benefits from it. The reality may be different, as one company found. Sterling was a large information technology consulting firm with more than ten thousand employees and more than one hundred offices scattered across the United States. It specialized in helping huge companies implement large, complicated information systems known as enterprise resource planning (ERP) systems, like SAP and Oracle. These contracts were big deals, sometimes worth $50 million in fees, and sales teams fervently pursued them in stiff competition with firms like IBM and Accenture. Typically, a sales team of four to six people would spend about two months pulling together a proposal for implementing an SAP system for a client like Walt Disney Company. To impress the Disney folks, the team would reach out to other SAP experts in Sterling to get their advice on how to perfect the bid.

Clearly, Sterling's senior people thought that all this collaboration was good. But no hard data existed to prove it. Helping to test it, my colleague Martine Haas and I pulled a sample of 182 teams and measured things such as hours of help received to test their effects on winning a bid (it was either won or lost, so no ambiguity there). We sat down in front of the computer in my office at Harvard Business School, stuffed all the data into a statistical program, and ran an analysis for a month. Figure 2-5 shows one of the charts that came up on the screen, showing the results for a sample of highly experienced sales teams.

Pause for a moment and inspect this chart. It shows something odd: the more these teams collaborated with colleagues in Sterling, the *less* chance they had of winning the sales contract. How could this be? It should have been the opposite: the more help, the more success.

We puzzled over this finding. As it turned out, the secret was to be found in the experience of the sales team itself. Highly experienced

FIGURE 2-5

The more help, the worse off

The relationship between receiving help and winning sales contracts for experienced teams in a large IT consulting company

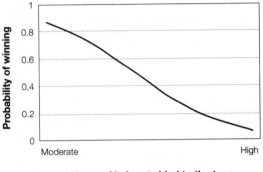

Hours of help provided to the team

Source: The results of this study are reported in Martine R. Haas and Morten T. Hansen, "When using knowledge can hurt performance: the value of organizational capabilities in a management consulting company," *Strategic Management Journal* 26, no. 1 (2005): 1–24.

Data: Regression analysis of a sample of 105 sales teams.

teams—those led by senior partners who knew everything there was to know about an SAP system—had no use for this outside help. They already had what it took to bid on an SAP job, and yet they assumed that collaborating with other SAP experts in Sterling would bring even more benefits. It didn't. In fact, it brought only pain—time and effort involved in collaborating, which was time and effort the sales team did not spend making an even better bid. They overshot: the benefit of collaborating with the experts in the firm was never there for experienced teams.[38]

Leaders also tend to overshoot when they estimate the benefit of placing different businesses under one roof.[39] When Daimler's boss, Dieter Zetsche, in 2007 sold Chrysler for a pitiful $1 billion, a company the German automaker had bought nine years earlier for $36 billion, he confessed that "we obviously overestimated the potential for synergies." A $35 billion mistake! Some studies have reported that between 39 and 66 percent of acquisitions fail to deliver on the promised value, and yet leaders keep overestimating the potential for synergies that are based in part on collaboration.[40]

Don't Undershoot

It's equally wrong to undershoot. When leaders believe—incorrectly—that there is little or no upside from collaborating across the company, they ignore a big opportunity. Sometimes they fear that it will kill the entrepreneurial freedom that each business unit enjoys. They believe, often wrongly, that the potential gains from collaborating will be overshadowed by the loss of entrepreneurship.

Bertelsmann, one of Europe's largest media companies, was stuck in this belief. Its leaders insisted that each business unit—book publishing, scientific publishing, magazines, music, music clubs, and television—should operate as an independent business and that there was no need to collaborate. "Bertelsmann has a strictly decentralized organization," said CEO Gunter Thielen. "Each profit center has a managing director who acts as 'an entrepreneur within the greater enterprise.' These directors—not the executive board—are the company's real drivers."[41]

Implicit in Thielen's thinking is a trade-off between entrepreneurial freedom and collaboration; companies can have only one of them. I disagree. Bertelsmann has left opportunities on the table by undershooting on the collaboration front.[42] Case in point: the company did not forge collaboration among its various divisions to respond to Amazon.com and launch its own online bookstore in a timely manner. As a result, the company is not really a player in the online bookstore market.[43]

Both overshooting and undershooting add up to undisciplined collaboration. The leader is not carefully calibrating the opportunity to collaborate.

When Do You Say "No!" to Collaboration?

Should you start a collaborative project or not? Managers need a rule to help them decide when to collaborate and when to say, "No, there is no business case. Let's not collaborate."

But this rule needs to be different from the usual go, no-go rule for projects. Managers need to take into consideration two additional costs: opportunity costs and collaboration costs. People should launch a collaboration project only if the net value of collaboration is greater than the return minus *both* opportunity costs and collaboration costs. I call this net value the collaboration premium, and the principle can be imagined as a simple equation:

Collaboration premium = return on project − opportunity costs − collaboration costs

Opportunity cost is the answer to the question, "What else could we do with the time, effort, and resources going into a collaboration project?" Maybe there are better uses of people's time and effort—projects with better returns altogether. The opportunity cost is the net cash flow that organizations forego by doing the collaboration project instead of something else.

Collaboration costs refer to the extra hassles of working across units and their consequences: extra time traveling, time spent haggling with the other parties over objectives, efforts to solve conflicts, and all the poor results that these complications create: delays, budget overruns, poor quality, and lost sales (and these can be huge). Collaboration cost is the negative cash flow that results from all these factors.

To see why the collaboration premium is important, let's revisit DNV and look at a collaboration that went sour.

DNV: The Opportunity

In 2006, an E. coli outbreak in spinach sickened two hundred people and killed a two-year-old boy in the United States.[44] The bacterium was later traced to Natural Selection Foods, a California company growing spinach and other vegetables. Because these kinds of disasters make food companies very nervous, they are eager to ensure safety in their production process, and they hire firms to help them with that

Given DNV's safety expertise, helping food companies produce safe food was an interesting opportunity. In 2003, two business units—certification and consulting—had come together to collaborate in the food area.[45] The certification business inspected food production chains and gave out "clean health" certificates. The risk management consulting business worked with food companies to help them reduce the risk in a food chain.[46] The initial estimates were promising: if the two businesses operated separately, they could grow revenues 50 percent from 2004 to 2008. If they collaborated, they could grow revenues 200 percent. The projected net cash flow would be $40 million.[47] It was a clear go.

The Real Costs

But the consulting unit hadn't really included opportunity costs— alternative ways of using available resources. As it turned out, food was not its best opportunity. The best one was risk management consulting for information technology. The consulting business would have been better off putting its efforts into that segment, which required no collaboration with other business units. By sticking with food, it had to forgo some of this opportunity—perhaps $25 million in net cash flow. (It's not difficult to estimate this number. It's the cash flow from the most attractive project not undertaken.)

The second problem was that collaboration costs were high; the organization wasn't set up to collaborate (for one thing, managers were measured only on the performance of their own business units). The cross-unit team quarreled, and the two parties grew suspicious of each other. "Many people were silo oriented," said one manager, referring to a myopic attitude. "Team members tried to protect their own customers." Said another, "Certification people were afraid to bring consulting people to their own customers." As a result, the two units couldn't agree on building a common database of customer information. The implication was that estimates—especially increased sales from selling services to each other's customers—had to be adjusted downward. (This number for collaboration costs is more difficult to estimate. In this case, it's primarily about lost sales as a result of the bickering—some $20 million in net cash flow.)

Following are rough estimates I made in writing a case study of DNV, but they reveal realistic dollar figures:

Collaboration Premium = return on project − opportunity costs − collaboration costs
   − $5 million = $40 million   − $25 million   − $20 million

Given that the collaboration premium was negative, DNV should not have gone ahead with the project.

The Fall

What happened? During the project, both costs haunted the team. The consulting business was not so committed to food after all, because it was getting better traction in the IT segment. Its opportunity costs were large, and it pulled the consultants away from the food project. Also, the frictions between the two teams rose, increasing collaboration costs in the form of lost revenues from cross-selling. By fall 2005, revenues were behind schedule, and the project was stopped. In reality, opportunity and collaboration costs doomed the project.

The lesson? Managers must carefully estimate opportunity and collaboration costs and clearly say "No, we will not collaborate" if the collaboration premium is negative, foreshadowing a loss. That's being disciplined about which collaboration projects to undertake and which not to start.

Now, you might think, "These numbers are really hard to estimate ahead of time. Only hindsight is 20/20." That is a good point. But managers already expend tremendous effort estimating the return from projects; is spending the same amount of energy on opportunity costs and collaboration costs too much to ask for, especially when they can fell a project?

The DNV example offers another important lesson. The last equation says that collaboration costs were $20 million, enough to make this a no-go project. But let's suppose collaboration costs had been very low. Suppose team members had not been suspicious of each other. Suppose they had not hoarded their customer relations but instead had sought to cross sell services. Suppose they had built that common customer database to enable cross-selling. If the collaboration costs had been very low, then the collaboration premium would have been positive, and the chances are that the project would have worked successfully.

Ultimately, collaboration costs are high in a company where there are barriers to collaboration—in this case, people hoarding their customer relations. The job of a leader, then, is to find those barriers, tear them down, and drive collaboration costs down to nearly zero.

Chapter 2: Key Points

Know when to collaborate, and when not to

- The goal of collaboration is not collaboration but greater results. Leaders have to infuse this discipline principle throughout the company so that people do not collaborate for the sake of collaboration but are able to say no to collaboration projects of questionable value. To be disciplined about collaboration is to know when not to collaborate.

- There is a compelling business case for collaboration in many companies. The upside can be large: collaboration improves sales, increases margins, and allows for efficient use of assets. Leaders can achieve much better return on equity as a result of collaboration.

- Leaders need to assess the potential in three areas: better innovation through collaboration (cross-unit product development and new business creation); better sales through collaboration (cross-selling and better customer service); and better operations (cost savings through transferring best practices and making better decisions). These potentials vary by company. Leaders need to calibrate the opportunity in their company and avoid both over- and undershooting the potential.

- To enforce discipline in collaboration projects, you must ensure that each project have a collaboration premium. Collaborative projects should be undertaken only if the value exceeds both opportunity costs (foregoing other projects) and collaboration costs (haggling across units, resulting in delays, budget overruns, lost sales, and poor quality). Managers must subject a collaboration project to a collaboration premium test before giving it a go.

- Leaders can drive collaboration costs down to nearly zero by tearing down barriers to collaboration. "Collaborate for results" becomes much easier if people know how to collaborate.

CHAPTER THREE

Spot the Four Barriers
to Collaboration

O N AUGUST 29, 2001, an FBI agent fired off an angry e-mail to a colleague Jane: "Whatever has happened to this—someday someone will die—and wall or not—the public will not understand why we were not more effective and throwing every resource we had at certain 'problems.'"[1] The livid agent wanted to hunt down a Saudi national named Khalid al Mihdhar. The agent thought Mihdhar was linked to the case he was working on—the investigation of the October 2000 bombing of the USS *Cole* in Yemen that killed seventeen sailors. But his FBI colleague, an analyst now known anonymously as "Jane," mistakenly invoked the "wall" at the FBI that she thought denied people working on criminal cases access to intelligence information. Hence the angry e-mail. Rather than urgently chasing Mihdhar, the FBI agent had to settle for a slow-moving routine request that Jane sent to the New York office. There, a novice agent started doing some research, but time was running out. On September 11, Mihdhar hijacked American Airlines Flight 77, which crashed into the Pentagon and killed 189 people.

The CIA had been in hot pursuit of Mihdhar before. The trail traced back to Kuala Lumpur, Malaysia.[2] In January 2000, agents from the Central Intelligence Agency learned that an al-Qaeda meeting was to take place there and that Mihdhar was staying in an apartment with an acquaintance. But the meeting broke off in a hurry, and Mihdhar and his companions, including Nawaf Hazmi, another 9/11 hijacker, flew to

Bangkok, Thailand, too quickly for authorities to track them. By the time the alert went out, "the travelers had already disappeared into the streets of Bangkok."[3] U.S. officials in Bangkok had to report that the trail had gone cold. They placed Mihdhar on a local watch list in Bangkok but, remarkably, did not alert the U.S. immigration services or the FBI. On January 15, Mihdhar and Hazmi flew to Los Angeles on U.S. visas, but no one knew they were coming.

Mihdhar and Hazmi rented an apartment in San Diego, opened a bank account under their real names, tried to learn English, and enrolled in school to learn to fly. Then in June 2000, Mihdhar made a tactical blunder when he left California for Yemen, only to return on July 4, 2001, about two months before September 11.[4] This could have derailed the whole 9/11 plot; he risked being detected, because he had to reapply for a U.S. visa in June 2001. But no one had put him on a watch list beyond the local one in Bangkok, so he was not detected.

In mid-May 2001, the Kuala Lumpur trail had again been picked up. "John," a CIA official in the United States, started to review some old reports and asked a colleague, "Mary," to look into it.[5] They soon discovered the old information, including that Mihdhar had been in Kuala Lumpur (and connected to al-Qaeda) and had obtained a U.S. visa. On August 24, 2001, Mary and Jane finally placed Mihdhar on the State Department's watch list. But it was too late, as Mihdhar had already entered the country on July 4. When the angry FBI agent investigating the USS *Cole* attack saw this information, he wanted to hunt down Mihdhar quickly. Instead, Jane launched the slow-moving search.

That wasn't the FBI's only missed opportunity. On July 10, 2001, in Phoenix, Arizona, FBI agent Kenneth Williams fired off an e-mail to FBI headquarters with the provocative title "Usama Bin Laden . . . supporters attending civil aviation universities."[6] Williams and colleagues had investigated a Saudi national named Zacaria Mustapha Soubra, along with two Algerian Islamic extremists. During an interview, Soubra told the investigators that he considered the U.S. government and U.S. military forces in the Gulf "legitimate military targets of Islam." Williams warned of the danger of having Islamic extremists learning to fly.

When Williams's memo showed up at FBI headquarters, two mid-level supervisors reviewed it but did not disseminate it.[7] They did not send it to top FBI managers, nor did they share it with other units in the FBI or the CIA. Williams had also sent the memo to the FBI's New York field office, but officials there did not distribute it, either. As a result, very few people knew of Williams' alarm.

On August 27, 2001, a heated phone conversation took place between a supervisor in the FBI's Minneapolis office and an FBI headquarters agent, who accused the supervisor of trying to get people "spun up."[8] The Minneapolis supervisor fired back that he was "trying to keep someone from taking a plane and crashing it into the World Trade Center." They were debating Zacarias Moussaoui, who had entered the United States in February 2001 and had begun flight lessons in Oklahoma and Minnesota. The flight school had tipped the FBI about this foreign national, who, with little knowledge of flying, "wanted to learn how to 'take off and land' a Boeing 747." The agents quickly learned that he was an Islamic extremist. As it turned out, Moussaoui had overstayed his visa, and the FBI arrested him.

The agents in Minneapolis suspected that Moussaoui possessed information on terrorist plots and wanted to search his laptop, but for this they needed a special search warrant. That was the source of the heated exchange: Minneapolis wanted the search warrant, but FBI headquarters ruled that there was not sufficient evidence.

Moussaoui escaped a full-blown investigation before 9/11, and that was a terrible missed opportunity, because as it turned out, there was a short trail from him to hijacker Mohamed Atta, the ringleader of the 9/11 hijackers and the suicide pilot on American Airlines Flight 11. Moussaoui received help from a person named Ramzi bin al-Shibh, who was operating from abroad and helping the other terrorists in the United States, including Atta.[9]

On August 6, 2001, President George Bush's daily security briefing had a shocking title: "Bin Laden Determined to Strike in the US."[10] For the intelligence community, as CIA Director George Tenet recalled, "The system was blinking red."[11] Intelligence officers throughout the world were picking up "chatter" and bits of information indicating that something major was afoot. According to the 9/11 Commission report, "A terrorist threat advisory distributed in late June indicated a high probability of near-term 'spectacular' terrorist attacks resulting in numerous casualties."[12]

On June 25, Richard Clarke, head of the Counterterrorism Security Group, warned National Security Advisor Condoleezza Rice that six separate intelligence reports showed al-Qaeda personnel warning of a pending attack.[13] By late July 2001, Tenet said, it could not "get any worse."[14]

The problem was, there was little specific information on where the attacks might occur and what kinds of attacks they might be.

Throughout this period, from January 2000 to September 11, 2001, no one connected the dots between these four pieces of information: the al-Qaeda terrorist Mihdhar entering the country and taking flying lessons; extremists learning to fly in Arizona; Moussaoui learning to fly Boeing 747 airplanes; and the system blinking red during the summer of 2001. Had someone connected the dots, he or she might have deduced that the high levels of general alert during the summer of 2001 were related to hijacking (al-Qaeda terrorists had taken flight lessons) and to certain individuals (Mihdhar, Hazmi, and Moussaoui). That's pretty close to knowing the "what" and the "who."

It is easier to see the connection among these pieces of information in hindsight than in real time amid an ocean of tips and data. But, the case of the 9/11 intelligence failure highlights the key message of this chapter: organizations—in this case the U.S. intelligence community—often develop barriers that hinder information sharing and collaboration. The failure of agents to disseminate information and connect the dots was a direct function of several barriers to collaboration. The job of a leader is to spot these barriers and tear them down so that better collaboration can take place.

The Enemy of Collaboration: Modern Management

Collaboration rarely occurs naturally, because leaders, often unintentionally, erect barriers that block people from collaborating. Many people, though not all of course, have a natural tendency to collaborate, but they are not left to their own devices. And the culprit is modern management.

Managers and management thinkers celebrate decentralization, which works like this: you delegate responsibilities for operations, products, business areas, and geographies to a group of managers. The clearer the lines of responsibility, the better. You then develop objectives and metrics for each manager so that he or she knows what to achieve each quarter and year. To improve the chances of success, you give the managers considerable freedom—they run their own unit. Then you hold them accountable for their results and put in place incentives to motivate them to reach the objectives. Bonuses, salary increases, stock options, and promotions go to those who deliver. Those who do not deliver are coached or let go. Predictably, managers of each unit work hard and focus on reaching their targets. You sit back and marvel at the beauty of this system.

This is the essence of modern management: a decentralized system with clear lines of responsibility, a great deal of accountability, and rewards for those who perform. It's a beautiful system, and it delivers very good performance—up to a point. The problem is that each manager becomes increasingly independent and tries to maximize his or her unit—after all, that is how the job is defined. Managers care about reaching their goals and have little interest in helping others achieve theirs. Over time, decentralization risks turning a company into a loose collection of units, which become fiefdoms or silos.

This is what happened with the U.S. intelligence community before September 11, 2001. It was a sprawling community, involving many units: the FBI, the CIA, the Immigration and Naturalization Service, the National Security Agency, the Defense Intelligence Agency, the National Reconnaissance Office, the State Department, the Federal Aviation Authority, the Counterterrorism Security Group at the White House, and the National Security Advisor. "The very phrase 'intelligence community' is intriguing," said 9/11 Commission vice-chair Lee Hamilton. "It demonstrates how decentralized and fragmented our intelligence capabilities are."[15]

The decentralized structure was sharply criticized by the 9/11 Commission, which noted that "the agencies are like a set of specialists in a hospital, each ordering tests, looking for symptoms, and prescribing medications. What is missing is the attending physician who makes sure they work as a team."[16]

The solution, however, is not to dismantle the decentralized system and go for the opposite—extreme centralization—where a few people at the top decide and filter information. That is throwing the baby out with the bathwater. After all, the decentralized approach produces large benefits. There is a better way—and a better model. *Disciplined collaboration requires that organizations be decentralized and yet coordinated.* To build this model, leaders need to detect the barriers to collaboration and overcome them without reducing the benefits of a decentralized structure.

Four barriers typically block collaboration. To gauge their prevalence in companies, I used the survey of 107 European and U.S. companies that I mentioned in chapter 2.[17] I developed an assessment tool and asked managers to assess the extent of these barriers (you can take this brief assessment, which is provided later in this chapter, and compare your results to this sample). Although the data is subjective, it indicates that all four barriers were present, although companies differed widely in which barriers they confronted and their severity. This means that leaders first need to spot the particular barriers they face.

1. The Not-Invented-Here Barrier

In Hewlett-Packard's European operations in the late 1990s, executives had created an internal benchmarking system that compared the time it took to process computer orders at factories in different countries.[18] The idea was to enable managers to measure their weak spots and learn from the best. But managers at the underperforming factories were not interested in learning from the others. It didn't help that the French factory was worse than the Belgian. The idea that they had to go to Belgium to learn from Belgian managers didn't sit well with the French managers. They did not believe that others could teach them useful practices, in part because they viewed their problems as unique. But they were not.

This example illustrates the not-invented-here barrier, which arises when people are not willing to reach beyond their own units to get input and collaborate.

Why don't people reach out to seek help? Of course, many times there is no need. But at other times people can reap great results by getting input from others—a piece of advice, a transfer of technology. Or there are opportunities to do joint work—develop a new product together or contact a customer with a joint offering. But even then, people do not reach out; they are not willing to do so. This is a *motivational* problem caused by several factors, as shown in figure 3-1.

Insular Culture

People who work together can develop an insular culture. As they spend time with each other to the exclusion of outsiders, they restrict the influx of new viewpoints and reinforce their own beliefs.[19] The

---

FIGURE 3-1

The first barrier: Why not-invented-here happens

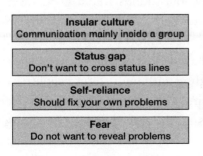

more close-knit a group becomes, the more the members turn inward and close themselves off from the world.

In my study of 120 product-development teams in Hewlett-Packard during the 1990s, I found some product-development teams that got into this predicament.[20] Members of these teams mingled only inside their own business units. Over time an insular network developed that consisted of informal relations among them. As a result, they preferred to find solutions to product-development problems on the inside. Their performance suffered as a result.[21]

Status Gap

If individuals think that they have higher status than others, they will not reach out to collaborate with those "less worthy" human beings. At Morgan Stanley, around 1998, people in the investment banking arm— elite bankers who often came from top universities—looked down on the "street smart" employees in the recently acquired retail brokerage arm of Dean Witter.[22] Shortly after the merger between these two entities, traders from the two sides had to start working together. The Morgan Stanley traders didn't conceal their disdain. According to a *Fortune* article, "One Morgan Stanley trader described the moment as bringing into his life 'guys named Vinnie in cheap suits.'"[23] The old worlds of Morgan Stanley and Dean Witter could not have been more different, and a status gap kept people from collaborating well.

But surely the "low-status" Dean Witter brokers would welcome the opportunity to mingle with the high-status investment bankers? Rubbing shoulders with high-status people sounds like a good idea, but evidence suggests otherwise. For members of low-status groups, reaching out to high-status groups ruins the comfort of being with people of the same status. It's acceptable to have low status if people in the same circle also have low status. But mingling with high-status people destroys this reassurance and reminds them of their fate. Economist Robert Frank calls this phenomenon "choosing the right pond."[24] Reaching out to high-status groups in a company is one of the last things low-status people want to do.

Status gaps run both ways: high-status people do not want to sully their image of themselves, and low-status people do not want to let high-status people make them regret their circumstances. Both attitudes create a barrier to collaboration.

Self-Reliance

When a norm takes hold that says, "You should fix your own problems," people tend to resist reaching out for input. It is not that people feel they are better than others; rather, it comes from the deep-seated belief that people need to solve their problems on their own instead of asking for help. When this attitude crops up among people in a unit, chances are that the not-invented-barrier will set in.

Fear of Revealing Shortcomings

Reaching out to someone and saying, "We're not doing well in this area and need help," can be interpreted by others as failure: "These guys are not very good." People sometimes fear exposing their weaknesses to others, especially to experts. By asking for input, people expose their vulnerability, allowing others to stand in judgment. As a result, people may decide that it's better not to reach out at all, or it's better to go to people they already know and trust (even if they're not the most knowledgeable).[25] Fear of revealing shortcomings becomes a barrier to collaboration.

Did the not-invented-here barrier play a role in the U.S. intelligence community's failure to uncover the September 11 plot? Although it was not the most important barrier, it did play a role.[26] Several agencies possessed a lot of information, and yet few analysts worked the phones, chasing other agencies for every bit of information. Although a few people tried, as when the angry FBI agent requested information from Jane, the 9/11 report reveals that the norm was *not* to reach out. For example, information that could be used to identify hijacker Hazmi had existed but was left undistributed. As the commission report points out,

"Someone had to ask for it. In that case, no one did."[27] At the FBI, agents rarely reached out to ask other federal agencies with potentially valuable information databases to assist in searches.[28]

2. The Hoarding Barrier

Have you ever wondered why some employees do not return phone calls from colleagues requesting their help? You may have thought, "Oh, they just forgot." Employees' motives might be more sinister. Some people deliberately do not want to share with others; they withhold their help, information, time, and effort. Sometimes they refuse to provide anything (even though they don't admit it openly), or they withhold parts of what they know. Or they may agree to cooperate on something and then drag their feet.

Unlike the not-invented-here barrier, where people do not want to ask others for input, the hoarding barrier concerns people in the opposite role: those who might provide help but do not offer it. Several factors lead to hoarding, as shown in figure 3-2.

Competition

Competition inside a company undermines people's willingness to collaborate. In the study of Hewlett-Packard in the 1990s, I asked managers

FIGURE 3-2

The second barrier: Why people hoard

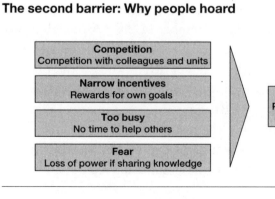

how competitive they thought their cross-business relations were; they categorized an astounding 30 percent of all interdivisional interactions as competitive. Why? Managers from different divisions frequently argued over who had the right to develop certain products. They were competing for the same opportunities, and it created hoarding behaviors. When the time came to transfer technologies from one division to another, engineers providing the technology would sometimes drag their feet. They were reluctant to help when they perceived a competitive relationship between their division and the requesting division.[29]

Narrow Incentives

When people are rewarded only for how well they do their jobs, they tend to focus attention on their jobs exclusively. Many companies operate with this form of unit-focused incentive system. This setup creates hoarding behaviors, because people pay attention to their own targets to the exclusion of helping people outside their unit.[30]

Being Too Busy

Paradoxically, the emphasis on performance management over the past decade has created what Harvard Professor Leslie Perlow calls a "time famine" at work.[31] As people are pressured to perform, they feel that they don't have the time to help others; reasonable requests for help are seen as burdens that put them behind in their own work. So people are faced with a trade-off—to do their own work (but not help others), or to help others (but get less work done). My study of project teams in Hewlett-Packard in the 1990s revealed this trade-off: team members who helped other projects ended up taking longer to complete their own project, because they spent their valuable time helping others and not finishing their own project.[32]

Fear of Losing Power

As the adage goes, "Knowledge is power," implying that a person is more powerful in an organization the more he or she knows about something and the less others know. So why share that knowledge with others and thereby make oneself less powerful and ultimately redundant? If people fear they will become less powerful and less valuable to the organization by spreading their wisdom, they will be inclined to hoard it.

Massive hoarding behaviors existed in the intelligence community before the 9/11 attack. Consider the examples in the beginning of this chapter. First, the CIA officials on the Kuala Lumpur trail didn't share what they knew with the FBI and the State Department. Second, in the Mihdhar case, FBI agent Jane refused to share information with the FBI agent assigned to the USS *Cole* investigation, citing the wall in the FBI. Third, agents who read the Phoenix memo decided not to distribute it further.

Incentives were extremely narrow in the U.S. intelligence community. At the FBI, each field office had its own performance metrics, including the number of arrests, indictments, and convictions. Officials cared about reaching these targets, and not about spending their time helping other field offices. Worse, there were incentives in place to discourage information sharing. As the 9/11 Commission report observed, "Each agency's incentives structure opposes sharing, with risks (criminal, civil, and internal administrative sanctions) but few rewards for sharing information."[33] Well, if people can go to jail for sharing information with other agencies, it is easy to see why they would tend to hoard information.[34]

The decentralized structure of the intelligence community, narrow incentives, and fear of revealing information all contributed to a climate of hoarding in the intelligence community.

3. The Search Barrier

Many companies are familiar with the adage, "If only we knew what we know." By that they mean that somewhere in the company, someone knows the answer to a problem, but the rub is that the one who has the problem cannot locate the one who has the answer. That's the search barrier. Unlike the first two barriers, where people are unwilling to collaborate, the search barrier concerns the *inability* to find information and people in a company.

FIGURE 3-3

The third barrier: Why search is difficult

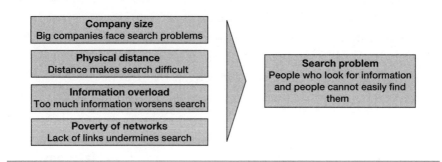

People can spend way too much of their time searching for the knowledge they need. In my study of Hewlett-Packard's measurement sector in the 1990s, innovation teams spent a great deal of their time asking around to find useful technical know-how and marketing information in other divisions in the company (this time amounted to 5 percent of the staff budget).[35] One team ended up spending 22 percent of its total engineering months on search; that's about one-fifth of the entire project budget paying for people searching! Several factors make search difficult (see figure 3-3).

Company Size

The bigger the company, the greater the search problems. My survey of 107 companies showed that managers in large companies judged the search barrier to be much higher than in small companies. And company size in turn is related to the number of business units, product groups, subsidiaries, and sales territories in a company: with larger size comes more units to search, worsening the problem.

Physical Distance

Companies that are spread across cities, regions, countries, and continents have bigger search problems than those that reside in one place.[36] People prefer to interact with others who are close by. In his famous study of an engineering company, Thomas Allen of MIT showed that the communication between two engineers was a direct function of the number of meters between their cubicles in the building: the closer the cubicles, the more communication there was. When the cubicles were twenty-five meters apart, the communication dropped to almost nothing.[37]

I found similar results when I studied the forty-one business units in Hewlett-Packard in the 1990s.[38] Business units communicated less with each other as the number of miles between them went up. In fact, the biggest drop in communication was from zero to one mile: as soon as two business units were not located on the same premises, their collaboration activity dropped. And beyond one thousand miles, the chances of collaborating withered. The main reason was that people found it inconvenient to look for knowledge and people in units far away.

Information Overload

At 7:02 a.m. on December 7, 1941, two military men who operated a radar station near Pearl Harbor detected something looking like an airplane 137 miles north of the island of Oahu in Hawaii. They telephoned the information center, where an inexperienced officer told the two to forget it. They did. The Japanese attack on Pearl Harbor, which drew the United States into World War II, occurred 53 minutes later.

The most vital pieces of information—like this bit about an incoming airplane—were drowned out by irrelevant information. According to Roberta Wohlstetter, who wrote the authoritative book on the warning signals at Pearl Harbor, "We failed to anticipate Pearl Harbor not for want of the relevant materials, but because of a plethora of irrelevant ones."[39] The noise ratio was simply too high. The same can be said for 9/11 intelligence; useful bits of information, like the four mentioned at the start of this chapter, were lost in a sea of data.

What a paradox! In a rush to help people get the information they need, companies have put in place databases, intranets, and knowledge-management systems, but these have created their own problem: too much information. As one manager in a large company told me, "Five years ago, business unit people complained that they did not get enough information; today they complain that they are drowning in information."[40]

Information overload makes search harder because of information noise—the ratio of the *total* amount of information available to the amount of *useful* information. Information systems, including knowledge-management systems, increase the noise ratio by making too much information available, and that complicates the search for the right type of knowledge or person.[41]

Poverty of Networks

A myth has taken hold in our society—that we live in a small world. Almost everyone can recount an anecdote of two strangers in a far-off place who happen to know someone in common. Psychologist Stanley Milgram of Yale University tells the tale of Fred Jones of Peoria, Illinois, sitting in a sidewalk café in Tunis in Africa and asking the man at the next table for a match. The stranger is an Englishman who spent several months in Detroit studying the operation of an interchangeable-bottle cap factory. Jones asks the Englishman whether by chance he has ever run into Ben Arkadian, an old friend who manages a chain of supermarkets in Detroit. The Englishman has. "Good Lord," Jones exclaims. "It's a small world, isn't it?"[42]

Milgram is famous for promulgating the belief in the small-world idea. His study showed it took people about six steps to pass a letter from the Midwestern state of Nebraska via acquaintances to reach a stranger—a stockbroker—in Boston fourteen hundred miles away.[43] The folklore of "six degrees of separation" and "It's a small world" took hold.

That the world is small should give us great comfort for search. But unfortunately, the world isn't always small. That two strangers might discover a common connection doesn't mean that we're always a few steps away from the information we need. In fact, Milgram found a huge difference in how well connected people were: the best connected Nebraskan reached the stockbroker by using only one intermediary, but the worst had to go through a whopping ten intermediaries (and 71 percent of the started searches never reached the stockbroker, so the searches failed completely).

That the world can be very big is also true for employees in companies. In one study of a 3,000-person global management consulting company, the best employees completed their search in one step, and the worst took as long as five steps.[44] That's a pretty long search chain, considering that the company is not very large. It may be a small world for a few well-connected people, but it's a big world for many others, and that's a formidable barrier to search.

———————

Search was an immense barrier in the intelligence community before the terrorist attack on September 11, 2001. The 9/11 Commission put it bluntly: "The FBI lacked the ability to know what it knew."[45] Much of the blame for this was put on the outdated information system. Director Robert Mueller acknowledged that, over the years, the FBI had "failed to develop a sufficient capacity to collect, store, search, retrieve, analyze, share information."[46] But the problem went well beyond having a poor IT system. All the other factors wrecked havoc: it was a large community that was spread out; oceans of information overwhelmed agents; and there was a poverty of networks among the agencies.

4. The Transfer Barrier

People run into problems in transferring expertise, know-how, and technologies when people from the different units do not know how to work together. This transfer problem is not about motivations but about abilities: people can be highly motivated to work together, but they find it difficult to do so.

The transfer barrier can be a massive problem. Some project teams at Hewlett-Packard in the 1990s, for example, ran into this barrier when they tried to transfer complicated technologies from other divisions in the company.[47] Project teams spent on average 10 percent of the staff budget transferring technologies, with one project racking up a whopping 57 percent! Several factors cause this type of transfer problems (see figure 3-4).

Tacit Knowledge

This type of knowledge makes transfer hard. Tacit knowledge refers to information that is hard to articulate orally—in writing, in manuals, in

FIGURE 3-4

The fourth barrier: Why transfer problems happen

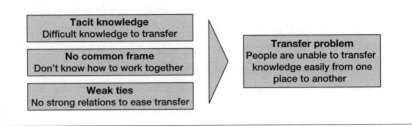

equations, and in software code.[48] Explicit knowledge, on the other hand, can easily be articulated. For example, consider this formula:

$$PR(A) = (1-d) + d \, (PR(T1)/C(T1) + \cdots + PR(Tn)/C(Tn))$$

Do you know what it is? That's the famous formula that Google uses for its search engine—a method of ranking pages on the Web. Google cofounders Larry Page and Sergey Brin wrote this up in an academic working paper in 1996, when they were graduate students at Stanford University.[49] This is highly explicit knowledge, now worth billions of dollars.[50]

Now, can you write down a formula for "how to close a tough sales negotiation"? Probably not. You could write tips for how to negotiate hard, but could you write down all the subtle moves that a masterful salesperson engages in to close the deal? No, because it is highly tacit knowledge.

It takes time to learn and master tacit knowledge. The great French chef Fernand Point, often considered the father of modern French cuisine, wrote in his book *Ma Gastronomie,* "What is a béarnaise sauce? An egg yolk, some shallots, some tarragon. But believe me, it requires years of practice for the results to be perfect."[51]

Several studies demonstrate the challenges of transferring tacit knowledge.[52] It's easier to collaborate when people deal in straightforward, well-documented, technical knowledge or clean and reliable market data. It's much harder to collaborate when people have to share novel technologies that are poorly understood, ambiguous market data, or intuitions about where markets might be going.

No Common Frame

People who do not know each other have no common frame—an understanding of each other's working habits, subtle ways of articulating something, a liking of each other, and an appreciation for each other's moods.

Lack of a common frame may not seem like a big deal, but it is. Consider the flip side—situations where there is a strong common frame between people who collaborate. Have you ever considered why there are long-lasting duos in sports (a coach and an athlete), in science (two scientists working together for nearly their entire careers), or in music (think Lennon and McCartney)?

Angelo Dundee coached the great boxer Muhammad Ali during his entire career and was Ali's corner man in all his fights. Kieran Mulvaney of ESPN wrote about the duo, "Theirs was a relationship that was founded on strong mutual respect that morphed into a deep and abiding friendship."[53] Dundee had developed a fine-grained understanding of how to treat Ali and how to improve his boxing. His approach was not to mold Ali but to "smooth out a lot of stuff." "The smoothing, though, had to be done in a particular way," Mulvaney wrote. "If he wanted Ali to jab, he wouldn't tell him to jab; he knew the boxer's ego wouldn't allow it. Instead, he started complimenting him on the way he was jabbing." Dundee had a deep understanding of Ali's way of taking input and working: "I made him feel like he innovated it. If I was the guy that gave him directions, he'd say, 'Hey, who's this midget to tell me what to do?' No, I never gave him a direct order."

Dundee and Ali worked well together because they had developed a strong common frame. Without it, people become strangers in the sense of lacking a deep understanding of how to work well together.

Weak Ties

People find it hard to transfer knowledge when they don't know each other well (a weak tie). They need strong ties—relationships where people talk often and have a close working association. Weak ties create havoc when people need to transfer tacit knowledge. That's what happened to some project teams at Hewlett-Packard in the 1990s: the teams wanted to transfer tacit and novel technologies from other divisions, but they had only weak ties to the engineers who knew the technologies.[54] They did not know how to work together and how to communicate subtle points, and they didn't share the same terminology and ways of phrasing problems. The result: some teams took 30 percent more time to finish when they had to transfer tacit knowledge with weak ties. Think about that: that's adding four months to a twelve-month project simply because people had only a weak tie between them.

The transfer barrier played hardly any role in the U.S. intelligence community before the 9/11 attacks. The knowledge that agents dealt in was by and large explicit—information about Mihdhar's whereabouts, for instance. Once someone shared information, the receiver would understand what that information meant ("al-Qaeda terrorist Mihdhar flew from Bangkok to Los Angeles on January 13, 2000" is highly explicit knowledge). Whether people understood the significance of this information and acted upon it is a different matter, but they understood its literal meaning.

From Barriers to Solutions

The first step in overcoming barriers is to accurately assess which ones occur in a situation. The second step is to tailor management solutions to each barrier.

Not All Situations Are Equal

Companies vary widely in their scores on the four barriers. In some companies, all the barriers are high. In a few others, no barriers are high. Most organizations experience a mix of barriers. For example, based on my assessment of the 9/11 intelligence situation, two barriers were huge: hoarding and search. The not-invented-here barrier played a limited role, and the transfer barrier was not important.

FIGURE 3-5

Which barriers are present in your company?

Step 1. Take a brief, subjective poll. Question: which barriers to collaboration are present in your organizational unit? Assess your unit from 1 (not at all) to 100 (to a large extent).

Barriers	Survey Question	Enter 1–100
Not-invented-here	1. Even when they need help, our employees are not willing to seek input from outside their organizational unit.	
	2. When faced with problems, employees in our unit strive to solve them by themselves without asking for help from outsiders.	
	3. There is a prevailing attitude in our unit that people ought to fix their own problems and not rely on help from outside the unit.	
	Total of responses to questions 1 to 3:	
Hoarding	4. Our people keep their expertise and information to themselves and do not want to share it across organizational units.	
	5. People in our unit are often reluctant to help colleagues in other parts of the organization.	
	6. Our employees seldom return phone calls and e-mails when asked for help from people outside our unit.	
	Total of responses to questions 4 to 6:	
Search problems	7. Our employees often complain about the difficulty they have locating colleagues in other units who possess the information and expertise they need.	
	8. Experts in our company are very difficult to find.	
	9. Our employees have great difficulties finding the documents and information they need in the company's databases and knowledge-management systems.	
	Total of responses to questions 7 to 9:	
Transfer problems	10. Our employees have not learned to work together effectively across organizational units to transfer tacit knowledge.	
	11. Employees from different organizational units are not used to working together and find it hard to do so.	
	12. Our employees find it difficult to work across units to transfer complex technologies and best practices.	
	Total of responses to questions 10 to 12:	

Step 2. Benchmark your score against a sample of 107 companies.

	Lowest quartile (lowest)	Second lowest quartile	Median	Second highest quartile	Highest quartile (highest)
Not-invented-here	3–105	106–159	160	161–200	201–300
Hoarding	3–60	61–99	100	101–140	141–300
Search problems	3–90	91–134	135	136–180	181–300
Transfer problems	3–110	111–167	168	169–210	211–300
Implication:	Barrier not a problem	Barrier might cause some problems	Barrier might cause problems	Barrier a problem	Barrier a big problem

Because organizations differ, leaders first need to identify the mix of barriers confronting them. What's the combination in your organization or unit? You can do a quick, subjective evaluation by answering the questions listed in figure 3-5 and then benchmark your score against the 107 companies that have done this exercise.

Tailoring Solutions

In the U.S. intelligence community, solutions need to be tailored to the two most important barriers: hoarding and search. Building extensive cross-agency networks or putting in place an IT system could help with search but not with hoarding (IT systems do not motivate people to share information). And changes in incentive systems—encouraging people to share information across agencies—would reduce hoarding barriers, but not search (which requires IT systems and networks). The upshot: to lower the two crucial barriers in the intelligence community, changes are needed in incentives (to lower the hoarding barrier) as well as networks (to lower the search barrier). That's tailoring solutions to specific problems.

Leaders who practice disciplined collaboration pick the right solution for the right barrier. The barrier-to-solution map, shown in table 3-1, illustrates which solutions are best for each barrier, and also which solutions won't work—the empty cells in the map.[55] Deploying a wrong solution to reduce a barrier is a waste of resources.

TABLE 3-1

The barrier-to-solution map

Pick a barrier and then read across to see which solutions fit best.

Barrier	Lever 1: Unification (chapter 4)	Lever 2: T-shaped management (chapter 5)	Lever 3: Nimble networks (chapter 6)
Not-invented-here	+++	+++	+
Hoarding	+++	+++	+
Search problems		+	+++
Transfer problems		+	+++

+++ = best solutions for a barrier + = modest effect

Notice that the first two barriers (not-invented-here and hoarding) concern motivational issues. The two barriers exist because people are not willing to collaborate. This means that management solutions must motivate people to collaborate. Two solutions do this:

- *Unify people:* Craft a unifying goal, state a core value of teamwork, and use the leadership pulpit to signal collaboration.

- *Cultivate T-shaped management:* Use recruitment, promotion, firing, and rewards to cultivate collaboration.

These solutions help select the right people—those who are motivated to collaborate in the first place—and change the attitude of others. Together, they reduce the not-invented-here and hoarding barriers.

In contrast, the other two barriers—search and transfer problems—concern people's abilities to collaborate well. Surmounting these two barriers has nothing to do with motivation and attitudes. A leader who preaches collaboration may motivate the troops but cannot by words alone help them locate experts. One solution is particularly potent to reduce search and transfer:[56]

- *Build nimble networks:* Encourage formation of the right kinds of cross-unit personal relationships to help search and reduce transfers problems.

———————————

The barrier-to-solution map is a road map for the next three chapters. Each chapter presents a solution to specific barriers. In chapter 4, I discuss how leaders can unify people. In chapter 5, I unpack the concept of T-shaped management. Then, in chapter 6, I describe how networks reduce the search and transfer barriers.

Chapter 3: Key Points

Spot the Four Barriers to Collaboration

- Modern management is the enemy of collaboration. Managers have installed extreme decentralization to foster entrepreneurship, individual freedom, and accountability. This is a great system that yields many benefits, but it is also hard to collaborate across a loose collection of units. The solution is not to centralize, but to spot barriers to collaboration among units and tear them down. That's a decentralized and yet coordinated model.

- Research shows that four barriers block collaboration among decentralized units.

  - Not-invented-here: People are not willing to seek input from others outside their unit.

  - Hoarding: People are not willing to provide information and help others when asked.

  - Search problems: People are not able to find information and people easily.

  - Transfer problems: People are not able to transfer complicated knowledge from one unit to another.

  The first two barriers are motivational problems—people don't want to collaborate. The latter two barriers are ability problems—people are not able to collaborate well.

- Different situations have different barriers. Leaders must first evaluate which barriers exist in their organization. Not doing so is the same as throwing darts in the dark; you have no idea what you're hitting.

- Different barriers require different solutions. No solution fits all situations. For example, installing an information system helps search but does not lower hoarding behaviors. Disciplined collaboration means first evaluating which barriers are present and then tailoring solutions to those barriers. This means that leaders have to be careful when they choose a mix of levers to implement disciplined collaboration. They need to fit their particular circumstance.

- Three levers need to be tailored to an organization's mix of barriers: unification mechanisms (detailed in chapter 4), T-shaped management (chapter 5), and networks (chapter 6).

PART TWO

Solutions

CHAPTER FOUR

Lever 1: Unify People

I N 1954, an unusual experiment happened in the United States, never to be repeated.[1] A colorful Turkish-born, Harvard-educated psychologist, Muzafer Sherif, stepped out of his usual role as professor and ran a summer camp in the Robbers Cave State Park in Oklahoma. He wanted to explore group behaviors and thought that a real-world experiment would offer better insight than some laboratory experiment on his university campus.

Sherif and four researchers—his psychologist wife and three doctoral students—recruited twenty-two eleven-year-old boys for a three-week summer camp.[2] The boys, who were not told that they were part of a giant psychological experiment, were broken into two groups called the Eagles and the Rattlers. They spent the first week of "camp" doing what kids usually do during summer camp in a beautiful nature preserve filled with lakes, forests, and campsites. The groups—separately—went on hikes, overnight trips, and canoe outings. They cooked together, swam, and performed skits around the campfire. By the end of the first week, the Rattlers had become a tight-knit group, and so had the Eagles. This was just what Sherif had intended—the formation of two independent and cohesive groups.

In the second week, the real experiment began. Shrewdly, the researchers induced conflict between the two groups. Camp staff announced a grand weeklong tournament between the two groups; the winner would be rewarded with a trophy, which had great appeal to the boys. Each team started practicing fervently for the upcoming competitions.

Then the games began. The first competition—a baseball game—
went to the jubilant Rattlers, who had shouted, "You're not Eagles,
you're pigeons!" In the second game, a tug-of-war, the Rattlers won
again, and the unhappy Eagles were left behind on the field wondering
what to do.[3] Upon leaving the field, an Eagle boy noticed a flag that the
Rattlers had proudly put up on the field and yelled that they should take
it down. Someone else cried out, "Let's burn it!" The boys promptly
burned the flag and hung the remnants back up on the pole.

When the Rattlers strode onto the field the next morning, they were
enraged about the burned flag. A Rattler grabbed the Eagle flag and ran
down the road, with several Eagles in hot pursuit. Meanwhile, another
Rattler seized an Eagle and held him in a wrestling hold, and a third
Rattler downed an Eagle in a fistfight. The adults had to jump in to
stop the fight. The next game of tug-of-war lasted forty-eight minutes—that is, twenty-two boys desperately pulling on the rope for
almost an hour to defeat the other group. The Eagles won.

A lot more was to come. That evening, the Rattlers, who had dark-
ened their faces and arms in true commando style, raided the Eagles'
cabin when the unsuspecting Eagles were fast asleep. The raiders turned
over beds and ripped the window screens. The next morning, while the
Rattlers ate breakfast in the canteen, the Eagles, armed with sticks and
bats, took revenge and raided the Rattlers' cabin, turning over beds and
messing up the place. Needless to say, the competition was fierce that
day, with the Rattlers winning two games and the Eagles one.

On the last day of the tournament, with the Rattlers behind by one
point and singing, "The enemy's coming," the Eagles prevailed and
were awarded the trophy.[4] As they ran off to celebrate, the Rattlers
again raided their cabin, savaging the beds and piling clothes into one
big heap. When the Eagles returned, a fistfight broke out, and the
adults had to jump into the fray and break it up again.

In the third week, Sherif and his fellow plotters started the third and
most intriguing part of the experiment. They now wanted to test
whether they could unite the warring groups. But how? They introduced a series of seven unifying goals that appealed highly to the boys,
but they could be achieved only if the boys worked together.

The professors made the water tank at camp "break down" by shutting off a valve and stuffing a sack in the faucet. Growing thirsty in the afternoon, the boys realized that they had to fix it to get water. Because the water was pumped from a reservoir via a long pipeline, searching for the problem required covering a large area, and that search had to be coordinated. All the boys volunteered; they searched together and eventually found the valve and the sack. Almost all of them gathered around the faucet to help fix it.

On an overnight hiking trip that followed, a staff member announced that he was driving down the road to get food for the boys. "The driver feigned great effort," Sherif noted. "The truck made all sorts of noises, but it just would not start."[5] Seeing that unless the truck started there would be no food, the boys began to help out. "Let's push it," one of the boys said. But it was heavy and required effort from more than one group. A Rattler said, "Twenty of us can." The boys proceeded to tie a rope to the back of the truck, and all twenty joined to pull hard.[6] As the boys chanted "Heave, heave" in rhythm, the truck "restarted" on the second try. The boys got their food, friendly talk and backslapping ensued, and four boys—two Eagles and two Rattlers—went to the pump and got water for each other.

Sherif and his colleagues introduced several more unifying goals over the next few days that dramatically lowered the animosity, turning hostility into friendliness. Around the campfire on the last evening, the groups took turn entertaining each other with skits and songs, and the majority of the boys suggested that they should return back home on one bus together (they had arrived in separate buses).

This astonishing experiment holds two profound lessons for leaders who want to unify a group. The first is that leaders can easily pit groups in their organization against each other and induce competition. What Sherif did was in fact benign: he divided the boys into clearly defined groups (Rattlers and Eagles). Like many executives overseeing organizational units, he created a modest level of rivalry between the groups, and that in turn took on a life of its own. Leaders can learn from this to beware how easily interunit rivalry can take hold and undermine collaboration.

The second lesson—and the key one for this chapter—is that leaders also have the power to unite separate groups by the actions they take. Leadership is, after all, ultimately about uniting people. In the Robbers Cave experiment, Sherif did this by creating unifying goals—that is, goals that both groups found appealing and that required both groups to pull together to achieve.

Just how does a leader unify groups so that they will collaborate with each other? Three fundamental *unification mechanisms* allow a leader to translate the lofty aspiration of unity into concrete measures: (1) creating a unifying goal, (2) inciting a common value of teamwork, and (3) speaking the language of collaboration. These mechanisms are effective in making people more willing to collaborate. They reduce the not-invented-here and hoarding barriers.

Create a Unifying Goal

On April 12, 1961, Americans were in shock. Yuri Gagarin became the first man in space that day, and the Soviet Union's dominance in space was made clear. Its Sputnik 1 spacecraft had also been the first to circle Earth on October 4, 1957. Now what should the United States do? President John F. Kennedy looked for a grand project that could prove U.S. leadership. In a memo to Vice President Lyndon B. Johnson, he asked, "Do we have a chance of beating the Soviets by putting a laboratory in space, or by a trip around the moon, or by a rocket to land on the moon, or by a rocket to go to the moon and back with a man?"[7] Johnson investigated the matter, and eight days later he wrote back that the Russians were ahead in several ways but when it came to manned trips around—or on to—the moon, "with a strong effort, the United States could conceivably be first in those two accomplishments by 1966 or 1967."[8]

As the Kennedy White House and the leaders of NASA debated, it became clear that landing a man on the moon was a challenge in which the Soviets didn't have an advantage. Kennedy quickly settled on this goal. Seven weeks after Gagarin had orbited Earth, on May 25, 1961,

Kennedy announced, "I believe that this nation should commit itself to achieving the goal, before this decade is out, of landing a man on the moon and returning him safely to Earth."

Kennedy's "man on the moon" is one of the best-known goals in the annals of leadership. But few people know about the fervent debates surrounding it, and not many people are aware of how the goal led scientists to make painful decisions in the name of unity.

On November 21, 1962, at an important White House meeting, President Kennedy gathered NASA head James Webb and several advisers to consider additional spending bills for the Apollo moon program. For Webb, the goal was preeminence in space: the Apollo moon program was clearly one important goal, but it wasn't the only one. For Kennedy, however, landing on the moon was the only goal. During the meeting, a heated exchange took place between Kennedy and Webb, as recorded in transcripts released thirty-nine years later:

President Kennedy: "Everything that we do ought to really be tied into getting onto the Moon ahead of the Russians."

James Webb: "Why can't it be tied to preeminence in space . . ."

President Kennedy: "I do think we ought get it, you know, really clear that the policy ought to be that this [landing on the moon] is the top-priority program of the Agency, and one of the two things, except for defense, the top priority of the United States government."

James Webb: "I'd like to have more time to talk about that because there is a wide public sentiment coming along in this country for preeminence in space."

President Kennedy: "If you're trying to prove preeminence, this is the way to prove preeminence . . . I think all these programs which contribute to the lunar program are . . . justified. Those that are not essential to the lunar program, that help contribute over a broad spectrum to our preeminence in space, are secondary."[9]

That was clear language. Landing a man on the moon was the number 1 space goal, and everything else in space was not as important. Webb got it.

The clear goal of landing a man on the moon also forged decisions that, had they not been made, could have wrecked the program. A crucial decision was to select the mode of entry to the moon—how to land a spacecraft on the moon without crashing and then get the astronauts back to Earth. Different parties proposed different modes: using a powerful rocket to send a spaceship directly to the moon (direct); starting by circling Earth and then catapulting a landing craft to the moon (Earth orbit); and circling the moon and sending in a small landing ship (lunar orbit).[10] This decision was fundamental, because it involved the basic approach for getting to the moon. Some people even suggested sending astronauts to the moon in a hurry and *then* working on figuring out how to get them back! At the outset, different organizations pushed different proposals, each wedded to a particular mode—a stance that could have ended in years of squabbling and derailed the whole enterprise.

The stage was set for rampant not-invented-here attitudes. The Marshall Space Flight Center, headed by Wernher von Braun, a towering figure in space exploration, had invested in one mode: the Earth orbit mode. "We have spent more time and effort at Marshall on studies of the Earth Orbit Rendezvous Mode (Tanking and Connecting Modes) than on any other mode," von Braun commented.[11] Both the Marshall Center and the other powerful NASA center, the Manned Spacecraft Center, were skeptical of the alternative ideas. In fact, one idea—the lunar orbit mode—had not been dreamed up by either the Marshall or the Manned Spacecraft Center, but by another agency.

But, looming large in the background was Kennedy's goal; it had to be done by the end of the decade. Putting aside different viewpoints, the various groups worked together to arrive at a decision. In a stunning reversal, von Braun and his team abandoned their quest for the Earth orbit mode and endorsed the lunar orbit idea. The Manned Spacecraft Center did the same. Von Braun stated that, when judged according to Kennedy's goal, the lunar orbit mode was more aligned with the goal: "We believe this program offers the highest confidence factor of successful accomplishment within this decade."

This story demonstrates the power of a unifying goal. Kennedy zoomed in on the goal of landing a man on the moon, and he relentlessly hammered the need to stick to it and not take on a bunch of other projects. This zealous pursuit led scientists to set aside their differing viewpoints and decide on an approach that could accomplish the goal in time. On July 24, 1969, eight years and two months after Kennedy's speech, Neil Armstrong and the rest of the crew returned from the moon and splashed safely into the Pacific Ocean. The goal was reached.

Why was Kennedy's goal so brilliant? Because it met the following four criteria for a compelling unifying goal (table 4-1 shows examples of unifying goals).[12]

Criterion 1: The Goal Must Create a Common Fate

A unifying goal has power only if all relevant groups need to pull together to make it a reality. Landing a man on the moon required the coordination of some 400,000 people, and this meant that, if one of the activities faltered, the whole thing could founder. Something as "mundane" as the Apollo space suits, for example, involved roughly 500 people working over several years to make space suits that could withstand the moon's searing 250-degree Fahrenheit heat in the sun and minus 250-degree chill in the shadows.[13] If the space suit malfunctioned, astronaut Neil Armstrong would have died.

Not all goals conjure common fates. Take Jack Welch's famous goal for General Electric when he became CEO: "Be no. 1 or 2 in every business globally."[14] This is a goal for each business unit, but not the whole corporation. It might have been a great objective for each unit, but it is not a common-fate goal.

During the 1990s, Airbus, the European aircraft maker, had one unofficial common-fate goal: "Beat Boeing."[15] This entailed a simple metric: the total number of new commercial aircraft orders received in a year.[16] In the beginning of the 1990s, Boeing had handily beaten Airbus in orders (273 versus 101 orders), so Airbus had a long way to go.

But during the 1990s, Airbus divisions pulled together and started to close in. By 1999, they passed Boeing for the first time, counting 476 orders against Boeing's 355. It was a great accomplishment. And Airbus maintained the number 1 spot from 2001 through 2005. The unifying

TABLE 4-1

Examples of unifying goals

Unifying goal	Common fate?	Simple and concrete?	Stir passion?	Competition outside?	Comments
Nissan: "Nissan 180"* 1 = one million more cars sold 8 = 8 percent operating margin 0 = zero net automotive debt	Yes	Yes	Probably	Yes	CEO Carlos Ghosn launched these goals in 2002, to be reached in three years.
Scandinavian Airlines: "To become the best airline in the world for the frequent business traveler."**	Yes	Yes	Yes	Yes	"Business traveler" means tourist segment is out (so not completely unifying). But this was a galvanizing goal for the company.
Morgan Stanley: "Our goal is to be world's best investment bank and the Firm of choice for our clients, our people, and our shareholders."†	Yes, for investment banking	Simple but not very concrete	A bit bland	Yes	The word *best* is not defined, and it can mean different things to different people (number 1 in market share, profitability, quality of advice . . . ?)
SAP: "We will define and establish undisputed leadership in the emerging market for business process platform solutions, accelerate business innovation powered by IT for firms and industries worldwide and thus contribute to economic development on a grand scale."	Yes	No	Not clear	Yes	Clearly unifies the company; they can get there only by working across functions and geography. But, at thirty-seven words, this statement is difficult to remember.

*See David Magee, *Turnaround: How Carlos Ghosn Rescued Nissan* (New York: Collins Business, 2003).

***Jan Carlzon: CEO at SAS (A)," Christopher Bartlett, Kenton Elderkin, and Barbara Feinberg, Case 9-392-149 (Boston: Harvard Business School, 1992).

†M. Diane Burton, Thomas DeLong, and Katherine Lawrence, "Morgan Stanley: Becoming a One-Firm Firm," Case 9-400-043 (Boston: Harvard Business School, 1999).

goal kept Airbus clearly focused. Beating Boeing became more important than squabbling over departmental goals, at least for a while.[17]

The greatest benefit of a common-fate goal is that it elevates the aspirations of people to something bigger than parochial group goals.

Criterion 2: The Goal Must Be Simple and Concrete

President Kennedy wanted to demonstrate U.S. world leadership, which could be manifested by preeminence in space. So why did he not just state that the United States should become preeminent in space? Preeminence could be shown in a variety of ways—say, in the number of satellites launched—but it wouldn't have had the same clear message. Kennedy wanted a simple, compelling goal, which for him meant landing a man on the moon. As he told James Webb, "That's the dramatic evidence that we're preeminent in space."[18]

Kennedy's moon goal is so memorable—so captivating—precisely because it is simple and concrete: every U.S. citizen could grasp it (see figure 4-1). It didn't need further explanation. "Preeminent in space" needs another page of explanation. And notice that Kennedy went from the abstract (preeminence) to the concrete (land a man on the moon), and from the complex (a variety of space initiatives) to something simple (land a man on the moon and get him back safely to Earth). Clutter is

FIGURE 4-1

From lofty aspirations to a concrete unifying goal

How President Kennedy went from the main objective of demonstrating U.S. world leadership to landing a man on the moon.

U.S. world leadership	=>	Preeminent in space	=>	Land a man on the moon
Abstract		●————————————▶		Concrete
Complex		●————————————▶		Simple
Many interpretations		●————————————▶		One interpretation
Difficult to measure		●————————————▶		Measurable

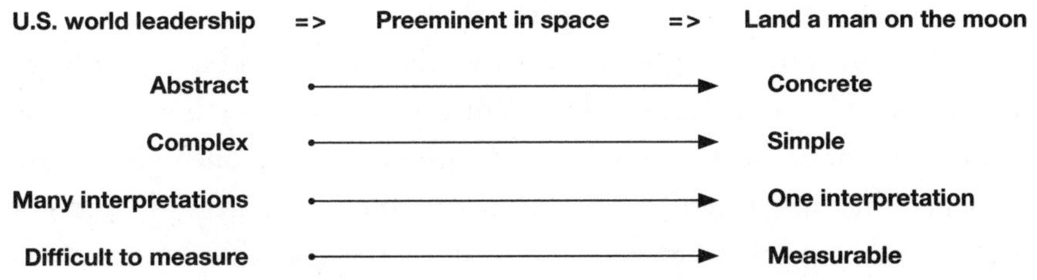

used to hide and hedge. Simplicity means stripping away clutter. One simple phrase ("land a man on the moon") beats many long sentences.

But, there is a problem with simplicity. Most leaders, when they try to be simple, turn out vague and abstract goals, not concrete ones. Once I was doing a seminar with a group of top executives from a company whose stated goal was to be "the world's premier provider" in its industry. I went around the table and asked, "Okay, what is your definition of 'premier'?" The first person said "biggest in revenues," another said "most reliable service provider," and someone else said "largest market coverage." There were at least three different interpretations in the top two hundred group of a very large company. Now imagine the interpretations by the next top one thousand employees, not to mention the next ten thousand!

Leaders who state a simple and concrete goal will do better, because people will know what it means. It is not open to interpretation. It also is measurable: worlds like *premier, preeminence,* and *superior* are open to many interpretations and hard to measure. In contrast, "bringing him safely back to Earth" is measurable. Did the astronauts come back safely? Yes, they did. Check.

Criterion 3: The Goal Must Stir Passion

"One of the things we had was a common goal," recounted Charlie Mars, who was a project engineer working on the lunar module at NASA. "We're going to go to the moon! We're putting a man on the moon! And that so captured our imagination, and our emotion, that we didn't want to go home at night. We just wanted to keep going, and we couldn't wait to get up and get back at work in the morning."[19]

Powerful unifying goals stir passion and inspire. They appeal to people's hearts and not only their minds.

So what inspires people? A worthwhile pursuit, such as landing a man on the moon, obviously does. But other things, such as achieving competence or doing a good job, also inspire people. In one poll of 2,509 managers in the United States, by far the most managers (45 percent) picked "knowing you did your job well" as the goal that got them out of bed in the morning.[20] Unifying goals need not appeal to a higher purpose (such as helping humankind) or noble pursuits (landing a man on the moon) to be inspiring. Leaders who appeal to high performance and excellence can also stir passion among people.

What about competition? "Competition is the thing that drives everybody to do their very best work," notes Steve Ballmer, Microsoft CEO. "I start with the fundamental premise that says competition is a great thing."[21] There's no doubt that the excitement of competing against others fires people up. It's a great inspiration. The question is, though, competing against whom?

Criterion 4: The Goal Must Put Competition on the Outside

Few things unite people better than having a common enemy. Beating Boeing galvanized the Airbus organization. One Airbus engineer told me, "We were so focused, so energized, it was the key thing we aimed for." The beauty of the goal was that it tapped in to competition as a motivator, and yet it placed the target of competition—Boeing—on the outside of the company.

This example shows something very important: the target of competition should be outside the company, not inside.[22] This important point has not been lost on Anne Mulcahy, CEO of Xerox. "Competition gives you a focus," she says. "Lots of times you need a mission, a bulls-eye that keeps you focused, and competition can do that. A passion for winning when it's focused on a strong competitor provides a lot of incentive and passion and pride for people."[23] That bull's-eye is a competitor on the outside, not fellow workers on the inside. Leaders can have it both ways: people are juiced up because they compete, but the company incurs fewer negatives by not having employees compete against one another.

Many executives blunder by stoking competition among employees—for example, by instilling rivalry between salespeople. In a special issue devoted to competition, *BusinessWeek* wrote, "Everyone likes to win. Beneath all the talk about teamwork and balance, all the books on being kind and cultivating emotional intelligence, people still crave to be the best."[24] The problem with this argument is that teamwork and "being best" are seen as mutually exclusive. But they are not. People can still crave to win, to be the best, but they can do so as part of a team that wins against an outside competitor. They unite in competing against an external force.

Leaders who practice disciplined collaboration get this straight: collaboration does not replace competition. They are not opposing forces. Competition should be directed to the outside. Collaboration on the inside, competition on the outside.

This separation has become a bit more complicated in recent years, because companies that are fierce competitors in one arena may collaborate in another. It's a bit difficult to fire up people at Airbus to "beat Boeing" if some of the same people also partner with Boeing.

Microsoft and German software giant SAP are in that situation. They are ferocious competitors in selling software to small businesses, and yet they collaborate on a joint product called Duet. Duet allows people to import data from SAP's software (which runs accounting information in many companies) into Microsoft's Excel spreadsheets. Keeping the balance between being enemies and being friends is not easy. It means that grand enemy goals ("Beat the Soviets," "Beat Boeing") don't work as unifying goals. For SAP's part, there is no grand "Beat Microsoft" goal that unifies all of SAP. As co-CEO Henning Kagermann put it, "Our larger customers don't tolerate vendors acting like children and fighting among themselves. There's a point where you step back from being too competitive."[25]

Create a Core Value of Teamwork

It was a fall day in Miami, and I was about to step on stage to address the top one hundred bankers in a large investment bank. I was quite nervous, because I feared the topic of my talk would be explosive. I was a professor at Harvard Business School at the time, and I had been asked to lead the group in a discussion of a case—themselves. To this end, the organizers had asked the hotel to build a large-scale blackboard on stage. So here I was on a stage in a fancy hotel in Miami, chalk in hand, to talk core values to a group of bankers who presumably cared more about money than soft stuff like values.

But I knew the topic was an attention-grabber. It was not because the bankers cared about the precise wording in a value statement. They cared deeply about two paradoxical beliefs about success. I started the discussion by asking, "Let's get some of your values up on the board. What are they?" A hand shot up: "Liberty."

"What do you mean?" I asked.

"We value the freedom to create our own success, that each of us do what is necessary to please our client." "Yeah," continued another, "liberty and freedom, that's what we stand for, that's why I am here." Heads nodded across the room.

I duly recorded the words *liberty* and *freedom* on the upper-right corner of the blackboard. Then I asked, "What else?" A confident-looking man to my left in the room answered in a loud but articulate way: "I see teamwork and cooperation as the foundation for our future success. If we don't help each other, we will not win deals."

Up went the words *teamwork* and *cooperation.* And then I lit the fire for the day: "Are these two sets of core values in conflict with each other?"

I might just have stood back and let the ensuing heated discussion run its course, but I had to work hard to contain the fire I had ignited. The arguments flew: "You bet they are in conflict; we have big problems because we have a bunch of selfish people who are more concerned about themselves than the franchise," one banker said. "Of course we have to stand for teamwork," another retorted. "How can we be successful if we don't return each other's phone calls?" Yet another argued, "I don't want to be part of a cult." "Liberty creates entrepreneurship and success."

As the discussion unfolded, I realized that there were very different people in the room; some had a core belief in the value of teamwork, but others fundamentally believed in the idea of individual liberty and freedom. These opposing beliefs were now coming out in the open and clashing big time.

Was one camp right and the other wrong? I don't think so. Companies can be successful by holding any of these values. But to create disciplined collaboration, both values are important. It is the combination of teamwork *and* individual ownership that leads to disciplined collaboration: without the value of teamwork, it is hard to collaborate. Without the value of individual ownership, people shirk.

What does teamwork really mean? It means working with others to accomplish a goal. People can work as part of a small team in which membership is clearly defined, or as part of a loose coalition of people from different parts of the company getting together briefly to accomplish a job (much collaboration is that way). As a core value, teamwork means that people believe that working with others is important and that they are willing to be part of teams and commit to common goals.

Leaders need to give voice to the value of teamwork. They need to pen it in a values statement. They need to write it up in a list of required leadership competencies (see table 4-2 for examples). But as they preach teamwork, they need to beware of three sins.

Sin Number 1: Small Teamwork Kills Collaboration

When leaders preach teamwork, they may just get what they ask for—the wrong kind of teamwork. When managers start instilling teamwork in their own units and not across the rest of the company, it leads to

TABLE 4-2

The value of teamwork

Examples of teamwork values, leadership competencies, and business principles

Morgan Stanley (value statement)	"We distinguish ourselves by creating an environment that fosters teamwork."*
SAP (leadership competencies)	"Ensure involvement of the appropriate people inside SAP (across roles, departments, and locations) to accomplish goals."
Goldman Sachs (business principles)	"We stress teamwork in everything we do. While individual creativity is always encouraged, we have found that team effort often produces the best results."***

*M. Diane Burton, Thomas DeLong, and Katherine Lawrence, Morgan Stanley: Becoming a One-Firm Firm," Case 9-400-043, (Boston; Harvard Business School, 1999).

**From Goldman Sachs business principle number 8 (http://www2.goldmansachs.com/our-firm/about us/business-principles.html).

pockets of local teamwork but not companywide collaboration. The company becomes "teamy" but not collaborative. This is precisely what happened in Sherif's experiment: he instilled great teamwork *within* the Rattler and Eagle groups, but no collaboration across them (not until he introduced unifying goals).

To combat this danger, leaders need to preach that teamwork means "teaming across the company." SAP has a statement that makes this clear. It demands that managers "ensure involvement of the appropriate people inside SAP (across roles, departments, and locations) to accomplish goals."

Sin Number 2: Everybody Do Teamwork Now (Except Those of Us at the Top)

When leaders give a sermon about the value of teamwork to the troops, and then ignore it themselves, they are not promoting collaboration. In one large company that was organized according to functions, managers needed to collaborate across product development, sales, marketing, and service. The top leaders duly preached the importance of teamwork. But there was a great deal of frustration among lower-level managers. "I spend endless amounts of time trying to work with product development, but to no avail," complained a sales manager in the United States. It turned out that a big part of the problem was in the top team; top executives didn't work together well. When conflicts escalated to the very top, they were not easily resolved, and people further down in the company knew this. The top team did not demonstrate the value of teamwork, leaving people in the company wondering whether it meant anything at all.

To unite a company, the top team needs to be united, too.[26] Top executives need to practice the value of teamwork that they preach.

John Mack, when he took over Morgan Stanley in the early 1990s, set out to cultivate teamwork in the company. To demonstrate that this included everyone, he applied the same standard to the top team—the operating committee. Tom DeLong, chief development officer for the firm at the time and now a professor at Harvard Business School, observed a clear change at the top: "Operating Committee members who normally did not share the important knowledge of their divisions realized that at the end of the year they would be evaluating one another. All of a sudden they began to share more information, knowing the consequences at year-end for their evaluations if they didn't."[27]

Sin Number 3: Teamwork Becomes the Point of It All

Teamwork, when practiced incorrectly, becomes the sole purpose: "The leader says we need to do teamwork, so we better do teamwork, all the time." People's judgment about when to work in teams—and when not to—gets corrupted by a norm that says, "You should do teamwork." As a result, people work in teams when they shouldn't, as when there is no compelling reason to team up (recall the point from chapter 2 of having a crystal-clear business case before starting a collaboration project).

The idea that teamwork means "teamwork all the time" works like a slow-moving disease. Little by little, people do more in teams, to the point that they start taking the practice for granted. They get into the office in the morning, and at 9 a.m., their shoes walk them to the conference room for a team meeting. When Steve Bennett took over as CEO of Intuit in 2000, he found a consensus-oriented culture with lots of teamwork. One day early in his tenure, he was walking around the halls and came across a team meeting with nearly thirty employees. He dropped in on the conversation and asked the attendees the purpose of the meeting. No one could give him a clear answer. Then he asked why everyone attended, and he was told, "I might miss something if I skip it." Apparently quite a few people had simply gone to the meeting because they were included on the invitation list. Seeing a chance to put more discipline into teamworking, Bennett replied, "Take a chance."[28]

Leaders who practice disciplined collaboration make a clear link between teamwork and performance. The point of teamwork is not teamwork but better results.

Create a Language of Collaboration

Students at Stanford University once undertook an experiment that involved a game called *the community game*. It's simple. In the first round, you choose to *cooperate* with the other player—let's call him

Peter—or *defect* from him (that is, compete against him). Peter makes the same choice. Neither player knows the other's decision before the outcome of the first round. If you both choose to cooperate, you both earn $40, as shown in figure 4-2.

As you can see, your payoff is best ($80) if you decide to defect and Peter decides to cooperate. But if you decide to cooperate and Peter decides to defect, you lose $20.

Let's play it for seven successive rounds. The goal is to earn the most money after round 7. After the first round, you will know what Peter chose, and he will know what you chose.

For the *first* round, which choice will you make—to cooperate or defect?

In a study running this experiment on Stanford students, Stanford professor Lee Ross and his colleagues found that 70 percent of students chose to cooperate, and 30 percent chose to defect.[29] Wow! That's a lot of cooperation!

You may recognize this game. It's a version of the famous prisoner's dilemma game that economists often use. But this is not the interesting story here. With another group of students, Ross and his colleagues played the same game, but now they named it the Wall Street game. That's it. Simply changing the name made a huge difference. In this group, only 30 percent of students chose to cooperate, while a whopping 70 percent chose to defect. That's the exact opposite!

FIGURE 4-2

Choices

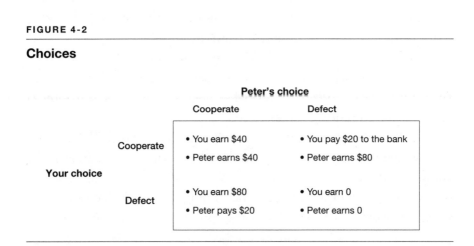

		Peter's choice	
		Cooperate	Defect
Your choice	Cooperate	• You earn $40 • Peter earns $40	• You pay $20 to the bank • Peter earns $80
	Defect	• You earn $80 • Peter pays $20	• You earn 0 • Peter earns 0

Think about this startling result. People chose a different behavior just because the game was called something different. When it was called "the community game," giving the impression that it was about communal values, such as cooperation, 70 percent chose to cooperate. When it became "the Wall Street game," suggesting market competition, 70 percent chose to compete.[30] The implication? The language a leader chooses matters a great deal in shaping behavior.

In a fascinating article, two Stanford University professors—Jeffrey Pfeffer and Bob Sutton—along with their colleague Fabrizio Ferraro, forcefully argued that the language of management has a sneaky tendency: it *becomes* true even if it isn't true at the outset.[31] To show this, they singled out a key assumption in economics: that people act according to their own self-interest. This is an assumption made by economics about how people behave. But is it true? Well, it *becomes* true: if you tell people that this is how the world works and how people should behave, then people start thinking and acting that way. They become self-interested.

In one study, college students were asked whether they thought it was appropriate for individuals to act in their self-interest.[32] Those students then took a course in economics, hearing about the virtue of self-interest. After they finished the course, they were asked again. The students now thought it was *more* appropriate to act in self-interest. The course had made them believe more in self-interest. An assumption—words—had shaped their beliefs. Thousands upon thousands of managers have taken courses in economics. We may just know what they believe about self-interest—and how they act. Words, language, and management theory shape behaviors—and become "the truth" as a result.

This is scary. How can we be that gullible and bendable? But it's a great tool for leaders. They can use language as a powerful tool for cultivating collaboration. After all, what goes for spreading self-interest also goes for promoting collaboration.

In 2006, when Henrik Madsen took over as CEO of DNV, the risk management services company described in chapter 2, he inherited a company where business units and country offices had become spread out, something he was dead set on changing. "I would like us to come together again after a period of being spread out. I want our leaders to think about the whole DNV and not just their own areas," he observed.[33] Madsen had a clear idea about what needed to be done and used his new pulpit to preach the language of collaboration, traveling to many of DNV's three hundred offices in one hundred countries, from Rio de Janeiro to Caracas to Houston to Beijing to Jeddah to London. "Every time I am talking, I challenge people: 'How can you help your colleagues?' We want people who can deliver their own results and collaborate across the organization when needed; I talk about this all the time." By his own estimate, Madsen spent about 20 percent of his time and effort promoting collaboration. That involved spending time on it in nearly every meeting, including meetings with customers. This relentless message—repeated hundred of times by Madsen and his top team—took hold. People got it.

Overdoing Unification

Leaders who create a compelling unifying goal, infuse a core value of teamwork, and talk the talk of collaboration inspire unity, allowing people to see the whole and not just their part. They become more willing to collaborate. The not-invented-here and hoarding barriers break down.

That's the good news. But there is a dark side to all this. Unification runs the risk of absolving the individual of responsibility. People can hide behind a unifying goal. They can participate in teams without pulling their weight. And they can interpret all the talk about collaboration as an excuse not to do their share.

To combat this danger, leaders practicing disciplined collaboration complement unification mechanisms with individual accountability mechanisms, as shown in table 4-3. They need to match unifying goals with individual goals, a value of teamwork with a value of individual responsibility, and the language of collaboration with the language of accountability (these issues are discussed in more detail in chapter 7). That's disciplined collaboration.

Leaders cannot move people by words alone. Words about goals, teamwork, and collaboration are crucial, but, by themselves, they can go

TABLE 4-3

Putting discipline into unification

To practice disciplined collaboration, leaders need to balance unification with individual accountability.

	Unification	Balanced with individual accountability
Goals	Unifying goal	Individual goals
Values	Teamwork	Individual responsibility
Language	Language of collaboration	Language of accountability

only so far. They need to be translated into action. That means implementing them in rules governing how people will be recruited, rewarded, promoted, and fired. Leaders need to cultivate T-shaped management, as discussed in chapter 5.

Chapter 4: Key Points

Lever 1: Unify People

- Leaders who practice disciplined collaboration translate their collaborative aspirations into concrete unification mechanisms: a unifying goal, a value of teamwork, and a language of collaboration.

- Leaders must craft a compelling unifying goal that makes people commit to a cause greater than their own individual goals. A crafty common goal meets four tests: it must create a common fate; it must be simple and concrete; it must stir passion; and it must place competition on the outside.

- Competition and collaboration are not opposites. Rather, these two powerful forces complement each other. But leaders must pair competition on the outside of the company with collaboration on the inside. People who unite to compete against a common foe are juiced up by competing and by collaborating.

- To unify people, leaders also need to create and demonstrate a value of teamwork. They need to articulate it and show it by practicing teamwork in their own top team. Teamwork means not only teaming within one's own group but also collaborating across units.

- A leader's language of collaboration sends a powerful signal. Leaders who talk competition will get competition (even among employees). Leaders who talk collaboration will get more collaboration. Leaders who talk "collaborate for results" will get more collaboration that yields results.

- Leaders can overdo unification. People stop being accountable. To temper this, leaders must balance unifying goals with individual goals, a value of teamwork with a value of individual responsibility, and the language of collaboration with the language of accountability. That's putting discipline into unification.

CHAPTER FIVE

Lever 2: Cultivate T-Shaped Management

No Lone Stars, Please

HERE'S A TOUGH DECISION confronting a leader. Paul Nasr, a senior banker at Morgan Stanley, had to decide whether to put his star performer, Rob Parson, up for promotion for the coveted position of managing director. This was a senior role that came with lots of money and prestige, so it was a big deal for both Morgan Stanley and Parson. As described in a best-selling Harvard Business School case by Professor Diane Burton, it's a hard decision because two criteria clash.[1]

On the one hand, Rob Parson was a star producer; over the past two years he had brought in valuable clients and built his product line: "Prior to Parson, the firm had been ranked tenth with a market share of 2 percent," writes Burton. "Now Morgan Stanley held the third rank position with a market share of 12.2 percent."[2]

Nasr himself had wonderful words for Rob Parson: "His clients love him. Every time they come to New York from anywhere around the world, they want to take him to dinner," Nasr remarked. "He is unique in his drive. He is unique in his pursuit of business. He is unique in his ambition. His knowledge of markets is excellent and he connects well with his clients."[3]

The annual performance review, which solicited comments by bosses and colleagues, also heaped praise on his performance: "Rob is a self-starter who is unusually aggressive in pursuing the business," read one comment. "He has made a big difference with several clients."[4]

It should have been an easy call: promote. The problem was, Parson was not a team player. "Rob goes from point A to point B within the time frame that the client has imposed, fulfills the client's demands, but in the meantime has broken every rule within Morgan Stanley to get there," Nasr explained. "So, people say, 'Wow, this guy is not following procedure. We work as a community, not individually.'"

"He has created a hostile environment around him," Nasr continued. "The syndicate guys are not happy with him basically questioning their prices. The traders are not happy with him questioning their knowledge of the markets."[5]

Comments from bosses and peers in the performance review reflected this second side of the assessment, which was as harsh as the praise was high:

"Lack of team player skills."

"Very difficult to work for or with."

"He'll have to learn to develop ability for teamwork."

"Sometimes, it is difficult to get a response."[6]

These were pretty awful statements, although Parson was not all bad in working with others; he had, for instance, helped cross-selling by introducing new products to his clients.

Professor Burton comments, "You come away with an impression of him as someone who wanted to try to fit in the culture, but didn't know how. Intolerant and impatient, he had difficulty delegating and collaborating, both of which were increasingly important skills for success at Morgan Stanley, but very difficult to learn in a vacuum."[7]

But shouldn't outstanding individual financial performance trump any concerns about teamwork? Not at Morgan Stanley, which had made teamwork a big deal. Two years earlier, Morgan Stanley's boss,

John Mack, had been troubled that fiefdoms prevented the firm from succeeding. As a result, he had launched an all-out effort to ensure that collaboration permeated the firm. His goal was to create a "One-Firm Firm."[8] To realize this goal, Mack had articulated a value of teamwork: "We distinguish ourselves by creating an environment that fosters teamwork." Recognizing that expressing the value was not enough, Mack put teeth behind it and rolled out a 360-degree performance appraisal, where "team player skills" and "contributions to MS [Morgan Stanley]" became new performance criteria. It was within this context that Parson's case came up.

If you were Nasr, would you put Parson up for promotion?

Lone Stars and Butterflies

When I pose this question in my executive education seminars, many managers say, "No way. He's ruining the culture of teamwork." Other people object. "He's needed, he is bringing in the deals," they argue. "You can't just let him go, and he will walk if he doesn't get promoted." Then I ask the question, "Would he get promoted in *your* company?" Even among those dumping on him, the answer most often is, "Yes, he would get promoted. We need the revenues, and leaders look the other way as long as the numbers are there."

The problem with Rob Parson is that he is a *lone star*. He delivers on his numbers big time, but several of his behaviors run counter to the teamwork that the firm is trying to install.[9]

Leaders cannot build a collaborative company with lone stars. Sure, in companies where individual performance reigns and where company performance is only the sum of individual performances, leaders benefit from having many lone stars. This is true for sales organizations where making the sale is an individual affair. But if executives want achievers who work across the organization, lone stars are not the right kind of star. Companies are better off cultivating another kind of star, those who excel at T-shaped management: people who simultaneously deliver results in their own job (the vertical part of the "T") *and* deliver results by collaborating across the company (the horizontal part of the "T").[10] They stand out from lone stars because they can perform two things well, and not just one.

T-shaped managers also differ from *butterflies:* people who work well across the company but who fail to do well in their own jobs. Butterflies are team players who flit from place to place and who willingly jet around the world to participate in committees, join seminars, and sit on task forces. They show up everywhere, while their own jobs suffer. Their individual performance numbers end up looking poor, the opposite of Parson's. Like lone stars, they can do only a single thing well (see figure 5-1).

Leaders who practice disciplined collaboration get rid of both lone stars and butterflies, either by firing them or transforming them into T-shaped managers. In 2000, Steve Bennett took over as CEO of California-based Intuit, then a five-thousand-person maker of tax and accounting software. He embarked on a process to transform the company from a highly siloed and entrepreneurial culture into a more collaborative organization.[11]

FIGURE 5-1

Cultivate T-shaped management

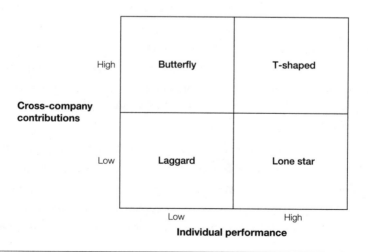

To implement his plan, Bennett followed a two-pronged change program, on one hand focusing on setting individual goals and holding people accountable and, on the other hand, fostering collaboration among product lines and functions. Bennett sought to cultivate T-shaped management and rejected people who worked only within their units or those who collaborated only, lacking a focus on performance: "In the old Intuit, we had some lone stars, and we had some people who collaborated too much," he noted. "We need to be in the middle."[12] During this process, many employees left or were let go, leaving fewer lone stars and butterflies and more T-shaped managers.

The idea of cultivating T-shaped management puts the whole business of "the war for talent" in a new light.[13] The idea is not to attract or develop anyone who is a star. It's a misplaced focus. The war for talent should not be about stars of all kinds but about T-shaped stars.

T-Shaped Management: The Power of Two Performances

To get an idea of what T-shaped management involves, let's take a look at an executive who practiced it well.[14] Soon after BP merged with Amoco, David Nagel was appointed general manager of BP's gas business unit in Egypt. Like all BP business unit managers, Nagel has a two-part job description. He is effectively CEO of his business unit, with responsibility for profitability, sales, costs, and capital expenses. There is no ambiguity here; he has signed on to deliver these numbers, and he'd better. This is the vertical part of the T—managing the individual business unit and communicating up the hierarchy.

At the same time, Nagel is expected to engage in a variety of cross-unit collaboration activities, which consume 15 to 20 percent of his time. That's the horizontal part of the T.

Nagel engages in four cross-unit activities. First, he collaborates in a cross-unit group comprising his business unit and seven others throughout the Mediterranean and Atlantic regions; like his, these units are focused on increasing gas production. The group does not have a boss but consists of the general managers of the units. They meet to coordinate work and decide on key issues common to all. In one instance, the group projected that it was likely to fall about 3 percent short of its goal for the year. Through intense discussions over the next two meetings, the group determined which business units were in the best position to close that gap.

Second, Nagel connects people from different parts of the company. For instance, he may get a call from a BP engineer seeking the name of an Amoco engineer who could offer advice in an area in which Amoco was known to have particular strengths.

Third, Nagel gives advice to other business units when asked. In one year, for example, he and his managers were involved in roughly twenty peer assists where people in his unit worked on projects and issues in other BP units. Nagel was personally involved in three of them.

Fourth, he takes advice from other units. In one year, his business unit benefited from roughly ten peer assists, in which people came from around the world to offer specific ideas on such issues as his unit's marketing plan. Sometimes the help comes more informally. Shortly after the merger with Amoco, for instance, an engineer in Nagel's unit tapped in to Nagel's network of BP contacts and determined within several days that the productivity of a particular type of well being drilled in Egypt could be tested without flaring it—that is, without opening it up and burning off gas. This technique allowed speedy evaluation of the well.

To ensure that collaboration doesn't undermine the goal of outstanding unit performance, Nagel must carefully manage his time (see figure 5-2). This means that he scrutinizes every effort to make sure it will improve performance. "We've tried to eliminate the peer group meetings that are held just for the purpose of saying, 'We had a peer group meeting,'" Nagel says. The dual demands of T-shaped management have also required him to delegate some business-unit responsibilities, particularly gas exploration and production, to two trusted lieutenants. That frees him for tasks extending beyond his business unit.

Nagel has been able to perform well in both dimensions: delivering financial performance for the gas business unit in Egypt and contributing across the company. That is, he delivers two performances.

T-shaped management as practiced by Nagel is especially powerful in obliterating two barriers to collaboration. T-shaped managers are

FIGURE 5-2

A T-Shaped Workweek

A typical workweek for David Nagel, BP's gas business unit head in Egypt, shows how he balances his vertical (business unit) and horizontal (knowledge-sharing) responsibilities. (The workweek in Cairo runs from Sunday through Thursday.)

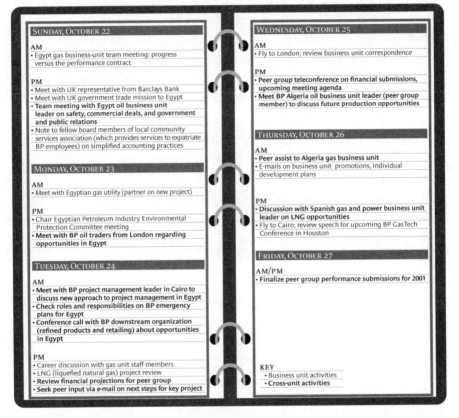

SUNDAY, OCTOBER 22

AM
• Egypt gas business-unit team meeting: progress versus the performance contract

PM
• Meet with UK representative from Barclays Bank
• Meet with UK government trade mission to Egypt
• **Team meeting with Egypt oil business unit leader on safety, commercial deals, and government and public relations**
• Note to fellow board members of local community services association (which provides services to expatriate BP employees) on simplified accounting practices

MONDAY, OCTOBER 23

AM
• Meet with Egyptian gas utility (partner on new project)

PM
• Chair Egyptian Petroleum Industry Environmental Protection Committee meeting
• **Meet with BP oil traders from London regarding opportunities in Egypt**

TUESDAY, OCTOBER 24

AM
• **Meet with BP project management leader in Cairo to discuss new approach to project management in Egypt**
• **Check roles and responsibilities on BP emergency plans for Egypt**
• **Conference call with BP downstream organization (refined products and retailing) about opportunities in Egypt**

PM
• Career discussion with gas unit staff members
• LNG (liquefied natural gas) project review
• **Review financial projections for peer group**
• **Seek peer input via e-mail on next steps for key project**

WEDNESDAY, OCTOBER 25

AM
• Fly to London; review business unit correspondence

PM
• **Peer group teleconference on financial submissions, upcoming meeting agenda**
• **Meet BP Algeria oil business unit leader (peer group member) to discuss future production opportunities**

THURSDAY, OCTOBER 26

AM
• **Peer assist to Algeria gas business unit**
• E-mails on business unit promotions, individual development plans

PM
• **Discussion with Spanish gas and power business unit leader on LNG opportunities**
• Fly to Cairo; review speech for upcoming BP GasTech Conference in Houston

FRIDAY, OCTOBER 27

AM/PM
• **Finalize peer group performance submissions for 2001**

KEY
• Business unit activities
• **Cross-unit activities**

Source: Reproduced from Morten T. Hansen and Belko von Oetinger, "Introducing T-shaped Managers: Knowledge Management's Next Generation," *Harvard Business Review* (March–April 2001).
Nagel's knowledge-sharing tasks are shown in boldface type.

willing to request input from others if needed (Nagel's unit requested ten peer assists from other units). In doing so, they overcome the not-invented-here barrier. And T-shaped managers are also willing to provide help to others (Nagel's unit provided twenty peer assists, with Nagel himself doing three). In this way, T-shaped managers overcome the hoarding barrier.

How to Expand T-Shaped Management in Your Organization

Steven Kerr, former chief learning officer at General Electric, wrote a famous article with the title "On the Folly of Rewarding A, While Hoping for B."[15] He observed that there was often an inconsistency between the behaviors that leaders desired in people and the reward system that the same leaders put in place—for example, by rewarding individual performance while hoping for teamwork. Similarly, it does not work for leaders to reward individual performance while hoping for T-shaped performance (something like, "rewarding I, hoping for T"). To cultivate T-shaped behaviors, leaders need to implement two-sided performance management: they need to reward people for individual results *and* for contributions to other units.

Two fundamental ways of growing the pool of T-shaped managers exist: *selection and change* (see table 5-1). Some leaders believe that people can't really change, so they focus on selecting the right kinds

TABLE 5-1

Two ways to enlarge the pool of T-shaped managers

	Select people	Get people to change
Belief	People don't easily change, if at all, so let's pick those who already exhibit T-shaped behaviors.	People *can* change to T-shaped behaviors if properly stimulated and helped.
Promotion (and firing)	Big effect: promote T-shaped, not others. Fire lone stars and butterflies.	Big effect: use T-shaped promotion criteria as a carrot for people to change their behaviors so that they are promoted.
Pay and bonuses	Small effect: pay more for T-shaped, hoping that some good people might be attracted to that.	Big effect: use T-shaped reward criteria as a carrot for people to change their behaviors to get better rewards.
Hiring	Big effect: recruit T-shaped, not others.	Does not apply (hiring is about selecting, not changing, people).
Leadership coaching	Does not apply (coaching is about change, not selection).	Big effect: provide support to help people change their behaviors to T-shaped.

of people—by recruiting and promoting them—and getting rid of the wrong kinds of people. In contrast, other leaders try to change their employees' attitudes and behaviors and turn them into T-shaped behaviors. They espouse the essentially optimistic view that people can change.

Which approach is best? In reality, a large organization will have a mix of people—some who resist personal change, and others who embrace it. For this reason, it's important to build a new human resource agenda that both selects for *and* develops T-shaped behaviors.

Promote T-Shaped, Not Other Behaviors

Disciplined collaboration requires that companies promote people who practice T-shaped management, and not others. Leaders who want to do this, though, are often frustrated, because data on cross-unit contributions is hard to come by. Executives must create a new mechanism that sets new criteria, collects data, evaluates performance, and rewards T-shaped management with promotions (see figure 5-3).

FIGURE 5-3

How to evaluate cross-unit contributions

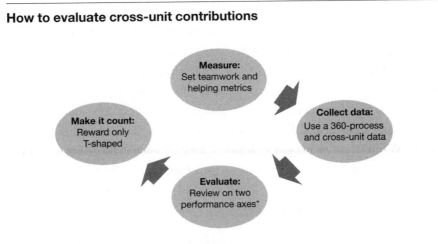

* Individual performance and valuable cross-unit contributions.

Collaboration Must Be Measured

To get any traction, leaders need to set criteria and metrics for cross-unit contributions. Overarching concepts—"teamwork"—need to be translated into concrete behaviors that are ranked from the least to the most desirable. Remember from chapter 4 that SAP, the large German software company, wanted its managers to collaborate better across functions. The company's new leadership requirement demanded that managers "ensure involvement of the appropriate people inside SAP (across roles, departments, and locations) to accomplish goals." Managers then defined three observable degrees of behaviors that could be used to evaluate performance.

1. *Needs development:* Misses opportunities to involve people from other businesses, functions, and locations across SAP

2. *Satisfactory:* Involves some people from other businesses, functions, and locations across SAP to accomplish goals

3. *Highly effective:* Ensures the involvement of the appropriate people from other businesses, functions, and locations across SAP to accomplish goals

At software company Intuit, managers also developed concrete metrics. Jennifer Hall, an executive who headed up the company's e-store, had to deliver on a key cross-unit metric: on-time marketing campaigns for the online store.[16] Did a campaign get started on the day it was supposed to start, and, if not, how many days of delay occurred? It was a cross-unit metric because she needed timely input from several business units (on product marketing), corporate marketing (order flow), corporate operations (manufacturing), and design resources (copy, graphics, etc.). The metric was a good measure of her ability to collaborate effectively with others. As she said, "While I was dependent on many groups, as the eStore's leader, I felt accountable for making sure all areas came together."[17]

Data Must Be Collected

The popular 360-degree tool is useful here, provided it is used correctly.[18] With this tool, superiors, subordinates, and peers get a chance to fill in a survey—anonymously—to evaluate a person. It's called "360" because evaluation is up (boss), down (subordinates), and across (peers). The power of this tool is the peer component. People not working directly with a person get a chance to evaluate how that person contributes across units. To do this correctly, those peers must come from other units.

Here's a great illustration of how to do it well. A large global investment bank put in place an online version of a 360-degree tool.[19] Once a year, some twenty-two hundred bankers were required to fill in an online survey (an impressive 93 percent did so). From a list of names, they were asked to identify and rank colleagues who had helped out. The instructions read, "When ranking your colleagues it is important to assign the ranks in terms of *usefulness to you* and not your perception of their contribution to the bank in general." To avoid grade inflation and prevent bankers from rating everyone "very useful," the system forced the bankers to allocate their picks into four buckets based on how useful they had been.

The bankers named seventy-eight colleagues on average as having provided input to their work. Now, armed with this data, top managers could determine how useful a person had been to other units in the bank. Suppose fifty people included "Robert" in their evaluation and ranked his usefulness to them. The system cranked out the ratings he received, and top managers then used the average rating that Robert received in determining his bonus for the year.

It Must Be Evaluated

There is no point in setting criteria and gathering data on cross-unit contributions if it doesn't count. At BP, David Nagel's annual review had two equally important conversations: one about his performance for the Egyptian gas production unit he was heading, and the other about cross-unit activities he had engaged in. "You might have spectacular individual business unit performance," noted Nagel. "But if you weren't seen to be making contributions beyond your own unit, you wouldn't be viewed favorably."[20]

It Must Have Consequences

Leaders pursuing disciplined collaboration practice consequence management: if people perform well both within and across their units, they are promoted. If they fall short on either dimension, they face the consequences. Leaders adopting this approach are tough on lone stars and butterflies who are unwilling or unable to change, especially after several annual reviews. They fire them or invoke less draconian consequences, such as delaying their promotions and reducing their bonuses.

Pay for Performance, but for What Performance?

Pay for performance is a powerful lever, whether it is in the form of salary hikes, bonuses, or stock options. But it's a mechanism plagued with problems.[21] It sounds easy: if leaders pay for the behaviors they desire, people will behave accordingly. But it isn't that straightforward. When it comes to collaboration, incentive systems often get in the way. Two popular schemes often undermine cross-unit collaboration.

Bad Incentive Number 1: Unit Performance Only

Incentives that reward unit performance only undermine collaboration. Imagine you run the London division of a decentralized global electronics firm, and your sole responsibility is to maximize the performance of your division. Your job performance and compensation are based 100 percent on your division's performance. In a budget meeting, you need to choose between two projects; you can't do both. Exodus is a solo project, and Yamba is a joint project with the Boston division. Here are the estimated net profits for the London division:

London Division

Project Exodus alone: $70 million profits

Project Yamba with Boston: $60 million profits (half of a total of $120 million)

You should pick Exodus, because it yields $10 million more in profit for London, and that's what you are responsible for.

Now imagine running the Boston division. It's the same setup: you're responsible for the Boston division, and that determines your job performance and bonus. Your team also must pick between two projects. Here are the estimated profits:

Boston Division

Project Stealth alone: $40 million profits

Project Yamba with London: $60 million profits (half of a total of $120 million)

You should pick Yamba, because it brings in $20 million more in net profits to the Boston division (and your performance is pegged to Boston's). But London will not do Yamba, so Yamba won't be happening. You have to settle for project Stealth.

Now imagine that you are CEO of the company, charged with considering what is best for the company overall. Yamba is best: it yields a total of $120 million in profits, compared with $110 million for the other two. What is best for the company overall is not best for the London division. London will make a decision that is optimal for itself but suboptimal for the company overall. This happens because you have devised an incentive system that encourages each division to maximize only its individual profits.

Bad Incentive Number 2: Corporatewide Incentives

Many leaders mistakenly believe that they will foster collaboration by pegging bonuses to the overall performance of the company. Consider a 30,000-person consumer-goods company, where bonuses can be up to 50 percent of salary. The company uses the following formula:

- 50 percent of bonus based on individual performance

- 50 percent of bonus based on overall company performance

Will managers become more collaborative as a result of this setup? "Yes" seems to be the answer. Their pay—up to 25 percent of their salary for a year (company performance is 50 percent of bonus, and bonus can be 50 percent of salary)—is determined by how well the company as a whole is doing. It is reasonable to assume that everyone will work hard to maximize the performance of the whole enterprise, because everyone will benefit. But this logic rests on two wobbly assumptions.

First, it assumes that employees believe that their contributions matter and that they will make an effort as a result. They would have to wake up in the morning telling themselves, "What I do today will affect the performance of the whole company, so I am going to work extra hard and do some collaboration!" Most people do not function this way. It is not that individual contributions—even if tiny—don't matter; many small *do* make one large. The problem is that each employee must believe that other employees will also make an effort: if employees don't believe this, they won't make their own small effort, because they assume that their effort alone is insignificant.

Second, it assumes that employees won't engage in what is called free-riding. People might believe that everyone else is making an effort to collaborate, but they might also be thinking, "Everyone else is making an effort, so I don't have to, because after all my contribution is too small to be noticed." The temptation to free-ride is huge in large companies.

Given these problems, I am baffled whenever I hear a senior executive extolling the virtues of this setup. "Compensation is based in part on how well the company does," they might say, arguing that "our people take a company view because of this." It's an argument resting on fragile assumptions.[22]

There is a much better way.

Good Incentive: Link Money Directly to Collaboration

Leaders will have more impact if they make a person's compensation (pay, bonus, stock options) dependent on his or her demonstrated collaborative contributions during the year. One modification to the formula does the trick. A bonus can be as much as 50 percent of salary, and the bonus has the following components:

- 50 percent of bonus based on individual performance

- 50 percent of bonus based on demonstrated individual collaborative contributions (and not the performance of the company as a whole)

This means that 25 percent of a person's salary is directly tied to how well she collaborates. If she collaborates well, and even if that is a tiny contribution in the larger scheme of things, she gets rewarded. This system requires that data on collaboration be collected, just as for promotion. Management consultancy Bain & Company has used this setup.[23] Partners are evaluated each year on a variety of dimensions, including how much help they have given colleagues (and data on this is collected every year). A partner's degree of high-quality collaboration with other partners can account for as much as a quarter of his annual compensation. That's a big deal—a full 25 percent of a partner's total annual compensation.

This incentive system is the correct way to stimulate collaboration.[24] It provides a direct link between a desired behavior—effective collaborative activities—and a person's financial rewards.

Recruit T-Shaped Managers, Not Stars and Butterflies

Leaders clearly need to insist on recruiting people who exhibit T-shaped behaviors. There is no point in putting in all sorts of mechanisms to try to change current employees if there is an influx of new people who couldn't care less about T-shaped behaviors.

If you interview to be a waiter for one of Roy's restaurants, a group of delightful restaurants in California and Hawaii, the interviewer may ask you this question: "What obstacles have you faced in a previous job that prevented you from doing a quality job? How did you overcome these obstacles?"[25] Many people will tell a heroic tale about how they took action and solved the problem by themselves. Unknown to the applicant, the interviewer is looking for evidence of the opposite behavior to this nonleading question: the right answer is to indicate that you didn't try to solve the problem on your own but that you asked for help and communicated the situation to others. That suggests a collaborative orientation, which Roy's seeks.

Southwest Airlines, the phenomenally successful U.S. airline, has for years vigilantly recruited people with a teamwork attitude and shunned lone stars. The company has invented techniques for revealing a person's real teamwork attitude. In one approach, recruiters ask a group of job applicants to prepare a short statement about themselves and to stand up and read it aloud in front of the group.[26] Job applicants might believe that they are being tested for their confidence and clarity in public speaking, but no. Instead, Southwest recruiters are observing how they listen, cheer, and clap for the *other* applicants. Do they pay attention to and support that person, or do they bury their heads in their own papers to prepare their own speeches? Those applicants who are other-focused go through to the next round, and the rest go home. According to longtime CEO Herb Kelleher, "We draft great attitudes. If you don't have a good attitude, we don't want you, no matter how skilled you are. We can change skill levels through training. We can't change attitudes."[27]

Coach for T-Shaped Behavior

"Do you really think he can change?" I asked my colleague Roger Lehman, a leadership professor at INSEAD and a sought-after executive coach in Europe. "I'm not sure—maybe," he replied.

We were talking about one of his clients, "Anthony," a high-flying forty-five-year-old executive in a large European retail company. His boss had referred him for coaching sessions, with a mandate for Anthony to become a more collaborative and less self-promoting executive (or else he would not be promoted to the most senior rank). So there was much at stake. It had fallen to Roger to work with Anthony.

I wanted to know more. "Why wouldn't he change?" I asked. "His dream promotion is dangling right in front of him."

"It's about his ingrained behavior," Roger replied. "He has spent his entire career looking out for himself and the team working for him, and for the first time in his life he is being asked to take a much broader view. This is a guy who can't help but say 'I' instead of 'we.' He's incredibly driven and ambitious for himself and constantly wants to prove himself."

As we talked, Roger explained that he had devised a two-part approach to help Anthony change: behavioral changes and systemic changes. The first part had to do with getting Anthony to change his *behaviors,* rather than his attitudes (especially in the beginning). This strategy followed the logic that changing behaviors is easier than changing deep-seated attitudes, and that a change in behaviors can change attitudes over time. (For more on this counterintuitive idea, see the box, "Should Leaders Try to Change People's Attitudes, or Their Behaviors?")

For example, at the most mundane level, Roger worked to get Anthony to recognize his self-oriented behaviors and his "I" statements. Training him to say "we" shifted the focus a little bit. Then Roger prodded Anthony to develop a small list of things he could do that would help other units in the company—things he would not normally do or see as valuable for his team but that would prove valuable for others. And this led to bigger things, such as proactively helping a few other colleagues put together a sales bid for a customer—tasks Anthony had always tried to avoid. Slowly, Anthony started to engage in a few more meaningful collaborative behaviors. The two met once a month, discussing progress and new techniques. Anthony continued to work to change his behaviors, meeting alternately with Roger and with his mentor at work (a senior executive). It went on like this for nine months.

Most executive coaching works this way. But as Roger points out, it is not enough: "All too often, executives go back to work trying to change their behaviors, but nothing has changed around them! The work is the same, the demands are the same, and colleagues expect the same old behaviors. The context has not changed. That's why it's important to combine individual coaching with systemic change."

When Anthony changed to "we," everyone at work expected him to say "I," and no one noticed the difference when he soon fell back on

Should leaders try to change people's attitudes, or their behaviors?

Leaders often think that they need to change people's attitudes—to convince people that they need to change. So they give pep talks to persuade people to change their attitudes. But research points to an alternative: concentrate on changing behaviors, not attitudes.

In a gripping experiment that took place at Yale University in the 1960s, researchers showed students pictures of patients with tetanus—a disease that causes severe muscle spasms, locked jaws, seizures, and possibly death (many people were not vaccinated against it in the 1960s).[28] To manipulate students' attitudes, researchers showed some of the students only a small amount of information. Others were shown horrific photographs of a patient with convulsions—"his back arched upwards, his head whipped back, mouth slammed shut." Afterward, all the students answered a question about their attitude: "How important do you think it is to get a tetanus shot?" Naturally, those who had seen the awful photos scored the highest.

The researchers then measured which students actually went to get a tetanus shot at the university's medical clinic. Amazingly, students who scored high on the attitude question were not more inclined than the others to get a shot. Different attitudes *did not* explain who went to get a shot! And here's the shocker: A portion of students received a detailed plan on how to get to the medical clinic;

---

saying "I." This was to be expected, because nothing had changed in the office. It's difficult to make personal changes when coworkers have come to expect old behaviors. Anthony's mentor then suggested an intervention in the office. People working directly with Anthony and his peers were told about his efforts to change; they now expected him to say "we" and to collaborate more frequently. When he fell back on they were told the times when shots were available; they were given a map with the clinic clearly circled; and they were asked to review their schedule to find a time. Of the students who received this detailed plan, 28 percent went to get a shot, compared with 3 percent of students without the plan. Think about that: attitudinal change had no impact on behavior, but a simple plan for action had a massive effect! The insight: work on changing specific behaviors, not only on changing attitudes. Later research has confirmed this finding.[29]

Some leaders practice this approach. Harvey Golub, the remarkable chief executive who saved American Express, is a believer in behaviors leading to attitude change. When he visited the MBA class that I taught at Harvard Business School in 2003, he pointed out that he tried to get his reluctant managers to change behaviors, and not only their attitudes, which he thought would change as a result. He worked hard to change from an environment replete with internal politics to more objective and analytical behaviors, such as "argues positions fairly and objectively" (a change from thinking about politics first); "supports agreed-upon decisions" (a change from undermining efforts); and "admits mistakes readily" (a change from blaming others).[30] It was as if he had read the tetanus experiment. The upshot: leaders should not only work to change attitudes about collaboration (and then hope that behaviors will follow) but should also work to instill collaborative behaviors regardless of attitudes. Both ways count.

"I" and didn't spend time helping others, his colleagues, including his assigned mentor, pointed it out to him.

This two-pronged approach of individual coaching and systemic change is powerful. It suggests that executive coaching, in isolation, may not be enough to change how the person behaves at work. The situation also needs to change.

In the case of Anthony, his superior hurled three forces at him to get him to turn collaborative:

- *Executive coaching:* Anthony received individual coaching sessions, focusing on collaborative behaviors.

- *Peer pressure and support:* There was an expectation in his immediate work environment that he would change to "we" and collaborate more.

- *Performance criteria:* His company did everything outlined in this chapter: its promotion and bonus criteria were clearly pegged to T-shaped behaviors (it was this that had prompted the coaching in the first place, because Anthony could not get through to the next level).

Importantly, executive coaching adds a dimension that the other forces lack. Changing promotion, compensation, and recruitment criteria demands T-shaped behaviors ("change, or else"), but it doesn't offer any help in how to change. In contrast, coaching helps the person develop skills and behaviors to be more successful at collaborating. This is crucial, because managers sometimes sincerely want to change; they just don't know how.

How Do You Transition an Existing Team?

Most leaders inherit a team when they assume a new role, and usually there aren't many team members who practice T-shaped management. If you're in this camp, your challenge is to transform your team. To see how it works, let's take a typical group of top one hundred managers in any large company and turn it into a team dominated by T-shaped behaviors.

The first step is to collect data to evaluate how well these people collaborate in the company. If you don't know whether people practice T-shaped behaviors or act like lone stars or butterflies, it's hard to start a change program. Let's suppose you've done this and are able to classify the top one hundred group as shown in the top portion of figure 5-4. Here you have

FIGURE 5-4

Transforming a team into T-shaped

One scenario: using HR levers to change a group of 100 managers.

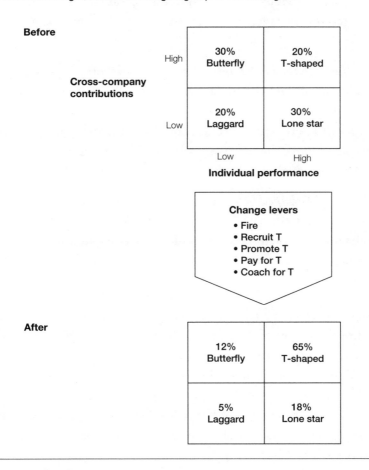

only twenty who practice T-shaped behaviors in a group of one hundred, so some real changes are needed.

You will need to use all the levers outlined in this chapter and take four steps.

1. *Fire laggards:* To create vacancies, which will allow you to add new collaborators, you can fire a few laggards. Also, encourage natural turnover among the laggards.

2. *Promote and recruit for T-shaped behaviors:* You can then begin filling these vacancies by promoting managers from the ranks. And you can recruit managers from outside the company. Obviously, you need to take great care to promote and recruit managers who exhibit T-shaped behaviors, not others.

3. *Pay for T-shaped behaviors:* Then you can work on changing the behaviors of the existing laggards, butterflies, and lone stars. You can put in place a pay-for-performance system based on two-sided performance. This should cause a few lone stars to become more collaborative, and a few butterflies to improve their individual performance.

4. *Coach for T-shaped behaviors:* You can also institute leadership development efforts aimed at changing managers' collaborative behaviors. You will need to single out those lone stars and butterflies you deem most willing and able to change.

The results of this combined effect can be dramatic. I have run a realistic simulation based on the starting position in figure 5-4. (It assumes that you fire 10 percent of the laggards per year for three years; that there is a 10 percent natural turnover in the group; and that you are able to cultivate T-shaped management in 10 percent of the remaining people each year—see the footnote for details.[31]) The result is the new mix shown in the bottom portion of figure 5-4. The team goes from having only twenty percent to having sixty-five percent of managers who exhibit T-shaped behaviors. That's a big change.

This group will reach a tipping point when it changes from being dominated by lone stars and butterflies to being dominated by T-shaped behaviors. When you have a top one hundred group where 65 percent practice T-shaped behaviors, the balance has tipped in favor of T-shaped management, and it becomes the dominant mode of operating. That's a lot of managers delivering two performances—and that's disciplined collaboration at its best.

Chapter 5: Key Points

Lever 2: Cultivate T-Shaped Management

- Managers practicing T-shaped management deliver two performances: results in their own job (the vertical part of the T) *and* results by collaborating across the company (the horizontal part of the T). They are willing to reach out and ask for input and also to help others when asked. But they are disciplined enough to say "no" to collaboration when it doesn't produce value.

- Leaders who practice disciplined collaboration do not tolerate lone stars—people who deliver outstanding individual performance but who do not help others outside their units. These leaders also discourage butterflies—people who are great institutional players but who do not perform well in their own jobs (the opposite of lone stars).

- To grow T-shaped management in their organizations, leaders can use two levers of change: selecting for T-shaped behaviors (through promotion and hiring) and changing behaviors (through pay, coaching, and promotion). Both levers work.

- To cultivate T-shaped management, leaders need to implement two-sided performance management: people need to be rewarded for individual performance *and* for contributions to others outside their own immediate groups. This criterion needs to be implemented in every key human resource activity: promotion, firing, pay, bonuses, hiring, and coaching. That's a radically different HR agenda from the one in most companies.

- Popular pay-for-performance systems often undermine collaboration. Leaders must eschew systems that are based on individual performance only and those that are based on overall company performance. The best incentives are based on a combination of individual performance and pay for collaboration: they link money (pay, bonus, stock options) directly to a person's own collaborative results during a year.

CHAPTER SIX

Lever 3: Build Nimble Networks

No Bloated Rolodexes

A T 4:30 P.M., Les Owen sat down in front of his Dell to go through his daily list of one hundred e-mails.[1] Owen, an engineer at BP's oil pipeline unit in Anchorage, Alaska, was used to fielding inquiries from colleagues in myriad faraway places—a result of his twenty-six years of employment all over the world. He figured he was a natural source of help to colleagues. Outside his unassuming office, the northern sky began to darken as he checked each message. One, about lightning, caught his eye. Big thunder-and-lightning storms were no friend of oil pipelines. One time when lightning struck a Koch Industries facility in Texas, a pipe exploded, spilling ninety thousand gallons of oil into the Gulf Coast over ten days.[2]

The e-mail garnering Owens's attention came from a colleague in Saratov, Siberia, some forty-five hundred miles away.

From: Larry Watson, BP Siberia
To: Les Owen, BP Alaska
Subject: Lightning Protection

Les,
We haven't talked in a while. Do you know anyone well versed in lightning protection equipment and practices? We've had a lot of problems recently with lightning strikes damaging our pumping facilities.

Not an expert in lightning protection, Owen knew where to turn—to Ian French, a colleague in Houston.

From: Les Owen, BP Alaska
To: Ian French, BP Houston
Subject: FW: Lightning Protection

How are things in Houston? I thought you might be able to help with the attached request for information, given your past experience in Larry's part of the world and with lightning-related problems.

French forwarded the inquiry to Nigel Wallace, who also worked in BP Houston.

From: Ian French, BP Houston
To: Nigel Wallace, BP Houston
Cc: Les Owen, BP Alaska
Subject: FW: Lightning Protection

Les Owen, who works for BP Pipelines in Alaska, has been asked by Larry Watson, an engineer at the pipeline unit in Siberia, about recommended practices for lightning protection. Before I follow up, could you respond with any thoughts?

Wallace promptly e-mailed back an answer.

From: Nigel Wallace, BP Houston
To: Ian French, BP Houston
Cc: Les Owen, BP Alaska
Subject: FW: Lightning Protection

There are many claims for exotic lightning protection systems. I prefer to approach the issue with good earthing and earth-bonding practice and the protection of particularly vulnerable components with surge diverter devices. I attach a copy of some useful presentation slides. Call if questions. I'm always happy to provide help in the area of lightning protection—often seen as black art, though it shouldn't be!

The next morning, Les Owen closed the loop, connecting Nigel Wallace, the expert based in Houston, with Larry Watson.

From: Les Owen, BP Alaska
To: Larry Watson, BP Siberia
Subject: FW: Lightning Protection

Received the following reply on lightning. I suggest you contact Nigel and Ian directly, who are both in Houston, if you have questions.

A request that started in a BP office in Siberia zoomed over to Les Owen in Alaska and then zipped to Texas, to hook up with a master of lightning. Then it sped over to Owen, who hurled it back to Siberia. Some 15,700 miles of e-mailing. What stands out here is not the extraordinary but the ordinary—that a routine question on a mundane issue was routed via Les Owen to someone else, located somewhere else, in BP. The success of networking in BP was a direct function of one person: Les Owen.

Owen is a *bridge*—someone who, by virtue of his network, can connect the many islands of a company by putting people in contact with each other. His boss at the time, Ann Drinkwater, understood Owen's invaluable role: "Les is better than a Web site. He's always helping other people connect. He knows everything that's going on."

Collaborative companies run on *networks,* those informal working relationships among people that cut across formal lines of reporting. If the formal org chart shows how work is divided into pieces, networks reveal the informal organization—how people actually work together. Good bridges like Owens are a key to terrific networks. And terrific networks are in turn a hallmark of disciplined collaboration.

Myths About Networks

And yet networks—or wrong ideas about them—often get in the way of disciplined collaboration. A fog of inaccurate perceptions often obscures how superb networks function. To better understand how networks can help collaboration, we must first dispense with these myths.

Networking Is Always a Good Thing

Few people dispute that networking is beneficial. Not many say, "Gee, I need to do less networking." But the idea that networking is *necessarily* a good thing can cause us to overlook the fact that networks can sometimes undermine performance. In the study of sales teams at Sterling, the consulting company I referred to in chapter 2, experienced teams that used many network contacts lost more competitive sales bids than others.[3] They didn't need these interactions, because their own experience was sufficient, but maintaining and using these relations represented a distraction from preparing the sales bids.

The More, the Merrier

Many people think that the more contacts they have, the better. They mistakenly see the person who knows lots and lots of people as a dream networker. This belief runs deep.[4] In his influential book, *The Tipping Point,* Malcolm Gladwell identified Dallas businessman and musical producer Roger Horchow as a supreme networker: "He keeps on his computer a roster of 1,600 names and addresses, and on each entry is a note describing the circumstances under which he met the person."[5] Gladwell goes on to assert that "the first—and most obvious" reason people such as Horchow are aces at connecting is that they "know lots of people."[6]

With all due respect to Gladwell, such beliefs are misplaced. Research shows that "the more, the merrier" does not necessarily yield the best results, at least not when it comes to networking in business. Why? Because networking is costly. It takes time and effort to nurture relationships. In my study of Hewlett-Packard in the 1990s (referred to in chapter 3), product-development teams that had many contacts took 20 percent longer to finish projects than those with few contacts. Team members spent time interacting with others at the expense of completing their own work.[7] For networks to be valuable, benefits need to be greater than costs. Building a bulging Rolodex can actually undermine performance.

Success Goes to the Socially Gifted

Conventional wisdom has it that great networkers are socially gifted. They are charming, socially adept, extroverted, good-looking, and charismatic. They crack good jokes, put people at ease, and claim the center of attention at dinner parties. They are more Bill Clinton than Al Gore, more Tony Blair than Gordon Brown, more Ronald Reagan than Bob Dole, more Andre Agassi than Roger Federer.

Vivi Nevo is such a guy. According to a *New York Times* article aptly titled "A Media Powerhouse Everyone and Nobody Knows," Nevo, forty-three, is networker supreme in the media investment world.[8] Having grown up in Israel and inherited some family money, Nevo settled in New York and transformed his modest inheritance into a sizable fortune through savvy investments in media and Internet companies during the 1990s. His uncanny networking ability and charm helped him establish relationships with important people and gain insight into investment opportunities. Engaged to Zhang Ziyi, a Chinese movie superstar best known for her role in *Crouching Tiger, Hidden Dragon,* Nevo mingles with billionaires and artists in the Hamptons, vacations on Rupert Murdoch's sailboat, attended Madonna's wedding, and frequents Bob Allen's retreat in Sun Valley for the who's who of the media world. There his charm wins people over. Bob Packer, an investment banker from Goldman Sachs, calls Nevo "a really affable, wonderful, loyal guy." Richard Parsons, Time Warner chairman and former CEO, recalls meeting Nevo at the duck pond in Sun Valley. "In typical Vivi Nevo fashion," Parsons recounts, "we shortly became best buds." When John Thornton, Goldman Sachs president, finished his 1999 Los Angeles presentation for the bank's public offering, he happened to sit down next to Nevo. "We just started talking and developed a nice rapport right then," he recounts.

How many people can show up at a duck pond in Sun Valley or at a presentation in Los Angeles and quickly establish a lasting connection to the chairman of Time Warner or the president of Goldman Sachs? Not many. Most of us just aren't like Nevo, and we assume that great networking is reserved for the club of the socially gifted.

But here's the reality: for every Vivi Nevo there are dozens of remarkable networkers who have none of his glamorous lifestyle or charm.

Research shows that personal traits related to being socially gifted, such as being extroverts, do not determine whether people are effective networkers.[9] Good networkers can be found everywhere. They can be introverts or extroverts, shy or gregarious, insecure or cocky.

Networking Is an Art

The final myth is that networking is an art, not a science. This myth reflects the belief that networks are hidden from view and evolve as employees work together rather than being the product of design. As a result, people believe that networks belong to the realm of company life that cannot be pinned down, measured in numbers, and changed.

Recent advances in the social science of networks have changed this premise. Researchers have begun to measure and analyze networks in organizations, much as doctors use X-rays to see fractures. New network maps show the strong links and the gaps. This means that we can pinpoint with some precision what networks look like and how to improve them. With the help of social science, networks can not only be measured but also better managed.[10]

Now that we have solid academic evidence, these myths about networking need to give way to reality. Too little networking dooms organizations, but so does too much: people choke on it, by spending too much time and getting distracted. So we need a set of rules based on the principle that people need to limit indiscriminate networking and instead build nimble, results-based networks. Indeed, the principles of networks follow the principles of disciplined collaboration: the goal of networking is not networking but better results.

Identify Opportunities, Then Capture Them

For the leader demanding disciplined collaboration, the first thing to ask is, "What are networks good for?" Research shows that networks provide two fundamental benefits. First, they help people identify opportunities; people use existing professional relationships to find resources—a technology, an idea, an expert, a collaboration partner. Second, networks help people capture value; people realize benefits from the resources they have identified.

This identification-and-capture challenge is everywhere in society: a teenager first needs to identify a desirable date, then convince him to go out. A college graduate first needs to hear about a job opportunity, then land the job. An entrepreneur first needs to find potential investors, then convince them to part with their money. An engineer first needs to identify who can help with a technical problem, then be able to work with that expert to transfer the knowledge. A manager first needs to find a marketing expert, then persuade the expert to share her knowledge.

These network benefits reduce barriers to collaboration. Networks reduce all four barriers outlined in chapter 3, although to different degrees.

- *The not-invented-here barrier:* Identifying opportunities requires that people be willing to look for them. If they spend most of their time talking to colleagues within their own units, they will not discover many opportunities elsewhere. Networks can help reduce this reluctance somewhat, because people who interact with others tend to be more open to input from the outside world.

- *The search barrier:* Once people are willing to look for opportunities outside their own units, they need to be able to search efficiently. Networks can have a huge impact by helping people search better.

- *The hoarding barrier:* Networks can help people overcome the hoarding barrier somewhat, because people are more willing to help those whom they know.

- *The transfer barrier:* Good networks can lower transfer problems. Good relationships among colleagues help overcome the difficulty of passing along complicated knowledge people need to do their work.

Six Network Rules

Six network rules help people identify opportunities and capture value (see table 6-1). The first four help people identify opportunities, and the last two help people capture value. The rules help people develop "just enough" networking, as opposed to indiscriminate globe-trotting.

TABLE 6-1

Six network rules help people identify opportunities and capture value

Key Activity	Barrier lowered	Network rules	Effect
Identify Opportunities	Not-invented-here	Rule 1: Build outward, not inward.	+
	Search	Rule 2: Build diversity, not size. Rule 3: Build bridges, don't use familiar faces. Rule 4: Build weak ties, not strong.	+++
Capture Value	Hoarding	Rule 5: Swarm target, don't go it alone.	+
	Transfer	Rule 6: Switch to strong, don't rely on the weak.	+++

+++ Great effect   + Good effect

Rules for Identifying Opportunities

Network Rule Number 1: Build Outward, Not Inward

As you saw in chapter 3, some people mingle predominantly with colleagues in their own units.[11] Companies whose employees build their networks inward become full of insular networks; business units and country operations become islands unto themselves, with few bridges spanning them. To alleviate this tendency, the first network rule—almost a foundational rule—is to build connections to other parts of the company.

Consider the European media company mentioned in chapter 2. Headquartered in London, the company publishes newspapers, magazines, videos, and books in eight countries from the United Kingdom to Sweden and Russia.[12] When the top two hundred managers completed a network survey about which country operations and business units they communicated with, they revealed that they communicated a great deal within the operations in their own respective countries but rarely between countries (except for regular contact with headquarters in the United Kingdom). Table 6-2 reveals that the frequency of communication *within* countries (shown in the shaded cells) far exceeds that

TABLE 6-2

Cross-country network

Communication patterns among top managers across countries in a European media company. Numbers indicate communication frequency between country units on a scale of 1 (no interaction) to 5 (daily interaction).

	Austria	Baltics	France	UK*	Russia	Spain	Sweden	Italy
Austria	5.0							
Baltics	0.2	3.9						
France	0.6	0.2	2.8					
UK*	1.9	1.0	1.0	4.1				
Russia	0.5	0.4	0.5	2.5	5.0			
Spain	0.4	0.2	0.5	1.5	0.5	4.3		
Sweden	0.4	0.4	0.4	2.2	1.3	0.4	3.9	
Italy	0.4	0.2	0.7	1.7	0.1	0.6	0.5	5.0

*Headquarters.

Question: Over the past 6 months, how frequently have you interacted with people in [country]? Scale: 0 = no interaction; 1 = once a month or less; 2 = about every other week; 3 = about once a week; 4 = about twice a week; 5 = daily interaction. 150 of the top 200 managers answered the survey. The numbers are the average of responses and displayed as symmetrical data (e.g., the average of responses of how frequently the French managers said they communicated with the Austrians and how frequently the Austrians said they communicated with the French).

with the other countries. For example, the French subsidiary communicated with almost no one else. Its frequency of communication ranged from a low score of 0.2 with the Baltic region (basically no interaction) to a modest score of 1.0 with U.K. headquarters ("once a month or less"). Clearly, top managers in this company need to make people connect better across country subsidiaries if they wish to collaborate better across geographies (which was the goal).

When we look at network connections across business units in this media company, we see a different story. The network is more outward-looking. As table 6-3 shows, people in each business unit still communicated a lot with each other (naturally), but people in some units also stayed in frequent touch with colleagues in other business units. For example, people in online newspapers communicated pretty frequently—about once a week—with people in television and film.

TABLE 6-3

Cross-business network

Network contacts across business units in a European media company. Numbers indicate communication frequency between business units on a scale of 1 (no interaction) to 5 (daily interaction).

	Newspaper print	Newspaper commercial	Classifieds	Online newspapers	Publishing	Television and film
Newspaper print	3.8					
Newspaper commercial	3.1	3.7				
Classifieds	2.0	2.3	3.1			
Online newspapers	3.2	3.1	2.4	4.0		
Publishing	2.1	2.5	2.0	2.8	4.2	
Television and film	2.6	2.7	1.5	3.0	1.9	3.8

Question: Over the past 6 months, how frequently have you interacted with people in [business unit]? Scale: 0 = no interaction; 1 = once a month or less; 2 = about every other week; 3 = about once a week; 4 = about week; 5 = daily interaction.

Armed with this kind of data, top executives can pinpoint obvious gaps (where people should build their networks outward) and where the gaps are fine as they are (where there is no need to interact more). Executives can then work to build more connections where needed to make the network more outward-looking.

The data also shows whether people engage in undisciplined collaboration—whether they network too much. By having too many connections outside their own units and too few inside, people tend to become butterflies, constantly on the road and in meetings with people in many parts of the company. Some people thrive on this outward orientation. But at some point, it tips over, and they lose the connections and communication inside their unit to the detriment of their work. Terrific networkers—those who practice T-shaped management— strive for a balance.

Network Rule Number 2: Build Diversity, Not Size

Research shows that it is not size—the sheer number of contacts maintained by a person—that counts. Rather, it's the *diversity of connections*—the number of different types of people, units, expertise, technologies, and viewpoints—that people can access through their networks.[13]

Take a look at how this worked at Hewlett-Packard in the 1990s. Ever since HP created an oscillator that was used for the Walt Disney movie *Fantasia,* the company had developed many measurement devices over the years (this business was later spun off as Agilent in 1999). By the mid 1990s, some forty-one units had cropped up in places like California, Colorado, New Jersey, Germany, France, and Japan. The units were home to experts in different measurement technologies, such as digital signal processing, quartz resonance, and analog-to-digital conversions. In all, twenty-two such technologies were spread across the forty-one businesses.[14]

This setup offered some nice opportunities for collaboration: engineers could develop new products by combining different technologies from different business units. For example, in the microwave instrument business in Santa Rosa, California, a project team was able to use connections in the vector signal analyzer unit in Lake Stevens, Washington, to access technical competence in high-speed digital design. This hookup contributed 50 percent of the software needed and saved the project eight person-years of work.

When I analyzed the network among these forty-one units as part of my PhD work at Stanford University, I started with a straightforward thought: the units with the most connections would create better recombinations, simply because they would know more people. So I plugged the data in to my computer and looked for statistical proof. But it didn't show up. The hypothesis was wrong—no effect. What did matter was diversity: business units that tapped in to many *different* technologies through their network did better. The trick was not simply to have many connections but to have the right ones that tapped in to diverse technologies. Such network diversity led to faster and more innovative product innovation.[15]

TABLE 6-4

Network size and network diversity in two business units at Hewlett-Packard

Business unit	Network Size Number of connections to other business units (max = 40)	Network Diversity Number of *different* technologies accessed by those contacts (max = 22)	Ratio Number of technologies/ Number of connections (the higher, the better)
Edmonton, Canada	3	11	3.7
Melbourne, Australia	3	5	1.7

Data based on my doctoral dissertation at Stanford University and collected in 1995, when the electronic instrumentation sector was still part of Hewlett-Packard (now part of Agilent). See Morten T. Hansen "Knowledge Integration in Organizations," Unpublished PhD dissertation, Graduate School of Business, Stanford University, 1996.

The difference between the Edmonton and Melbourne business units illustrates this point (see table 6-4). Each unit had connections to only three other business units. In the case of Edmonton, those three connections provided access to eleven different technologies. In contrast, "poor" Melbourne accessed only five different technologies through its three contacts. Edmonton and Melbourne had the same network size (three contacts), and yet the diversity of technologies each was able to access differed a great deal (eleven versus five).

When managers build network diversity, they first need to decide which factors matter. For engineers in the measurement business at HP, tapping in to different technologies mattered. Here's a list of factors to consider:

- Contacts with different cliques of people (who don't talk across cliques)[16]

- Contacts with different technologies

- Contacts with different types of experts

- Contacts with different types of customers

- Contacts with different consumer trends

- Contacts with colleagues of different ages (old and young)

- Contacts with colleagues of different tenure (new and old-timers)

- Contacts with colleagues of different gender

- Contacts with people of different nationalities and ethnicity

- Contacts with different styles (those wearing suits, a Mohawk haircut)

- Contacts with different manufacturing sites

- Contacts with different sales offices

- Contacts with different country operations

The rule is simple: when investing in new professional relationships, you need to ask, "What additional diversity does this new contact bring me?" Disciplined collaboration means adding contacts that bring more diversity into your network.

Network Rule Number 3: Build Weak Ties, Not Strong Ones

I attended high school in Oslo, Norway, where I had a friend, Arne, who seemed to know everyone. Students hung out in fifteen or so cliques, which organized parties on Friday nights at someone's house when parents were away. There were two or three parties every week, and the trick was to know who was throwing the party where. Arne always knew. I always wondered how. Looking back, I now realize that he had weak links to a number of students; he knew many students only a little bit, by talking to them once every week or two. They were neither close friends nor strangers. Because they were *weak ties* (infrequent and not personally close), he could keep up a great number of them, maybe fifty or so. Information about the whereabouts of the parties would flow to him through these weak ties.

Intuitively, one would think that close friends—*strong ties*—would help us most, because we know them well and talk to them frequently.

But research shows that weak ties can prove much more helpful in net-working, because they form bridges to worlds we do not walk within.[17] Strong ties, on the other hand, tend to be to worlds we already know; a good friend often knows many of the same people and things we know. They are not the best when it comes to searching for new jobs, ideas, experts, and knowledge.

Weak ties are also good because they take less time. It's less time-consuming to talk to someone once a month (a weak tie) than twice a week (a strong tie). People can keep up quite a few weak ties without them being a burden.

For these reasons, people should build networks replete with weak ties, which are especially good for identifying opportunities. They allow people to have connections into different groups and to know what's going on and who can help. In Hewlett-Packard's measurement sector, for example, project teams with weaker links spent less time searching for useful technologies. They spent only 50 percent of the time that strongly tied teams spent to obtain the same amount of technical expertise.[18]

Network Rule Number 4: Use Bridges, Not Familiar Faces

People should use *bridges* when they network, and managers need to develop bridges in their company's network. Les Owen at BP is a bridge. My friend Arne, with all his weak high school ties, was a bridge. Bridges are uniquely placed by virtue of their networks to help other people search. They direct queries. People use them for *whom* they know, not for *what* they know.

Most people are not good bridges (in fact, some people are bridges to nowhere). Most of us ask colleagues who happen to be familiar and near to us—the ones we happen to chat with in the hallways ("Hey, I'm look-ing for lightning protection for pump facilities—do you know who knows about that?"). We ask our peers in the office building, our bosses, our direct reports, our close colleagues, our assistants, and our office buddies. The problem is, these familiar faces are usually just as clueless about finding that pump-lightning-protection expert as we are.

Research shows that people naturally stick to people who are near and familiar. We have a strong desire to mingle with people who are like ourselves—birds of a feather flock together.[19] This desire for sticking with the familiar spills over to search. In one study, four hundred consultants in a large management consulting company were asked whom they would contact as a bridge to find an expert on a specific topic such as "transfer pricing."[20] Senior people—partners—often knew who the experts were or at least pinpointed a real bridge such as Les Owen. But the interesting part was how junior people reacted. One would think that they would name someone well connected or a senior employee, because these contacts presumably would be most helpful. But no. They chose colleagues like themselves—junior people who were equally bad at finding an expert.

Good networking means knowing who the real bridges are and using them. Who makes good bridges? Take Les Owen. He has worked at BP for twenty-six years, in many places around the world, and in various types of jobs. As a result, his network has a wide range, and he knows something about many topics—not enough to be an expert, but enough to know who might be. To spot bridges, look for long-tenured people who have worked in different places in the company and who know about a broad range of topics.

Leaders who build powerful companywide networks ensure that there are enough people performing the bridging role. Having only a few connections across units in a company indicates a fragile network that is in danger of collapse. For example, in the network-mapping exercise among the top two hundred managers in the European media company mentioned earlier, results showed that very few were bridges.

- Only seven managers had frequent interactions across the eight country operations.

- Only twelve managers had frequent ties to all six business areas.

- Only one person had frequent links across all these countries *and* business units.

If these people left the company, there would be little bridging left. Clearly, the leaders of this company need to get more bridges going. To cultivate them, leaders should first identify who might be good bridges in the company—senior partners (in the case of the consulting company), and longtime engineers who have moved around (in the case of BP). Executives should then create room for some of these people to perform the bridging role. At BP, Ann Drinkwater, Les Owen's boss, had informally ensured that he had time to be a bridge: "I was careful when we agreed on work allocation that I didn't fill 100 percent of his time."[21] Leaders can also expand job rotation programs across units in their companies. People who spend time in different parts of the company often become excellent bridges, because they develop good contacts in every unit where they work.[22]

Rules for Capturing Value

Network Rule Number 5: Swarm the Target; Do Not Go It Alone

One snowy, freezing Friday night during my junior year in high school, I approached the doorstep of a home in suburban Oslo, hoping to get into a party. Two friends and I had heard about it from Arne, my buddy with so many weak ties. I was especially eager to get in because a cute Norwegian girl I was interested in was there. We rang the doorbell, and the guy running the party opened the door. Unfortunately, we didn't know him personally, and he wouldn't let us in. I mentioned Arne's name, but that wasn't enough (and he wasn't there to help). We had to turn around, heads bowed, with nothing much else to do (and no date). We had made a successful search for the right house, but we had failed to realize the opportunity.

What went wrong? We had no network of friends or influence to bring to bear on the target. We went alone; Arne had not mentioned me to the host ahead of time; he was not there to introduce me; and there was no one else at the door who knew both me and the host—a third party who might influence the host. Also, Arne didn't really know the host very well; after all, he had only a weak tie to him.

A silly example, perhaps, but it illustrates an important network principle: if you believe that the target identified in a search may not be forthcoming, you need to enlist the help of others to convince the target—ahead of time. You need to *swarm the target* with influencers—people who are in a position to exert influence on the target in service of your request.[23]

Malcolm Gladwell tells the story of how Roger Horchow landed the rights to revive the musical *Girl Crazy,* by George Gershwin, retitled *Crazy for You.* This wasn't a search problem, because Horchow knew who had the rights—Lee Gershwin. But convincing her to give them to him was another matter, as Horchow told Gladwell.

> I had lunch with a fellow called Leopold Godowsky, who is the son of Frances Gershwin, George Gershwin's sister . . . So they said—well, why should we let you have the rights to *Girl Crazy?* . . . So then I started pulling out my coincidences. Your aunt, Emily Paley. I went to her house . . . I pulled out all the little links.

> Then we all went to Hollywood and we went over to Lee Gershwin's house and I said, I'm so happy to meet you. I knew your sister . . . Oh, and then I pulled out my Los Angeles friend . . . Mildred Knopf. Her husband was Edwin Knopf . . . Well, it turns out Edwin Knopf was George Gershwin's closest friend . . . We mentioned that we had just been to see Mildred Knopf. She said—You know her? Oh, why haven't we met before? She gave us the rights immediately.[24]

This is not name-dropping but invoking common links; Mildred Knopf is a common link because she knew both Horchow and Lee Gershwin. Horchow invokes his connections to Emily Paley and Mildred Knopf to swarm Lee Gershwin with common contacts in order to influence her.

Mentioning the names of common contacts is the lightest swarming tactic. A more forceful one is to get common contacts to work on your behalf—if, say, Mildred Knopf had visited Lee Gershwin to put in a good word for Roger Horchow. In a company, swarming targets also involves enlisting bosses to get people to collaborate: Jim talks to his boss, who talks to Janet's boss, and Janet suddenly becomes a lot more cooperative with Jim.[25]

Swarming tactics are part of the a more general set of influence tactics that managers need to use to enlist the cooperation of others.[26] When working across the company, people can also influence others by appealing to the common good ("We're working for the same company") and invoking reciprocity ("If you help me, I will help you"). All these tactics help you ensure the cooperation of people who do not belong to the same organizational unit as you do and over whom you have no formal authority.

Network Rule Number 6: Switch to Strong Ties; Do Not Rely on Weak Ones

Sun Ho, an engineer working on a software project in a California office equipment company, didn't mince his words: "Basically, our newly hired U.S.-based engineers don't want to work with the Indian team anymore," Ho told his boss, Howard Chang, in a meeting. "They have told me they prefer working with people in the same location and that they don't trust the Indians."

Howard Chang had just taken over as head of an important software project code-named Shield.[27] The innovative project involved sophisticated technology and required a lot of creativity and problem-solving. The team was virtual, with one group of engineers based in the firm's Los Angeles lab and another group located in Bangalore, India.

Startled by Ho's comment, Chang called a team meeting in the Los Angeles lab, only to hear the same thing. Said an engineer about his colleagues in India, "They're nine thousand miles away, and there's a twelve-hour time difference. And frankly, I don't know what's on their mind. They may send me a twenty-page document, and I'm so busy I can't be bothered to read it."

As Chang listened, reality hit. This was a big mess. The Los Angeles and Bangalore groups had to work together on complicated technology requiring many back-and-forth interactions. Wanting to hear what the other side had to say, Chang hopped on a plane to Bangalore to meet with the thirteen engineers working on Shield. There was no shortage of complaints there either. The first developer grumbled: "The most difficult thing about working with the American team is the delay in response. The lack of rapid answers and clarifications hinders collaboration." Chang was outraged to hear that the Indians were estranged from the Shield team in Los Angeles. There was a complete failure of collaboration.

What happened here? This project team got itself into a classic trap: strangers started to work together in a virtual team, sitting in two different locations, and soon they ran into collaboration issues.[28]

Worse, their work was not of the plain-vanilla type but involved complicated technologies and emerging, rather than well-understood, technologies. It involved tacit or complicated knowledge—knowledge that is hard to articulate orally and in writing. As we saw in chapter 3, weak ties and complicated knowledge create a transfer barrier.

The Shield team found itself with what I refer to as a Molotov cocktail exploding in their midst—a lethal combination of hardly knowing each other *and* exchanging complicated knowledge.[29]

Molotov cocktail = weak ties x complicated knowledge

The network rule to solve this problem is to engineer strong ties between the team members:

Easier transfer = strong ties x complicated knowledge

In the Hewlett-Packard study I conducted in the 1990s, product-development teams that had strong ties when transferring complicated knowledge were able to avoid the Molotov cocktail from exploding and transferred technologies well.[30]

Getting people to know each other on short notice sounds difficult, but it is easier than you might think. I have found that teams of strangers can, with active team building, develop sufficiently strong ties and perform well. I sometimes do this in executive education courses, with excellent outcomes.

In one such course at INSEAD, France, twenty-eight executives were divided into five teams to investigate an important business issue and present recommendations to their CEO and the board, so the stakes were high. We deliberately mixed up the teams, which included people from different company units who did not know each other. Then, to engineer strong ties between them, we hauled the teams to the Fontainebleau forest just outside Paris—the emperor Napoleon used to hunt for wild boars there—for an afternoon of exercises that required them to work together.

One team had a rough start. When I first met these six independent-minded executives who did not know each other, I thought, "Oh boy, this is going to be some conflict-ridden team." They were six mini Napoleons trying to work in a cross-unit team. Sure enough, the team ran into trouble in the forest. Although each exercise was supposed to be group work, each person tried to figure out the solution alone. After the team members sweated in the forest for three hours, a coach debriefed them. Plenty of conflict came out, with one person barking at another, "I didn't like the way you always tried to do it your way!" The following day, the team worked with an executive coach the whole day, discussing their individual styles and approach to teamwork. Although they had spent only a day and a half together, the team members started to get to know each other, aired conflicts, and agreed on a method for working together. They built trust.

Two months later, when I met the team during one of its meetings, I was struck by how functional it seemed—a far cry from that day in the forest. In the end, the executives had managed to develop a one-team culture. One person told me, "We really came together as a team because of the work we put into getting to know each other."

Managers must act forcefully when they see a situation involving weak cross-unit ties and complicated knowledge. They must switch the team to strong ties immediately, by bringing the cross-unit team together at the beginning of the project in one location for a few days and building a one-team culture.[31]

Build Companywide Networks

Pursuing the six network rules allows leaders to build nimble networks that are effective and do not waste people's time. Such networks follow the principle of disciplined collaboration. The rules help people identify opportunities and capture value from those opportunities:

Nimble network = identify opportunities x **capture value**

- Built outward
- Diverse
- Many weak ties
- Many bridges

- Swarming targets
- Switching to strong ties

Individuals can use these rules to improve their own networks. But that's not enough. This book is about creating collaborative organizations and not only collaborative individuals (see table 6-5). Leaders can apply these rules to the company, asking, "How well do we as company do vis-à-vis these rules?" Three steps help.

Map the Network

If a bird flying high looked down at the myriad relationships among people in your company, what would it see? Would it look down on a map of islands with very few connections between them, or would it see a good number of relationships across the islands? To gain a bird's-eye view of their networks, leaders need to first create a network map. A cross-unit network map consists of all informal relations spanning units. You can identify these relationships by administering a network survey to people in the company.[32] The sum of their answers will show where there are many cross-unit interactions and where there are few or none.

Evaluate the Network

How well does the companywide network stack up against the six network rules? The European media company did not score well against some of the rules. Consider, for example, rule number 1. As the tables earlier in this chapter show, there were very few links between country subsidiaries and only a few good links between business units. Although the leaders knew this intuitively, the network map confirmed their suspicion.

TABLE 6-5

How the rules apply to individual and company networks

Principle	Individual network (connections to colleagues in other units)	Company network (connections across all units)
1. Build outward.	Build relations to other units. • Metric: percent of all your ties that are to people outside your own unit	Connect pairs of units. • Metric: number of pairs of units well connected
2. Build diversity.	Build ties to *different* types. • Metric: number of *different* ideas, skills, technologies, expertise, offices etc. that you get through your network	Connect units that are *different*. • Metric: number of *different* types of units, ideas, skills, expertise, etc. that are connected
3. Build weak ties.	Build a good number of weak ties. • Metric: percent of contacts in your network that are weak	Encourage people to communicate occasionally (not always often). • Metric: percent of cross-unit ties that are weak
4. Use bridges.	Find the best bridges and use them for search. • Metric: number of good bridges you know and use	Cultivate many bridges everywhere. • Metric: number of people in the company who are bridges
5. Swarm the target.	When needed, enlist support of others to persuade the target. • Metric: number of times you successfully swarmed the target	Coach people to rely on informal persuasion (swarming) across units. • Metric: number of times people fail to get things done cross unit
6. Switch to strong ties.	When needed, invest in strong ties. • Metric: number of times you invested up front in building relationships in cross-unit teams	Encourage up-front investments in strong ties. • Metric: number of times cross-unit teams fail due to lack of strong ties

Tailor the Intervention

Disciplined collaboration means identifying the weak spots in a companywide network and designing specific solutions for each one. If the problem is lack of connections among isolated units, then it's best to work on developing more bridges (e.g., by starting a job rotation program). If the problem is lack of diversity, then you should get people from different kinds of units to mingle. If the problem is lack of connections between technical areas, then start communities of practice focused on a technical area that involves people from across the company—and so on. This approach is vastly different from saying, "Let's do an annual retreat to help our people network." That's a shotgun approach that only adds costs without pinpointing specific problems.

Managing company networks has evolved from an art to a science: we know a lot about what makes networks work and how they can help disciplined collaboration. Networks are manageable: managers can collect network data, assess it based on network rules, and implement specific remedies. Leaders who pursue disciplined collaboration retire aimless networking lunches and annual networking retreats and apply the six network rules in a scientific way.

Chapter 6: Key Points

Lever 3: Build Nimble Networks

- Many people hold the wrong beliefs about networks, believing that networking is always a good thing (in fact, it can be bad); big networks are better than small ones (that is not always the case, because networking takes time); only the socially gifted network well (many others build good networks); networking is an art, not a science (it can be measured). These beliefs are dangerous: networking will run amok, destroying results.

- These off-base beliefs can be replaced by six network rules that infuse discipline into networking and form nimble, not bloated, networks. The rules provide two fundamental benefits: they help people identify opportunities outside their own units, and they help people capture value from those opportunities.

- The six network rules are especially powerful for reducing two barriers to collaboration—search problems and transfer problems. They also help with the not-invented-here and hoarding barriers, although in limited ways.

- Four network rules help people identify opportunities: build outward (not inward), build diversity (not size), build weak ties (not strong), and build bridges (do not use familiar faces).

- Two networks rules help people capture value: swarm targets—colleagues, other units—by enlisting help from others who can influence them; and switch to strong ties when the transfer of knowledge across units involves tacit and complicated knowledge.

- Leaders need to move from treating networks in a company as annual gatherings to carrying out rigorous network analysis: map the network, evaluate the network, and target the interventions. Such disciplined networking is a hallmark of disciplined collaboration.

PART THREE

A Personal Challenge

CHAPTER SEVEN

Grow to Be a Collaborative Leader

O N AUGUST 31, 2004, two months before the U.S. presidential election pitting George W. Bush against John Kerry, Arnold Schwarzenegger strode on stage to speak at the Republican convention in Madison Square Garden. The California governor had become one of the most improbable political leaders in the United States. A seven-time Mr. Olympia bodybuilding champion by 1980, Schwarzenegger had reinvented himself as a Hollywood movie star, famously uttering in his thick Austrian accent, "Hasta la vista, Baby" in *Terminator 1, 2,* and *3.* Then, in 2003, when California held a special election, the terminator had seized the opportunity to run as a Republican. He became the governor—or the "governator" as he is often called—of the eighth largest economy in the world.

Now, at the Republican convention, Schwarzenegger created an uproar. The audience was ecstatic, and Schwarzenegger clearly relished his newfound role. All summer, the governator had been at war with his opponents in California. The lone action hero was battling all those liberal Democrats who had blocked his $103 billion state budget— what a great drama to bring to the Republican convention. Gazing at the audience of some five thousand delegates, Schwarzenegger built to his climax, punching his index finger in the air. He thundered, "To those critics who are so pessimistic about our economy, I say: don't be economic girlie men!" The audience erupted in a wild roar, standing and waving "Arnold!" banners.[1]

Naturally, the "girlie men" were livid. Democrat John Burton, the California senate president, fumed, "I don't know what the definition of 'girlie man' is. As opposed to his being a he-man? I can't think of a way to have the he-man and the girlie men join hands around the Capitol and sing 'Kumbaya.'"[2] The atmosphere in Sacramento, California's state capital, wasn't exactly ripe for collaboration.

How had California politics devolved to this dire state? After he had been sworn in as governor in November 2003, Schwarzenegger had been lauded for working with the Democrats. But it didn't last long. Come June 2004, when he met resistance to his budget, Schwarzenegger turned nasty. In mid-July, he broke off negotiations and departed on a road trip to mobilize Californians, calling the Democrats "girlie men" and urging voters to terminate them on "judgment day" in November: "I want you to go to the polls . . . You are the terminators, yes!"[3] In a rally at the Cheesecake Factory restaurant in San Diego, Schwarzenegger "spread his arms, hunched his shoulders, and struck a bodybuilding pose," rallying the crowd: "We're here to pump you up!"[4]

The Democrats fired back. "We can't get a budget done at the Cheesecake Factory. We can only get it done here," declared Kevin Murray from the state senate floor.[5] Senate President John Burton piled on: "I was a little bit worried about whether Arnold thought he was elected God or elected governor."[6]

By the time of the election in November 2004, the Democrats were not terminated. But the partisan fight took an even nastier turn the following year. Schwarzenegger warned that if the Democrats wouldn't play along with his agenda, he would call a special election to put his proposals directly to the voters (California law allows for this). And he did just that, backing four proposals to be voted on in November 2005.[7]

Election day in November 2005 was indeed judgment day. By this time the voters themselves were the terminators—of Schwarzenegger's proposals, that is. In a bitter repudiation of the governator, all four measures were soundly defeated. His 60 percent approval rating in January 2005 had tanked to 33 percent by September 2005. Voters detested the warfare.

Now what should Arnold do? As in *The Terminator,* he had fashioned himself as a lone hero crusading against his enemies. His autocratic style and heated rhetoric had poisoned the atmosphere in Sacramento. One option was to continue on this path and come back stronger, with more ammunition. But instead Schwarzenegger made a U-turn: he reached out to collaborate with the Democrats. After his defeat, he declared, "I also recognize that we also need more bipartisan cooperation . . . And I promise that I will deliver that."[8] In January, he confessed, "I've thought a lot about the last year and the mistakes I made . . . I have absorbed my defeat and I have learned my lesson."[9]

The Economist wrote, "Defeated, the governor abruptly apologised and turned benign, like the reprogrammed hero of 'Terminator 2.'"[10] So began Schwarzenegger's new collaborative leadership phase. To put talk into action, Schwarzenegger replaced his Republican chief of staff with Democrat Susan Kennedy.

Everything Schwarzenegger does comes with a strange twist. He loves to puff on a cigar, but because smoking is banned in official buildings, he had erected a large smoking tent in the courtyard outside his office, complete with chairs and a clubby atmosphere. The tent turned out to be a great place for the former he-man and girlie men to bond, including the two most important Democrats: Senate President Don Perata and Speaker Fabian Núñez. As the *Wall Street Journal* wrote, "The 59-year old governor and the 40-year old speaker often talk over cigars in the smoking tent. Amid continuing criticism from their own parties, they're tackling thorny areas, including health-care reform."[11] One time while puffing cigars in the tent, Speaker Núñez mentioned a proposed law that aimed to cut greenhouse gases: "I told the Governor, 'Here's what I want to do.'" The governor's eyes lit up; "I'm a Republican, but I'm a Hollywood Republican!"[12]

The personal bonds that developed among Schwarzenegger, Núñez, and Perata allowed them to find common ground. That's how they were able, for example, to agree on an increase in the minimum wage for California workers. Schwarzenegger had twice before vetoed proposals to increase that wage above $6.75 per hour. Many Republicans did not want an increase, arguing that it would hurt small businesses. On the Democratic side, workers wanted a big increase and an automatic adjustment pegged to future inflation. Rather than let these narrow agendas define their work, Schwarzenegger and the Democrats focused on the bigger goal: getting a reasonable adjustment for California's workers. This entailed some compromises. Schwarzenegger agreed to a higher increase—an increase of $1.25 per hour—but he insisted that it not be indexed to inflation. The Democrats got a larger increase, but they relented on the automatic adjustment. And with that, they solved the problem together.

The results were dramatic. In 2006, Schwarzenegger signed laws that increased the minimum wage, sought to reduce greenhouse gases, and allocated huge pots of money to improve roads, bridges, and schools.[13] According to one newspaper, the year will go down in history as "one of the most productive legislative sessions in decades."[14] Not only did their collaborative efforts solve important problems, but also the governor's and the Democrats' approval ratings soared in late 2006 (see figure 7-1). They both won.

FIGURE 7-1

The fall and rise of Governor Arnold Schwarzenegger

Percent Californians with favorable approval

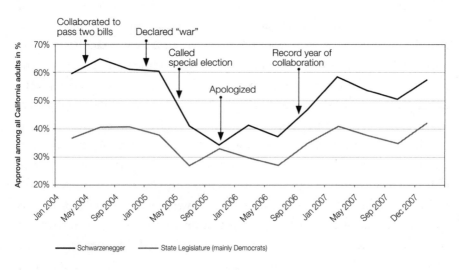

Source: Public Policy Institute of California, http://www.ppic.org.

Like Arnold Schwarzenegger, leaders can change their leadership styles from autocratic to collaborative behaviors. You might object, "He's only a politician, and all politicians do whatever they need to do to get their way. He didn't really transform himself." True, we don't know whether Schwarzenegger truly transformed himself. He may well fall back into the terminator role next time there is a budget crisis. But consider two facts: we know that he behaved collaboratively in 2006; even his opponents acknowledged it. We also know that this collaboration led to major legislative successes rarely seen in California politics. Whether his collaborative style is temporary or lasting is secondary: it happened, and it led to great performance.

This book has so far concentrated on how leaders can cultivate collaboration among people in an organization. I have offered tools a leader can deploy, such as setting a common goal or creating a human resource system that fosters T-shaped management. But tools alone are not enough. Leaders who implement disciplined collaboration successfully also walk the walk—they exemplify a collaborative leadership style. In this closing chapter, I shift the focus from the organization to the individual leader, and I examine what it takes personally to be a collaborative leader. It's a personal challenge for leaders to change not only others but also themselves.

Three behaviors define a collaborative leadership style: redefining success, involving others, and being accountable (see table 7-1). Figure 7-2 offers an assessment tool you can use to score yourself or others.[15] Because a collaborative leadership style works in any organization— whether business, nonprofit, government, or political—this last chapter focuses equally on political leaders like Schwarzenegger and on CEOs.

Redefining Success: From Narrow Agendas to Bigger Goals

When Arnold Schwarzenegger changed his leadership style in November 2005, one of the first things he did was to redefine success. Before, when he pushed the ballot initiatives, success was clearly defined as

TABLE 7-1

The three behaviors of a collaborative leadership style

Behavior	What it means
Redefining success: from narrow agendas to bigger goals	Collaborative leaders redefine success and focus on goals bigger than their own narrow agendas. They seek common ground, look for pragmatic solutions, and compromise.
Involving others: from autocratic to inclusive decision making	Collaborative leaders involve others in decision making and exhibit an open mind—to alternatives, divergent views, dialogue, and working with others.
Being accountable: from blaming to taking responsibility	Collaborative leaders hold themselves accountable, and they also demand accountability from others.

FIGURE 7-2

Do You have a collaborative leadership style?

Step 1. Take a brief, subjective poll. Pick a person to rate: yourself, your boss, your subordinate, or someone else. Please assess this person according to his or her behaviors and characteristics. Enter a number from 1 (not at all) to 7 (to a large extent) that best describes the person.

Behavior	Survey Question	Enter 1–7
Redefining success as bigger goals	1. Puts own goals as secondary and the company's overarching goals as primary.	
	2. Is preoccupied with own agenda to the exclusion of larger company goals. (Score 1–7, then take 8 minus your score and enter that number.)*	Enter 8 – your score =
	3. When confronted with a situation where people disagree, is able to get people to look at the bigger picture.	
	4. Is good at finding common grounds among people who have different goals and agendas.	
	A: Total of responses (sum 1 to 4):	
Involving others	5. Empathizes with people who have different views.	
	6. Encourages open discussion and debate of issues early in the process.	
	7. Often makes decisions alone or overrules the team's decisions. (score 1–7, then take 8 minus your score and enter that number).*	Enter 8 – your score =
	8. Thinks "How do I involve people?" as opposed to "I will tell people what to do."	
	B: Total of responses (sum 5 to 8):	
Being accountable	9. Takes responsibility for a mistake	
	10. Frequency used language like, "I am responsible."	
	11. Demands accountability in others.	
	12. Makes sure others take responsibility for their actions.	
	C: Total of responses (sum 9 to 12):	
	Total Score (sum A + B + C):	

*You need to reverse your scores for questions 2 and 7. For example, if your score is 5, then do: 8 – 5 = 3. Enter 3 in the column to the right.

Step 2. Benchmark the scores against a sample of 162 high-performing executives. Plot your scores to benchmark them against a sample of executives who were rated a top 50 percent performer in their company.**

	Lowest quartile (lowest)	Second lowest quartile	Median	Second highest quartile	Highest quartile (higest)
1. Redefine success	4–16	17–19	20	21–23	24–28
2. Involve others	4–13	14–17	18	19–22	23–28
3. Accountability	4–17	18–19	20	21–23	24–28
Total score	12–49	50–57	58	59–64	65–84
Implication:	Not a collaborative leadership style	A fairly low collaborative leadership style	A modest collaborative leadership style	A pretty good collaborative leadership style	An excellent collaborative leadership style

Total score is the sum of scores from redefine success, involve others, and accountability.

**Note that this is not a random sample of managers in companies. 185 participants from six different executive education courses were asked to select one executive they knew really well and to assess this person according to this instrument. 162 picked someone whom they rated as a top 50 percent performer in their company, forming the basis of this sample. The rated individuals were senior managers in large companies: 15 percent were business unit heads, 26 percent functional managers, and 48 percent senior executives in various roles, with another 11 percent in other capacities (corporate, etc). The sample is highly biased in terms of gender (93 percent men), with a mean age of 47 years, with an average tenure in their company of 15 years. 90 percent had a college or master's degree.

achieving *his* goals. Each initiative was a declaration of war against a constituency. In his new collaborative style, Schwarzenegger played down his own agenda and focused on finding common ground with the Democrats.

All leaders face Schwarzenegger's dilemma. You can push your own narrow agenda above all else, or you can redefine success as achieving bigger goals.[16] CEOs can define success in personal terms—maximizing their compensation, celebrity status, and prestige on the world stage—or they can redefine success by pursuing goals bigger than themselves, such as focusing on the company, not themselves, and leaving behind a strong organization that will do well when they are gone.

Unless you're in retail, you may never have heard of Robert Ulrich. Chances are, though, that you know the company he has led for the past fourteen years—Target, the Minneapolis-based retail chain. Under his stewardship since 1994, Target's sales went up 197 percent to reach $63 billion in 2007. The stock price soared 750 percent over the same period.[17] These numbers are even more impressive when you consider the competition: Wal-Mart.

Ulrich grew up in retailing in the Midwest. From the time he started out as merchandising trainee in 1967 with Dayton department stores, he was hooked on retail. He rose quickly through the ranks at Dayton Hudson (the antecedent to Target) and eventually became CEO in 1994. Known to kick back with a Coors Lite and a game of poker with pals, Ulrich exudes a Midwestern reserve.[18]

The emblematic company man, Ulrich likes to fly under the radar. It helps that headquarters are in Minneapolis, away from the busy media circuits of New York and London. And he does his part to remain a recluse. Not until March 2008, when *Fortune* managed to do a cover story on Target, did the company or Ulrich grace the cover of a major business magazine, something that is highly unusual for a company of its size. In 2003, Ulrich showed up at Target's annual stockholder meeting, offered a few prepared remarks, and disappeared behind the curtains without taking a single question. That performance earned him a raspberry award for "Worst Annual Meeting Behavior" from a shareholder advocacy group.[19] But that didn't ruffle him. Nor is Ulrich one to stoke a personality cult inside the company: when he walks through his stores twice a month, his own employees often do not recognize him. One former Target executive dubbed him the "Silent Sam Walton," referring to the iconic founder of Wal-Mart.[20]

Being publicity-shy in itself doesn't mean that a leader is putting company interests first. But in Ulrich's case the two are related. In 1993, when his peers voted him Discounter of the Year, Ulrich had this to say to a journalist: "I love this job, I love this company. My personal goals are pretty much wrapped up with Target."[21] Anne Mulcahy, CEO of Xerox, has known Ulrich for a long time and is a board member of Target. Describing him and his groomed successor, she observes, "Their ambition is about the company; it is not about themselves as individuals." When a *Fortune* reporter in 2008 committed the sin of focusing too much on personas, asking Ulrich how his successor differs from him, the journalist noted, "The room grows silent, his mouth gets thin. Arms cross. 'This isn't about me,' he says. Long, awkward pause. 'We're all a little bit nervous when we are talking too much about [ourselves].'"[22]

Perhaps the most telling indication is Ulrich's view of how much the company depends on him. After all, isn't it a great testimonial to one's own genius if the company falters after the leader departs? "I know there are some people who have sort of this twisted concept that they can't do it without me," Ulrich says, "but that would obviously be the worst legacy that one could possibly leave." For Ulrich, it's about Target, not him.

Arnold Schwarzenegger and Robert Ulrich reveal two dimensions of a leader's ability to go beyond narrow agendas and focus on bigger goals.

Putting Personal Goals and Interests Second

The collaborative leader has the capacity to subordinate his or her own goals to the larger goals of the institution.[23] Of course, in most situations, there is no conflict between personal interests and those of the enterprise. But sometimes self-interest and the interests of the enterprise diverge. Collaborative leaders follow a clear rule in these situations by prioritizing the bigger goal.

Getting Others to Transcend Their Own Agendas

Collaborative leaders seek common ground among people who have different goals and agendas. Schwarzenegger, Núñez, and Perata pursued this behavior in 2006. Some of the tools that I described earlier in this book—such as setting a unifying goal—are useful here, but the effort needs to start with the leader's own willingness to seek out common ground with others.

Redefining success is the first part of a collaborative leadership style. But it is not enough. Collaborative leaders also need to involve others in deciding how to achieve broader goals.

Involving Others: From Autocratic to Inclusive Decision Making

At nine o'clock at night on October 18, 1962, Robert Kennedy squeezed into the front seat of his car together with the CIA director, the chairman of the Joint Chiefs of Staff, and a driver. Six more passengers crowded into the backseat. The packed car secretly sped off from the State Department and headed for the White House, where President John F. Kennedy awaited.[24]

Three days earlier, President Kennedy had learned that the Soviets were placing nuclear-armed missiles on Cuba—missiles that "within a few minutes of their being fired" would kill eighty million Americans.[25] The president had immediately asked his brother, Attorney General Robert Kennedy, to hurry over to the White House, where senior members of his team had hastily convened. The U.S. military commanders didn't blink. As Robert Kennedy recalled, "The members of the Joint Chiefs of Staff were unanimous in calling for immediate military action."[26] That meant a massive surprise air strike to obliterate the missile sites. But then someone suggested an alternative: a naval blockade in which U.S. warships would surround Cuba and prevent Soviet ships from entering. The generals didn't buy it. "We don't have any choice except direct military action," General Curtis LeMay said bluntly.[27]

President Kennedy was in a bind. But instead of hastily making a decision, he took his time and instructed his brother to lead a thorough deliberation where all viewpoints could be aired. The president did not want to repeat the earlier Bay of Pigs fiasco, in which cabinet members had supported an ill-conceived covert operation to unseat Fidel Castro. When some fifteen hundred Cuban freedom fighters landed on the shores of Cuba, they were quickly killed or captured. Historian Arthur Schlesinger, who took part in those deliberations, later wrote, "Our meetings were taking place in a curious atmosphere of assumed consensus . . . not one spoke against it."[28]

In the aftermath, President Kennedy had introduced four changes to how his top team made decisions.[29] First, he demanded that each participant function as a "skeptical generalist," focusing on the problem as a whole rather than approaching it from his department's standpoint. Second, to stimulate freewheeling discussions, Kennedy wanted to use informal settings, with no formal agenda and protocol. Third, he introduced the idea of subgroups: the team would be broken into groups that would work on alternatives and then reconvene. Fourth, he wanted some leaderless sessions, without him present, so as to avoid people simply following his views. The result was an inclusive approach, which could now be put to use in this new crisis.

In the unfolding days of the Cuban missile crisis, the group of more than a dozen met in an unassuming office at the State Department and shuttled secretly back and forth to the White House. The informality surrounding their meetings inspired frank dialogue. "During all these deliberations, we all spoke as equals," Robert Kennedy recalled of the group, which included Secretary of State Dean Rusk, Secretary of Defense Robert McNamara, CIA Director John McCone, and General Maxwell Taylor (chairman of the Joint Chiefs of Staff). "There was no rank, and, in fact, we did not even have a chairman," said Robert Kennedy. "The conversations were completely uninhibited and unrestricted. Everyone had an equal opportunity to express himself and to be heard directly."[30] The president did not attend all the meetings. "I felt there was less true give and take with the President in the room," Robert Kennedy said. "There was the danger that by indicating his own view and leanings, he would cause others just to fall in line."[31]

By the third night, the group had moved in the direction of a blockade. Now ready to involve the president in the discussions, they crowded into one car and hurried over to the White House.[32] But, as the evening went on, and with probing questions from the president, opinions started to shift. Some favored an air strike, others a blockade.

The following morning, back at the State Department, the group deployed the subgroup procedure. One group drafted the argument for an air strike and a detailed recommendation for how to implement it. Another group did the same for the blockade. The groups then swapped papers, dissecting and criticizing each other. The papers were returned to the original group, which responded to the critique and developed further answers. In this way, the group was able to surface most pros and cons.

Two days later, the group presented the two fully developed alternatives to President Kennedy, who chose to pursue the blockade rather than an air strike. Immediately, the Navy sent 180 ships to the Caribbean. The B-52 bomber force was sent up in the air, loaded with nuclear weapons. As one bomber landed, another took off. The president was to speak to the nation on Monday evening at 7 p.m. One hour before the speech, Secretary Rusk called in Soviet Ambassador Dobrynin and told him about the blockade; the ambassador left considerably shaken.

It worked! A week later, on Monday, October 29, Soviet leader Khrushchev announced he would remove the missiles from Cuba.

President Kennedy had chosen an *inclusive approach* to making the decision, involving a wide group of people. Fundamentally, leaders who, like Kennedy, practice inclusiveness have an open mind by following three practices.

Openness to People

Inclusive leaders invite a fairly diverse group of people into their decision-making process. The opposite is to be unilateral—that is, to make decisions alone, with little regard for other people's views. Being open to people's input can be difficult, especially because it runs counter to a natural tendency to swoop in, take charge, and make decisions. Kevin Sharer, CEO of Amgen, the large biotech company based in Los Angeles, is careful not to let this tendency prevail. "When I go into what I call my submarine mode—when I go very, very deep into a problem—I tend to think I can solve it myself," he admitted, "and am at risk of ignoring the advice of experts and closing down debate. I've paid a price for this—for example, in forging ahead with a product that others were telling me didn't have sufficient commercial promise."[33]

Openness to Alternatives

Inclusive leaders give serious consideration to different views. They listen well: they seek to understand what others think and why. This requires leaders to be empathetic—to put themselves in the shoes of others and see things from their perspectives. Being open in this way is rare in leaders. New York columnist David Brooks singled out then-presidential candidate Barack Obama as someone who can do this: "He still retains the capacity, also rare in presidents, of being able to sympathize with and grasp the motivations of his rivals."[34]

They also ask questions instead of talking all the time. A. G. Lafley, CEO of Procter & Gamble, fits this mold. Jeffrey Immelt, CEO of General Electric, describes Lafley as an "excellent listener. He's a sponge."[35] Lafley also creates room for others to talk. Not long after he became CEO, he rearranged the furniture in the conference room: out went the rectangular table, and in came a round one, with no place for the CEO at the head. In his weekly meetings with his senior team, people could sit where they liked. "At one of those meetings, an outsider might have trouble distinguishing the CEO," observed Robert Berner of *BusinessWeek*. "He occasionally joins in the discussion, but most of the time the executives talk as much to each other as to Lafley."

Openness to Debate

Inclusive leaders encourage debate and make it safe to voice opinions. Professor Amy Edmondson of Harvard Business School calls this "psychological safety": leaders need to behave in such a way that people feel safe to speak up without fear of retribution.[36] Leaders who praise dissent and alternative suggestions (even if they were not followed) help create this safety.

One risk of an inclusive approach to decision making is that leaders debate endlessly without forging decisions and moving ahead. To combat this risk, collaborative leaders also need to be decisive. They make the final decision. This approach is not the same as a consensus process, in which everyone must agree on a decision. Inclusiveness means that people take part in coming up with alternatives, supplying information, and debating, but it stops there.

It is the combination of being inclusive and decisive that makes collaborative leadership powerful. Nowhere is this better illustrated than in the TV footage of President Kennedy alone at his desk at 7 p.m. that October 22, 1962, addressing the nation. He had made the decision.

Collaborative leaders who master this inclusive style make better decisions and get better buy in. It ensures that alternative views are considered and that flaws in thinking are exposed. Autocratic leaders, in contrast, risk running with preordained views that may be wrong. Including others also leads to better support: people who are part of the decision making will work harder and be more committed to implementing the decision.[37]

Involving others means that a number of people participate in the decision-making process.[38] But that raises another issue: when everyone is involved, who is accountable?

Being Accountable: From Blaming to Taking Responsibility

On the night of March 13, 1964, in New York City, a psychopath named Winston Moseley sneaked up on a twenty-eight-year-old woman, Kitty Genovese, and violently stabbed her twice in the back. Genovese had just stepped out of her car after work to walk the one hundred feet to her apartment building in the Kew Gardens section of Queens. When she screamed out, "Oh my God, he stabbed me! Help me!" several neighbors heard her cries. One shouted from afar, "Let that girl alone!" and Moseley ran away. Genovese, seriously injured, struggled toward her apartment. No one came out to help. Moseley returned and found Genovese barely conscious in a hallway. He stabbed her several more times, sexually assaulted her, stole about $49, and left. When police arrived, it was too late: she died in the ambulance on the way to the hospital.[39]

Two weeks later, after *The New York Times* published a piece with the headline "Thirty-Eight Who Saw Murder Didn't Call the Police," public anger flared about the callousness and apathy it described. Although the headline exaggerated the number of witnesses, police investigations identified about a dozen of them. This notorious murder led to much soul-searching and to a stream of research that highlighted a disturbing phenomenon: the *bystander effect,* in which people who are part of a large group often do not reach out and help.[40]

In a very different setting, in the safety of an experiment run by professors at the University of Massachusetts, Carl and his fellow students were asked to do something simple: pull as hard as they could on a rope.[41] In the first round, Carl went up to the rope, fastened his hands around it, firmly planted his legs on the floor, held his breath, pulled until his face turned red, and then let go. A device measured how hard he had pulled, a respectable 130 pounds (59 kg), which was the average among the participants. In the second round, Carl pulled together with Adam (as a duo), then with two others, and finally as a team of six people.

Now, pulling a rope is one of those activities where people's effort should simply add up; if Carl pulled 59 kg and Adam 41 kg, then their team score should be 100 kg.[42] But odd things happened in those team settings: their efforts went down! Carl and Adam together didn't score 100 kg; they scored 91 kg when the two of them pulled as a duo. That's 91 percent of the sum of their individual efforts. And when Carl pulled as part of a trio, the team score dropped to 82 percent. The worst drop happened when Carl was part of a six-person team; it scored a miserable 78 percent of the sum of the individual scores. These studies gave rise to what is called *social loafing:* people tend to contribute less in a group setting.[43]

The bystander effect and social loafing point to a vital problem in collective work: when people can hide, they often do. People working in teams can shirk and get by because individual output is not being measured, only team output. Who hasn't been on a team where some people didn't pull their weight?

The antidote to this malaise is the third behavior found in collaborative leadership: a high degree of individual accountability. Accountability is important in all kinds of management, of course, but it is especially important in collaborative organizations because of the tendency to hide behind the collective.

Collaborative leaders who take responsibility do so in two ways.

Assuming Individual Accountability

Collaborative leaders hold themselves accountable even though collaborative work often leads to a diffusion of responsibility. A striking example is Carlos Ghosn, the French-English-Portuguese-Italian-Spanish-speaking globe-trotter who took over Nissan in April 1999, when the company was on the brink of disaster. When he landed in Japan and reviewed the company, he found a culture void of accountability: "If the company did poorly, it was always someone else's fault. Sales blamed product planning, product planning blamed engineering, and engineering blamed finance. Tokyo blamed Europe, and Europe blamed Tokyo."[44]

To break this culture of blame, Ghosn first took personal responsibility. On October 18, 1999, on the eve of the Tokyo Motor Show, Ghosn presented the now famous Nissan Revival Plan to a cynical audience of the world's press and, via video, to company employees worldwide.[45] And then he did something highly unusual: "When I announced the revival plan, I also declared that I would resign if we failed to accomplish any of the commitments we set for ourselves."[46] These commitments were three crystal-clear objectives: return to profitability by 2000; increase operating margins to more than 4.5 percent by 2002; and reduce debt to less than $5.8 billion by 2002. So was his language: "Don't judge me on a good speech. Judge me on my results. Be very cynical. Be very cold. Look at the profits, the debt, the market share, the appeal of the cars. Then judge me."[47] This is clear language. No hedging. No vague objectives he could finesse in case things weren't going well. Instead, he stood there, in public, naked: three hard metrics, to be achieved in three years, for everyone to track and judge.

Holding Others Accountable

Collaborative leaders also demand that others be held accountable. After all, collaborative work involves different people, with each one responsible for her part. This is not the same thing as blaming others; there is a difference between saying, "We are all accountable" and saying, "They are at fault."

This is the second revealing part of Ghosn's approach: he declared that the entire executive committee had to resign with him if the three goals weren't met![48] And he held everyone in the company accountable: "I made it clear that every number had to be thoroughly checked. I did not accept any report that was less than totally clear and verifiable, and I expected people to personally commit to every observation or claim they made."[49]

So here we have an unusual situation in business: a CEO who says publicly that he and his entire executive committee will resign if they do not reach three transparent and measurable targets. That is holding oneself and everyone accountable.

On March 31, 2002, Ghosn could breathe a sigh of relief when he announced record profits for the company: "We have achieved the goals set in the Nissan Revival Plan a year ahead of schedule."[50]

Collaborative leaders who hold themselves and others accountable engage in a few key practices. As Ghosn did, they spell out what they are accountable for—which targets, what kind of job. You can't hold yourself and others accountable if you don't know what to be accountable for. They then accept responsibility for mistakes and poor performance, no matter the circumstance and whether or not others mess up a collaborative effort.

Tearing Down Personal Barriers

If a collaborative leadership style is so powerful, why don't we see it more often? The benchmark data that my colleague Roger Lehman and I collected on 162 top-performing managers shows that only 16 percent of these managers scored high on all three behaviors that make up the collaborative style. This is what the data shows:

- 39 percent scored high on redefining goals ("high" means greater than 5 on the 1-to-7 scale shown in figure 7-2).

- 25 percent scored high on involving others.

- 40 percent scored high on being accountable.

- Only 16 percent scored high on redefining success, involving others, *and* being accountable.

Why is a collaborative leadership style rare? Leaders often blame the system: politicians are only actors in a corrupt system favoring special interests; business leaders are rewarded for individual performance above all, so they are not encouraged to collaborate. Some of this is true. But leaders often face another barrier—themselves. Powerful *personal barriers* can make it difficult for leaders to assume a collaborative leadership style. Spotting these and tearing them down promote a collaborative leadership style.

In our research, we found that five personal barriers matter (see figure 7-3).[51] You can measure yourself or someone else on these barriers by taking the brief assessment in figure 7-4.

Hunger for power. Leaders who seek power—who want others to depend on them—do less well in moving beyond their narrow agendas and redefining success as bigger goals.[52] This makes intuitive sense: giving up part of one's agenda to focus on a bigger goal can be felt as

FIGURE 7-3

How five personal barriers block a collaborative leadership style

This chart shows which personal factors block the three collaborative behaviors. For example, power hunger has a big negative effect on a leader's ability to redefine success: the more hungry leaders are for power, the less they go beyond narrow agendas and focus on bigger goals.

	Redefining success	Being inclusive	Being accountable
Power hunger	Biggest Negative	Negative	Small Negative
Arrogance	Negative	Biggest Negative	No Effect
Defensiveness	Big Negative	Big Negative	Biggest Negative
Fear	Small Negative	Small Negative	No Effect
Ego	Small Negative	Small Negative	No Effect

Data: These are conclusions from a statistical analysis of a sample of 185 managers. Correlation and regression analyses were used.

FIGURE 7-4

Do personal barriers block your collaborative leadership style?

Score yourself or someone else on the five personal barriers that prevent leaders from developing a collaborative leadership style.

Assess the person according to his or her behaviors and characteristics. Use the following scale:

1 ············ 2 ············ 3 ············ 4 ············ 5 ············ 6 ············ 7
Not at all   Somewhat   To a large extent

	Enter 1 to 7:
1. Wants others to depend on him/her	
2. Wants power for its own sake	
3. Has an attitude that "I know best"	
4. Thinks he/she is a much smarter person than others	
5. Has a hard time taking criticism	
6. Has an attitude that problems tend to lie outside him/herself	
7. Is afraid of losing	
8. Takes defeat personally	
9. Is worried about being humiliated	
10. Likes the limelight	
11. Is self-absorbed	
12. Cultivates an "aura of personality" around her/him	

Scoring sheet:*

Personal barrier	Compute sum of items	Compute final scores
Power hunger	Sum items 1+2: ___ (enter 2 to 14)	Divide score by 2: ___ (enter 1 to 7)
Arrogance	Sum items 3+4: ___ (enter 2 to 14)	Divide score by 2: ___ (enter 1 to 7)
Defensiveness	Sum items 5+6: ___ (enter 2 to 14)	Divide score by 2: ___ (enter 1 to 7)
Fear	Sum items 7+8+9: ___ (enter 3 to 21)	Divide score by 3: ___ (enter 1 to 7)
Ego	Sum items 10+11+12: ___ (enter 3 to 21)	Divide score by 3: ___ (enter 1 to 7)

Interpretation:

Each score ranges from 1 to 7, with 7 indicating a very high personal barrier:
- You can assess the absolute levels of these scores (a score of 4 or above is cause for concern).
- You can also compare the five barriers—which ones are high, which ones are low?
- You can find out how each of these personal barriers prevent a collaborative leadership style from emerging by looking at figure 7-3. For example, a high score on "power hunger" indicates difficulties in redefining success.

*This test has been developed by using the sample of 185 managers. Questions have been tested so that they form clear scales for each of the five personal barriers. The Cronbach Alpha—a measure of how well these scales work—is as follows: Power (CA=0.84); Arrogance (CA=0.86); Defensiveness (CA=0.67); Fear (CA=0.83); Ego (CA=0.76). A CA above 0.70 is good.

relinquishing power. When leaders have a strong craving for power, they tend to stick to their own narrow agendas.

Furthermore, leaders who crave power are less inclusive: letting others play a part in decision making can be seen as giving up power. The drive for power, it seems, is no friend of a collaborative leadership style.

Arrogance. This was the biggest block to involving others in our data. Arrogant leaders—those who have an attitude that "I know best" and think they are smarter than others—do not involve people in their decision making as much as others. After all, if I think I am the smartest person in the room and know it all, why bother asking lesser mortals for their opinions? Also, arrogant leaders don't seem very good at focusing on bigger goals: "I know best, so my goal should be the best one" seems to be the train of thought here.

Defensive Attitude. This is a huge personal barrier. Defensive leaders have a hard time taking criticism and believe that problems tend to lie outside themselves. They are not the ones who stand up in a room and say, "I am accountable here." Furthermore, defensiveness is not the best attitude for redefinition of success: the more defensive a leader is, the less that leader goes beyond narrow agendas. And the more defensive an attitude leaders have, the less inclusive they become. They somehow believe that if they open up to other people, they would be admitting they are wrong. The reality is different, of course: letting others participate in the decision-making process is not the same as admitting to one's own shortcomings.

Fear. A leader's fear of losing and fear of humiliation if defeated also matter, although not as much as other factors. Fear leads to the tendency to stick to one's own narrow agendas rather than focus on bigger goals. When one's identity is tied to one's agenda instead of the broader goal, defeat becomes personal. The same goes for inclusiveness: opening up decision making to other people can be seen as increasing the risk of defeat. Leaders may fear that other people's views will prevail, and not their own.

Big Egos. This did not have as strong an effect on collaborative behaviors as we had thought and plays only a modest negative role. Leaders who build a cult of personality seem to be less apt at transcending their own agendas and involving people in decision making.

Can Leaders Change?

You may look at the list of personal barriers and ask, "Can leaders really tear down these personal barriers and become collaborative?" For some personalities, change is indeed difficult. This is likely to be the case when these personal barriers have become *personality traits*; they are so deeply rooted in a leader's personality that they are nearly permanent. But many times these factors are not yet cemented in a person's personality, and change is possible. Leaders need to recognize these personal barriers, reflect on why they exist, and embark on a personal transformation.

Many leaders have developed a certain leadership style that worked for them in the past or in certain situations. They have grown accustomed to their style, and as they have been promoted up the ranks, they may have come to believe that the style was a contributor to their success. But as more companies turn collaborative, a collaborative leadership style becomes more important. This requires a change for leaders whose style is not collaborative.

John Chambers, longtime highly successful CEO of Cisco, a $35 billion high-tech company based in Silicon Valley, recognized that he had to change his style to become more collaborative. In a video interview with *Financial Times* editor Chrystia Freeland, Chambers talked about his own personal transformation:

> *John Chambers:* Most successful CEOs are command and control. Make no mistake. I am, and I am pretty good at it. That's not the future. It's about collaboration.
>
> *Chrystia Freeland:* How have you had to change the way you work?
>
> *John Chambers:* Well, the hardest thing you do as a leader is to change something that is working well. And yet I believe that

companies and leaders who do not change will get left behind. And so I had to move from a command-and-control leader.

Chrystia Freeland: Would you say that your basic personality is to be that way?

John Chambers: Yes . . . Yes! But you have to learn that you make better decisions through collaboration. And while you might spend more time discussing it than you'd like, once the team has discussed it with different backgrounds, then they can build upon that base much faster than before. And it's also as you watch this be successful, you say, "Why didn't I do that earlier?" And then you realize that you yourself can adjust very quickly.[53]

Arnold Schwarzenegger changed from terminator to collaborator. John Chambers changed from command-and-control to collaborator. Clearly, many people can develop a collaborative leadership style.

Chapter 7: Key Points

Grow to Be a Collaborative Leader

- A collaborative leadership style is defined by three behaviors.

  - Redefining success: Collaborative leaders transcend narrow agendas and define success as a bigger goal.

  - Involving others: Collaborative leaders are open to input, different viewpoints, debate, and working with others in the decision-making process.

  - Being accountable: Collaborative leaders see themselves as responsible for reaching goals and accountable for decisions made. They also hold others accountable.

- A collaborative leadership style is not common. In a sample of 185 managers, only 16 percent exhibited a clear-cut collaborative leadership style.

- One reason there aren't more collaborative leaders is the existence of five powerful personal barriers that block the three collaborative behaviors from emerging: a hunger for power, arrogance, defensiveness, fear, and big egos.

- These personal barriers may be deeply rooted personality traits in some leaders and therefore very difficult to change. But they may be changeable in many others. By reducing these personal barriers, more leaders can take on a collaborative leadership style.

Journey's End (for Now)

This book has now come full circle. While the final chapter highlights how leaders *themselves* can lead with a collaborative style, the other chapters outline how leaders can shape their organization and cultivate disciplined collaboration in *others*. Leaders who practice disciplined collaboration work at all levels: they cultivate collaboration by transforming themselves, their organization, and people working in the organization.

I began this book by relating my research journey of discovering how collaboration can lead to better performance. As I consolidated fifteen years of research, I was surprised by a few things. When I started my research on collaboration in the early nineties, the topic was not that important. Managers saw it as one of many things to get right, but it didn't climb to the top of their agendas. This has changed considerably. I have witnessed collaboration becoming a top priority in large multi-unit companies in the United States, Europe, and Asia. The focus on collaboration will continue, as companies become larger, more complex, more efficient, more global, more decentralized, and more open to working with other parties—all demand disciplined collaboration. And this emphasis continues in a recession, as leaders strive to get more out of existing assets by collaborating. More broadly, collaboration will remain a key part of leadership, for leaders will always need to unite disparate parts within and across organizations. In some sense, that is the essence of leadership. The very job of leaders is to unite people to pursue a common goal.

Another surprise was the importance of distinguishing between good and bad collaboration. A hallmark of my research has been to analyze when collaboration produces good performance and when it leads to terrible results. Many people were taken by the idea that collaboration can be bad, because that idea runs counter to the collaboration hype. Somehow we have come to believe that collaboration is a positive thing and therefore that managers ought to promote it. Pointing out that collaboration can be damaging and can destroy results is a bit like saying that the emperor has no clothes. Of course, criticizing the idea is not enough. This book details *disciplined collaboration* as a solution to understanding the difference between good and bad collaboration.

While finishing this book, I have been thinking about the journey ahead—where will collaboration go? One area has the potential to take collaboration to a much higher level of performance: online collaboration. This book has not focused on the uses of information technology to enable collaboration, such as video-conferencing, social networking tools for business, company blogging, electronic "ask-me" features, and so on. My aim was first to formulate the underlying "management architecture" of collaboration. But with this basic building block in place, we can postulate how online collaboration can help—or destroy—performance. In this book, I have warned against the danger of believing that more collaboration is necessarily good. Likewise, I warn against the belief that more *online* collaboration is necessarily a good thing. We need to ask the same critical questions: What is the difference between good and bad *online* collaboration? When does online collaboration destroy value? There is a huge pot of gold for software firms that can answer these questions and offer tools that avoid the traps of collaboration and lead people to perform better.

———————————

While writing this book, I took a few days off to go to Barcelona, Spain, to give a talk on disciplined collaboration to more than a hundred senior executives from various countries. I asked for a show of hands: "How many here own an Apple iPod and use iTunes?" 95 percent of them put their hand up—that's 95 percent market penetration! When I asked,

"How many of you have owned a Sony Walkman at one point in your life?," 100 percent—100 percent!—of the hands came up. Then I asked, "How many of you have used Sony's Connect?" Not one hand crept up.

Sony, not Apple, should have given us the iPod. Sony failed miserably because it couldn't collaborate across its many decentralized divisions. It could deliver only one kind of performance—wonderful products coming out of independent business units that had a great deal of freedom. But it couldn't add another level of performance—great products resulting from collaboration across its divisions. It failed to move its performance to a higher plateau—to gain the best of both worlds—by keeping the benefits of having independent business units *and* reaping big results from collaboration. It lacked disciplined collaboration.

Leaders who successfully pursue disciplined collaboration avoid the fate of Sony and take their organizations to higher levels of performance. They know where the opportunities for collaboration exist and when to say no to lesser projects. They avoid the traps of overestimating benefits and overcollaborating. They tear down the barriers that separate their employees. They set powerful, unifying goals and forge a value of teamwork. They cultivate T-shaped management. They help employees build nimble, not bloated, networks. They look within themselves and work to change their own leadership styles. In cultivating collaboration in the *right way*, they set their people free to achieve great things not possible when they are divided.

The Research Behind the Book

The principles laid out in this book are based on my fifteen years of research on collaboration. In a snapshot, my findings are based, in addition to company-specific case studies, on the following studies.

The Hewlett-Packard Study

In the mid-1990s, as part of my PhD dissertation work at Stanford Business School, I studied Hewlett-Packard's electronic measurement sector (later spun off as Agilent in 1999). This sector consisted of forty-one decentralized business (product) units that specialized in various measurement products. They were also spread out across the world. After negotiating access to HP, I interviewed fifty managers, engineers, and marketers in more than ten business units in order to gain a deeper understanding of collaboration issues and design the study. (Because this was my dissertation, I gained invaluable advice from my PhD committee, including professors Jeffrey Pfeffer (chair), Joel Podolny, William Barnett, Robert Burgelman, and James March.

The study was a large-scale social network study at three levels of analysis.

- *New-product development projects:* The sample consisted of 120 projects. Using the firm's databases and a survey instrument,

I collected data on team composition, duration, innovativeness, management, technical requirements, and use of knowledge from other units in the instrumentation sector and the rest of HP.

- *Individual project team members:* Using a network survey, I collected social network data on a sample of 250 engineers in these projects.

- *Business units:* Using the firm's databases and a survey instrument, I collected social network data and information on technological competencies for the forty-one business units in the sector.

This data allowed me to analyze the conditions under which project teams benefited from collaborating with other units and thereby obtained valuable software, hardware, and advice. It was especially helpful for developing ideas about search and transfer barriers (outlined in chapter 3) and effective networks (chapter 6). Project measurements included time to market, knowledge obtained, and degree of innovativeness.

Later, I collaborated with others to conduct further analyses of this rich data set, including with Jeffrey Pfeffer, Joel Podolny, Bjorn Lovas, and Louise Mors. Published articles include the following.

- Hansen, Morten T. "The Search-Transfer Problem: The Role of Weak Ties in Sharing Knowledge Across Organization Subunits." *Administrative Science Quarterly* (1999). Winner of the ASQ 2005 Scholarly Contribution Award for best article.

- Hansen, Morten T., Joel M. Podolny, and Jeffrey Pfeffer. "So Many Ties, So Little Time: A Task Contingency Perspective on the Value of Corporate Social Capital in Organizations." *Research in the Sociology of Organizations* (2001).

- Hansen, Morten T. "Knowledge Networks: Explaining Effective Knowledge Sharing in Multiunit Companies." *Organization Science* (2002).

- Hansen, Morten T., and Bjorn Lovas. "How Do Multinational Companies Leverage Technological Competencies? Moving from Single to Interdependent Explanations." *Strategic Management Journal* (2004).

- Hansen, Morten T., Louise Mors, and Bjorn Lovas. "Knowledge Sharing in Organizations: Multiple Networks, Multiple Phases." *Academy of Management Journal* (2005).

The IT Consulting Company Study

With my colleague Martine Haas, who was then a doctoral candidate at Harvard Business School (now a professor at Wharton), I conducted an in-depth study of a large multinational consulting company that at the time had more than ten thousand consultants. Senior executives had launched a knowledge-sharing initiative a few years earlier, and they were interested in conducting statistical analysis of the effects of knowledge sharing in the organization. In addition to interviewing fifty managers about their collaborative activities, we undertook two statistical studies.

- Drawing on a sample of 180 sales teams, we analyzed the effects of cross-company collaboration on these teams' performance (including whether or not they won the bid).

- We collected data on database usage for the ten thousand consultants and the content in the firm's knowledge databases run by the firm's forty-three practice groups (where they had stored consulting documents to be used in subsequent client work). We analyzed how much consultants used the information provided by their colleagues through these databases.

This study led us to understand when collaboration is helpful and when it is detrimental (as discussed in chapter 2, under the disguise of "Sterling"). The results were published in the following academic articles.

- Hansen, Morten T., and Martine R. Haas. "Competing for Attention in Knowledge Markets: Electronic Document Dissemination in a Management Consulting Company." *Administrative Science Quarterly* (2001).

- Haas, Martine R., and Morten T. Hansen. "When Using Knowledge Can Hurt Performance: The Value of Organizational Capabilities in a Management Consulting Company." *Strategic Management Journal* (2005).

- Haas, Martine, and Morten T. Hansen. "Different Knowledge, Different Benefits: Toward a Productivity Perspective on Knowledge Sharing in Organizations." *Strategic Management Journal* (2007).

The Global Executive Study

With Bolko von Oetinger, a senior partner at the Boston Consulting Group and head of the BCG Strategy Institute, I conducted a series of in-person interviews on collaboration with fifty executives in large multinationals in the United States, France, Denmark, Germany, the United Kingdom, Hong Kong, and Singapore. Companies included (among others) Apple, BP, EMAP, Genentech, Goretex, Ispat (now Mittal Steel), ISS, Jardine Pacific, Levi Strauss, Motorola, Seagram, and SmithKline Beecham. After the first round, and with great help from *Harvard Business Review* editor Paul Hemp, we conducted ten more interviews with business unit managers at BP.

In this study we developed the idea of T-shaped management (as outlined in chapter 5). The study also provided insight into the notion of a collaborative leadership style (chapter 7). The key article from this study is as follows.

- Hansen, Morten T., and Bolko von Oetinger, "Introducing T-Shaped Managers: Knowledge Management's Next Generation." *Harvard Business Review* (2001).

The Collaboration Survey of 107 Companies

Along with professor Nitin Nohria at the Harvard Business School, I analyzed a survey of 107 managers working in various multiunit companies in the United States and Europe. The managers were asked about the level of barriers in their companies, the level of collaborative activities, and the potential upsides from collaboration.

This analysis helped develop insights into the areas of potential upsides from collaboration (as discussed in chapter 2) and the extent of barriers in organizations (chapter 3). It also gave insights into the unification lever (chapter 4). This study was reported in the following articles.

- Hansen, Morten T., and Nitin Nohria. "How to Build Collaborative Advantage." *Sloan Management Review* (2004). Winner of the PwC/Sloan Management Review for Best Article.

- Hansen, Morten T., and Nitin Nohria. "Organizing Multinational Companies for Global Advantage." In *The Global Market: Developing a Strategy to Manage Across Borders,* edited by John Quelch and Rohit Deshpande (San Francisco: Jossey-Bass, 2004).

The Knowledge Management Strategy Study

Together with Nitin Nohria at the Harvard Business School and Thomas Tierney, then worldwide managing partner at Bain & Company, I conducted a small-scale analysis of knowledge management in six companies, including Bain, Accenture, Dell, Hewlett-Packard, Memorial Sloan-Kettering Cancer Institute, and Access Health. This included a contrast analysis of different ways of sharing knowledge, namely through databases or through direct personal networks.

This project was helpful in understanding the various ways of sharing knowledge and the motivational and incentive systems behind them (as discussed in chapters 4 and 5). This effort was written up in the following article.

- Morten T. Hansen, Nitin Nohria, and Thomas Tierney. "What's Your Strategy for Managing Knowledge?" *Harvard Business Review* (1999).

The Search Network Study

With Professor Joel Podolny at Yale School of Management, I launched a study of search networks in a large multinational management consulting company. Jasjit Singh of INSEAD also joined the project. We conducted a field experiment, asking 400 consultants to name the person they would go to for advice or for help in finding an expert. We then asked the same question of the person they had named, and so on, until we arrived at the "true expert" on a particular topic (in all, 580 consultants were surveyed).

From this study came greater insights into the search barrier (chapter 3) and ways a person's network affects the search process, including the use of bridges (chapter 6). The results are reported in the following working paper.

- Singh, Jasjit, Morten T. Hansen, and Joel Podolny. "The World is Not Small for Everyone: Pathways of Discrimination in Searching for Information in Organizations." INSEAD working paper (Fontainebleau, France: INSEAD, 2009).

The Innovation and Collaboration Study

With Julian Birkinshaw at London Business School, I conducted a study of innovation in large multinationals. This work included interviews with managers in several companies, including Shell, Procter & Gamble, British Telecom, and Sara Lee, as well as a survey of managers in 121 companies.

This study provided insights into the idea of innovation as a recombination of talent, knowledge, and technologies from different units in a company, as discussed in chapter 2. This study led to the following publication.

- Hansen, Morten T., and Julian Birkinshaw. "The Innovation Value Chain." *Harvard Business Review* (2007).

All this research has combined three approaches: in-depth case studies to understand collaboration at a detailed level; in-company interviews to further uncover disciplined as opposed to undisciplined collaboration; and large-sample statistical analysis to verify that the hypotheses withstand scrutiny.

No research is perfect, of course, and there are incomplete parts of this body of work. In some places the evidence is mixed or weak, even speculative. In other parts there is only qualitative evidence, and no hard numbers. In addition, my research does not exist apart from that of other scholars, and my work is only a small boat floating on the ocean of outstanding prior work. I have referenced relevant work in the footnotes accompanying each chapter.

NOTES

Chapter 1

1. "Sony Celebrates Walkman 20th Anniversary 1 July 1999; 186 Million Units Sold as of the End of the Fiscal Year Ended March 31, 1999," press release, Sony, July 1, 1999.

2. For a brief history of Stringer's career, see Catherine Griffiths, "The Interview: Sir Howard Stringer, US Head of Sony: Sony's Knight," *Independent* (London), September 18, 2004.

3. *Sony Annual Report 2003; Apple Computer Inc. Annual Report 2003.*

4. For more about Sony Music, see "Details Prove Devilish for Sony, BMG Merger," *Billboard,* November 22, 2003.

5. Quoted in Phred Dvorak, "Out of Tune: At Sony, Rivalries Were Encouraged, Then Came iPod," *Wall Street Journal,* June 29, 2005, A1. Much of the account of the fate of Connect is taken from this article.

6. The quotation from the October 23, 2001, presentation comes from the video, downloaded from YouTube, on November 27, 2007: http://www.youtube.com/watch?v=kN0SVBCJqLs. "Hint: It's not a Mac" is from Steven Levy, *The Perfect Thing* (New York: Simon and Schuster, 2006), 7; As a journalist Levy received an invitation. This is the most detailed look at the development and introduction of the iPod, and I rely on it extensively for this story.

7. A good history of Apple is provided by Jim Carlton, *Apple: The Inside Story of Intrigue, Egomania, and Business Blunders* (New York: Collins, 1998, paperback).

8. Levy, *The Perfect Thing,* 137, documents the introduction of the Rio player (Rio PMP300), produced by a Korean company called Diamond (see also the Wikipedia Web site: http://en.wikipedia.org/wiki/Rio_PMP300). Other companies followed soon thereafter. For example, Compaq worked on a personal jukebox (PJB 100), which got started at Digital Equipment Corporation (DEC) but continued at Compaq when it acquired DEC. Compaq then licensed it to an obscure Korean company, HanGo, which introduced it (*The Perfect Thing,* 45).

9. Quoted in Leander Kahney, "Straight Dope on the iPod's Birth," *Wired,* October 17, 2006.

10. Erik Sherman, "Inside the Apple iPod Design Triumph," *Electronics Design,* Summer 2002. Also see Levy, *The Perfect Thing,* chapter titled "Origin."

11. Levy, *The Perfect Thing,* 92.

12. Quoted in Levy, *The Perfect Thing*, 64.

13. This story is described in Jeffrey Young and William Simon, *iCon Steve Jobs: The Greatest Second Act in the History of Business* (New York: Wiley, 2005), 92.

14. Quoted in Levy, *The Perfect Thing*, 70.

15. Dvorak, "Out of Tune: At Sony, Rivalries Were Encouraged, Then Came iPod," A1.

16. Ibid.

17. Walt Mossberg, "The Mossberg Solution: Sony's iPod Killer—New Digital Walkman Offers Longer Battery Life, but Apple's Player Still Rules," *Wall Street Journal*, July 28, 2004.

18. Dvorak, "Out of Tune."

19. "How Sony Failed to Connect, Again," CNET News.com, May 31, 2006.

20. Ibid.

21. "100 Million iPods Sold," press release, Apple, Cupertino, California, April 9, 2007.

22. Sources: sales of iPod and iTunes for 2001 to 2006 from Apple's annual reports 2002–2006. Sales on Sony's audio business from Sony's annual reports 2003–2006. Sony's audio business includes portable (the Walkman), car, and home audio sales. Share price data from Thomson securities (TOPIX is the stock market index on the Tokyo stock exchange where Sony is listed).

23. Information on Sony's and Apple's stock prices were taken from Datastream via Thomson Internet Interface, downloaded November 29, 2007 (stock prices adjusted for stock splits and capital changes).

24. In fact, Steve Jobs might have dictated the collaboration. That brings up another question: is it true collaboration if the CEO simply dictates it and everyone falls in line? Yes it is, although it is a somewhat unusual situation when a CEO has sufficient power that people dutifully collaborate all they can (collaboration is, after all, one of those things that people can quietly undermine if they don't like it). In my view, the way to think about the Apple situation is this: if you were an outsider and knew nothing about the company, you could look through the windows and observe people working together on the iPod. You would observe that they collaborated. Then you would ask, What makes them do it? One answer might be that Steve Jobs dictated it. Nevertheless, you would still observe collaborative behaviors among the iPod developers; whether the cause of that collaboration was an order by Steve Jobs or other things, such as a culture of collaboration, is a different issue. (This book focuses on how leaders build a culture of collaboration.)

25. Morten T. Hansen and Bolko von Oetinger, "Introducing T-Shaped Managers: Knowledge Management's Next Generation," *Harvard Business Review* (2001).

26. Robert F. Bruner, *Deals from Hell: M&A Lessons That Rise above the Ashes* (New York: John Wiley & Sons, 2005), 160.

27. Quoted in "Global Entertainment (A Special Report): Hollywood—Missing Links: Synergy Benefits Have So Far Eluded the Entertainment Giants," *Wall Street Journal*, March 26, 1993, R9.

28. There are numerous books on how to manage a team. Richard Hackman, one of the leading researchers on teams, has written a research-based, highly practical

book, *Leading Teams: Setting the Stage for Great Performance* (Boston: Harvard Business School Press, 2002). A few books on teams focus on how teams can work with others outside the team, such as *X-teams: How to Build Teams That Lead, Innovate, and Succeed,* by Deborah Ancona and Henrik Bresman (Boston: Harvard Business School Press, 2007). The focus in these works, however, is on the team itself—how team members can work across boundaries—and not so much on how leaders can design organizations so that people will work effectively across boundaries.

29. "PepsiCo at Consumer Analyst Group of New York 2008 CAGNY Conference," Voxant Fair Disclosure Wire, February 20, 2008.

Chapter 2

1. Robert Berner, "P&G: New and Improved," *BusinessWeek,* July 7, 2003.

2. Ibid.

3. The "Organization 2005" initiative and the subsequent events are well described in Mikolaj Jan Piskorski and Alessandro L. Spadini, "Procter & Gamble: Organization 2005," Case 9-707-519 (Boston: Harvard Business School, 2007).

4. This biographical sketch of Lafley is taken from Berner, "P&G: New and Improved."

5. "Getting Procter & Gamble Back on Track." Speech given by A. G. Lafley, Rotman School, April 21, 2003.

6. Katrina Brooker and Julie Schlosser, "The Un-CEO: A.G. Lafley Doesn't Overpromise, He Doesn't Believe in the Vision Thing, All He's Done Is Turn Around P&G in 27 Months," *Fortune,* September 16, 2002, 88.

7. "Getting Procter & Gamble Back on Track." Speech given by A.G. Lafley, April 21, 2003.

8. Berner, "P&G: New and Improved."

9. This effort was labeled "Connect & Develop" and is well described in Larry Huston and Nabil Sakkab, "Connect and Develop: Inside Procter & Gamble's New Model for Innovation," *Harvard Business Review* (March 2006).

10. "At P&G, It's 360-degree Innovation," *BusinessWeek,* October 11, 2004, www.businessweek.com.

11. http://www.whitestrips.com/en_US/press_releases/career.jsp.

12. Morten T. Hansen and Julian Birkinshaw, "The Innovation Value Chain," *Harvard Business Review* (June 2007). See also "At P&G, It's 360-degree Innovation"; Jennifer Reingold and Jia Lynn Yang, "What's Your OQ?" *Fortune,* July 23, 2007; John Foley, "Selling Soap, Razors—And Collaboration," Informationweek.com, November 14, 2005; and A.G. Lafley and Ram Charan, *The Game Changer: How You Can Drive Revenue and Profit Growth With Innovation,* New York: Crown Business (2008).

13. "Getting Procter & Gamble Back on Track." Speech given by A.G. Lafley, April 21, 2003.

14. P&G 2008 annual report. Profitability margins equal operating income divided by sales.

15. A substantial body of academic work has pointed to the recombination mechanism behind innovation. See Lee Fleming, Santiago Mingo, and David Chen,

"Collaborative Brokerage, Generative Creativity, and Creative Success," *Administrative Science Quarterly* 52 (2007): 443–475. For an academic study inside organizations, see Jeffrey Martin and Kathleen Eisenhardt, "Creating Cross-Business Collaboration: A Recombinative View of Organizational Form," working paper, The University of Texas, Austin, November 2005. This logic can also be found in several management books on innovation in general. See Andrew Hargadon, *How Breakthrough Happens: The Surprising Truth About How Companies Innovate* (Boston: Harvard Business School Press, 2003).

16. This account is based on "It All Started with Candles," chief technology officer Gordon Brunner's description in P&G's 1999 annual report.

17. Ibid, pages 3–5.

18. Procter & Gamble 2008 Annual Report.

19. Filippe Goossens, "Procter & Gamble Co.," Credit Suisse, November 28, 2007.

20. "No Errors? No Progress: The Kovacevich Approach to Risk," *RMA Journal,* September 2003; and Greg Farrell, "CEO Profile: Wells Fargo's Kovacevich Banks on Success as a One-Stop Shop," *USA TODAY,* March 26, 2007.

21. "Wells Fargo and Norwest to Merge," press release, Wells Fargo, June 8, 1998.

22. Farrell, "CEO Profile: Wells Fargo's Kovacevich Banks on Success as a One-Stop Shop."

23.

Year	Number of products per retail household*	Source	Year	Number of products per retail household*	Source
1998	3.2	Annual Report 1998	2003	4.3	Annual Report 2004
1999	3.4	Annual Report 1999	2004	4.6	Annual Report 2004
2000	3.7	Annual Report 2004	2005	4.8	Annual Report 2005
2001	3.8	Annual Report 2001	2006	5.2	Annual Report 2006
2002	4.2	Annual Report 2002	2007	5.5	Annual Report 2007

* Household defined as consumer banking household

24. Wells Fargo Annual Report 2006.

25. Farrell, "CEO Profile: Wells Fargo's Kovacevich Banks on Success as a One-Stop Shop."

26. Since the merger in 1998, the bank has grown its revenues 166 percent, reaching $54 billion in sales by 2007. Wells Fargo is also one of the most profitable banks: even in the difficult banking year of 2007, it clocked a robust 15 percent profitability compared with an average of 10 percent for peer banks. Wells Fargo numbers are taken from its 2007 Annual Report. Peer bank data from 2007 comes from Thomson One Banker. According to Thomson One Banker, sales for all banks is defined as interest income plus noninterest income. Profitability is defined as net income over sales. Bank of America had 12.4 percent, Citigroup had 2.2 percent, JP Morgan had 13.2 percent, and Goldman Sachs had 13.0 percent net income margin, for an average of 10.2 percent in 2007.

27. We estimated this number in the following way:

Consumer finance in millions	1999 revenues	1999 net income	Number of customers	Profit per customer	Sales per customer
Community Banking	11,103	2,864	10.8	265	1028
Norwest Mortgage	1,408	277	2.5	111	563
Norwest Financial	1,625	247	4	62	406
Combined	14,136	3,388	17	196	817

Source: Wells Fargo 1999 annual report.

Sales = interest income + noninterest income; revenues = net interest income + noninterest income

Norwest Mortgage and Norwest Financial are today combined under Wells Fargo Financial, which, according to the 2007 annual report is defined as follows: "Wells Fargo Financial provides real estate-secured lending, automobile financing, consumer and private-label credit cards and commercial services to consumers and businesses."

Community Banking: 10.8 million households (1999); Norwest Mortgage: 2.5 million households; Norwest Financial: 4 million households (annual report 1999).

The Community Banking Group offers a complete line of diversified financial products and services to consumers and small businesses, with annual sales generally up to $10 million, in which the owner generally is the financial decision maker. Community Banking also offers investment management and other services to retail customers and high net worth individuals, securities brokerage through affiliates, and venture capital financing. Norwest Mortgage's activities include the organization and purchase of residential mortgage loans for sale to various investors as well as servicing of mortgage loans for others. Norwest Financial includes consumer finance and auto finance operations. Consumer finance operations make direct loans to consumers and purchase sales finance contracts from retail merchants.

28. These are 2007 numbers, which we estimated as follows:

Consumer finance	2007 revenues ($m)	2007 net income ($m)	Number of customers (m)	Sales per customer ($)	Profit per customer ($)
Wells Fargo					
Community Banking	25,538	5,293	11.1	2,301	477
Financial	5,511	481	7.9	698	61
Combined	31,049	5,774	19.0	1,634	304
Bank of America GCSBB	47,682	9,430	59	808	160

Source: Wells Fargo 2007 annual report and www.wellsfargo.com/about/today 2. For Bank of America: 2007 annual report.

For correct comparison, two divisions of Wells Fargo must be included. The Community Banking Group offers a complete line of diversified financial products and services to consumers and small businesses (11.1 million households). Wells Fargo Financial provides real estate-secured lending, automobile financing, consumer and private-label credit cards, and commercial services to consumers and businesses (7.9 million households).

At Bank of America, Global Consumer & Small Business Banking (GCSBB) serves consumer households through checking, savings, credit and debit cards, home equity lending and mortgages. It also serves mass-market small businesses with capital, credit, deposit and payment services.

29. http://en.wikipedia.org/wiki/Hong_kong.

30. This example is from Morten T. Hansen and Bolko von Oetinger, "Introducing T-Shaped Managers: Knowledge Management's Next Generation," *Harvard Business Review* (2001), 6.

31. Martine R. Haas, 2005. "Cosmopolitans and locals: Status rivalries, deference, and knowledge in international teams." Research on Managing Groups and Teams, 7: 203–230.

32. This number is an estimate by the United Nations, http://www.un.org/Pubs/chronicle/2006/issue2/0206p24.htm.

33. Assumptions: in the first year, the company has $1 billion in sales, net income is 10 percent of sales, and equity is $700 million. Over three years, sales from collaboration go up 9 percent (3 percent per year), operating costs go down 2 percent, and asset requirements go down 2 percent, lowering the need for equity by 2 percent (also, the additional sales require only 80 percent of equity due to economies of scale). Return on equity goes from 14 percent to 18 percent, a 25 percent increase.

The following table shows the calculations leading to a 25 percent increase in return on equity.

($ in millions)

	Year 1	Changes	Year 3
Sales	$1,000	9%	$1,090
Net income margin	10%	2%	12%
Net income	$100		$131
Equity	$700		
Equity as % of sales	70%	–2%	68%
Equity required for adtl sales*		$50	
Equity adjusted for 2% gain**			$735
Return on equity	14.3%		18%
Return on equity change			25%

* Additional sales of 90m require only 80% of usual equity due to scale: 0.70 × 90m is equity requirement and then 0.80 scale factor => 50 million.

** Total equity required = (700m + 50) × 0.98 = $735 million

34. The following table shows the actual financials for Procter & Gamble for 2002 and 2005 (taken from the annual reports from 2002 and 2005). The benefits due to collaboration (versus other improvements) are assumed to be 15 percent revenue growth from 2002 to 2005 (total revenue growth was 41 percent). Net income margin is assumed to have improved 1 percent due to collaboration (due to cost reductions and productivity in research and development). Net income improved 2.0 percent during the period. Total equity as a percentage of sales is assumed to drop 1 percent due to collaboration (versus actual total drop of 3.3 percent). With these benefits of collaboration, we can now isolate the increase in return on equity (ROE) due to collaboration: it goes from 31.8 percent to 35.7 percent, a 12.6 percent increase. The bottom line: P&G's collaboration effort had a significant impact on ROE. This very simple simulation suggests a 12 percent increase in the three years 2002 to 2005.

	2002 (actual)	2005 (actual)	Change (actual)	Collaboration in 2005 (assumed)	2005 due to collaboration (estimated)
Revenues	$40,238	$56,741	41.0%	15%	$46,274
Opert. margin	16.6%	19.3%	2.7%		
Net income	10.8%	12.8%	2.0%	1%	$5,468
Equity	$13,706	$17,477			$15,299
Equity/sales	34.1%	30.8%		–1%	33.1%
ROE	31.8%	41.5%			35.7%
ROE growth		30.8%			12.6%

35. The names of the countries are altered to protect the identity of the company.

36. The information on *MS Estonia* was taken from http://en.wikipedia.org/wiki/MS_Estonia.

37. The information on DNV's collaboration matrix comes from the following case. Morten T. Hansen, "Transforming DNV: From Silos to Disciplined Collaboration Across Business Units—Changes at the Top," Teaching Case 08/2007-5458 (Fontainebleau, France: INSEAD, 2007).

38. The analysis also showed an opposite result for novice teams. For teams with little experience in the topic they were working on, receiving help from colleagues improved the chances of winning a bid.

39. It's interesting to note that Wall Street operates with a "15 percent diversification discount"; the stock value of multibusiness companies is 15 percent *less* compared with specialized firms. Research indicates that the discount is probably there but that it is smaller—no more than 10 percent. A great summary of all this can be found in Belen Villalonga, "Research Roundtable Discussion: The Diversification Discount" (Boston, MA: Harvard Business School, 2003), http://ssrn.com/abstract=402220. This article has a summary of findings and commentaries from sixteen leading academics.

The magnitude of the diversification discount depends on the kind of multibusiness firms we're talking about: research has found that companies whose diverse businesses are related, as in Apple's hardware and software products, fare better than firms whose businesses are unrelated, as in General Electric's jet engines and lightbulbs. See V. Ramanujam and P. Varadarajan "Research on Corporate Diversification: A Synthesis," *Strategic Management Journal* (1989): 523–551, for an extensive review of decades of research on this topic. Some research has confirmed the hypothesis that moderate related diversification may enhance performance. See, for example, Costas Markides, "Consequence of Corporate Refocusing: Ex-ante Evidence," *Academy of Management Journal* (1992): 398–412. A growing body of research argues that this depends on whether we're talking about developed economies (with mature and efficient financial markets) or developing ones. The argument is that in developing economies, conglomerates—companies operating in many different businesses—perform well because they perform functions that markets normally do: they have an internal market for capital that allocates money to their businesses and an internal labor market, moving people around according to needs in the different businesses. See Tarun Khanna and Krishna Palepu, "Why Focused Strategies May Be Wrong for Emerging Markets," *Harvard Business Review* (1997); and Abhirup Chakrabarti, Kulwant Singh, and Ishtiaq Mahmood, "Diversification and Performance: Evidence from East Asian Firms," *Strategic Management Journal* (2007): 101–120.

40. Several studies have tried to assess the number of acquisitions that fail. A KPMG study ("Beating the Bears," 2003), based on a sample of major deals in 2000–2001, found that 66 percent failed (based on the change in share price before the deal and one year later). Mercer Management Consulting, now Oliver Wyman, ("Trans-Atlantic Merger and Acquisition Activity Delivers Shareholder Value," *Canadian Corporate News,* May 28, 2002) analyzed 152 acquisitions and used as the success metric returns higher than the average of the industry over two years. It found that 39 percent under-performed (study results obtained through Oliver Wyman on November 25, 2008, in a slide presentation titled "How successful are transatlantic mergers and acquisitions at creating value?" Press breakfast, Paris, March 21, 2002). A study by Accenture ("Accenture/Economist Intelligence Unit 2006 Global M&A Survey," 2006) surveyed 420 senior executives and found that 55% thought that expected cost synergies had not been achieved while 50% believed that expected revenue synergies had not been achieved in their most recent acquisition. The books *The Synergy Trap: How Companies Lose the Acquisition Game,* by Mark Sirower (2007), and *Deals From Hell: M&A Lessons That Rise Above the Ashes,* by Robert Bruner (2005), reveal how the pursuit of synergy can reduce shareholder value. Other studies have come up with similar findings.

Some studies have shown that acquisitions can pay off. For example, a KPMG study ("The Determinants of M&A Success: What Factors Contribute to Deal Success?," 2007) examined 510 deals announced between January 1, 2000 and December 31, 2004 and found that acquirers' stock price had gained 10.8% more than non-acquiring industry peers after two years.

These are average results, however, with a wide distribution of outcomes within the sample. What all these studies have in common is that they reveal that there is a wide distribution of post-acquisition performance, with a large proportion revealing poor results. It would seem that acquisitions is a game fraud with uncertain—and oftentimes—poor outcomes.

41. Gunter Thielen, "Growth as an Entrepreneurial Challenge," speech, University of St. Gallen, St. Gallen, Switzerland, May 14, 2004.

42. This emphasis on decentralization is likely to continue. Hartmut Ostrowski, the company's new chairman and CEO, who took over from Thielen on January 1, 2008, will likely follow this approach: "To generate enduring organic growth, especially in mature media markets, Ostrowski feels it is more important than ever that every executive take advantage of their entrepreneurial freedom and strive for ambitious goals with maximum individual responsibility." "Bertelsmann Readies for Growth," press release, December 13, 2007, www.bertelsmann.com (accessed December 16, 2007).

43. Bertelsmann's problems in developing an online bookstore are well documented in the following case and teaching note: J. Barsoux and C. D. Galunic, "Bertelsmann (A) Corporate Structures and the Internet Age," Case 06/2007-4907 (Fontainebleau, France: INSEAD, 2000); and J. Barsoux, "Bertelsmann: Corporate Structure *and* the Internet Age" Teaching Note 06/2007-4907 (Fontainebleau, France: INSEAD, 2000).

44. Libby Quaid, "Some Seek a Single Agency to Ensure Safety of All Produce," *San Diego Union Tribune,* October 10, 2006, www.signonsandiego.com (accessed December 17, 2007).

45. Morten T. Hansen, "Transforming DNV: From Silos to Disciplined Collaboration Across Business Units—The Food Business in 2005," Teaching Case 08/2007-5458 (Fontainebleau, France: INSEAD, 2007).

46. Obviously, the certification business could not certify the consulting work of the other unit, but there were ample other opportunities for selling new services to existing clients.

47. This and other numbers in this case are altered for confidentiality reasons.

Chapter 3

1. All the information about 9/11 is taken from two sources: (1) The National Commission on Terrorist Attacks Upon the United States, *Final Report of the National Commission on Terrorist Attacks Upon the United States* (New York: W.W. Norton & Company, 2004). This is informally known as "the 9/11 Commission report" and "the 9/11 report." "Jane" is a disguised name used in the report (page 271). (2) The House Permanent Select Committee on Intelligence and the Senate Select Committee on Intelligence, *9/11 Report: Joint Congressional Inquiry. Report of the Joint Inquiry into the Terrorist Attacks of September 11, 2001,* July 24, 2003, http://news.findlaw.com/hdocs/docs/911rpt/. This is not the same as the 9/11 Commission report and contains testimonials not in the latter.

In addition, Jan Rivkin, Michael Roberto and Erika Ferlins have written a Harvard Business School case on the national intelligence situation before 9/11, and it provides summaries of some of the content in the 9/11 Commission report. J. Rivkin,

M. Roberto and E. Ferlins, "Managing National Intelligence (A): Before 9/11," Case 9-706-463 (Boston: Harvard Business School, 2006).

2. *Final Report of the National Commission on Terrorist Attacks Upon the United States,*159.

3. Ibid., 354.

4. Ibid., 267.

5. Ibid., 269–270.

6. Ibid., 272. The full memo can be obtained at http://www.thememoryhole. org/911/phoenix-memo.

7. The 9/11 Commission report devoted very little space to this memo, but it received a lot of attention during the hearings. And others have acknowledged its importance, including FBI Director Robert S. Mueller, who said about the memo and other information that "we did not have the people who were looking at the broader picture to put the pieces in place." Quoted in David Johnston and Don Van Natta Jr., "Traces of Terror: The F.B.I. Memo: Aschroft Learned of Agent's Alert Just after 9/11," *New York Times,* May 21, 2002.

8. *Final Report of the National Commission on Terrorist Attacks Upon the United States,* 275.

9. Ibid., 276.

10. Ibid., 260.

11. Ibid., 277.

12. Ibid., 257.

13. Ibid.

14. Ibid., 259.

15. Quoted in *9/11 Report: Joint Congressional Inquiry Report,* 78. The FBI practiced extreme decentralization. Former FBI Director Louis Freeh believed that the work should be done independently in the fifty-six field offices scattered around the United States. To make sure this happened, he had cut staff at headquarters and had given a great deal of power to the field offices. As a result, "the special agents in charge gained power, influence, and independence" (*Final Report of the National Commission on Terrorist Attacks Upon the United States,* 76.) Each field office was also measured on how well it did, using metrics such as number of arrests and convictions. In this structure, individual cases were assigned to a specific field office (New York handled the bin Laden case), but because the field offices operated independently, there was little motivation to collaborate on a case.

16. *Final Report of the National Commission on Terrorist Attacks Upon the United States,* 353.

17. Number of employees varied from 50 to 150,000 (mean = 11,076). Industries included manufacturing, financial services, high-tech, consumer goods/retail, healthcare, professional services, and energy. It is a fairly representative sample, but it is not a random sample, so caution must be exercised in drawing conclusions.

18. Quoted in Morten T. Hansen and Nitin Nohria. "How to Build Collaborative Advantage." *Sloan Management Review* (2004).

19. Psychologists have labeled this an "in-group" bias, where group members systematically overvalue group members and undervalue nonmembers. See R. Katz and

T. J. Allen, "Investigating the Not Invented Here (NIH) Syndrome: A Look at the Performance, Tenure, and Communication Patterns of 50 R&D Project Groups," in *Readings in the Management of Innovation,* 2nd ed., edited by M. L. Tushman and W. L. Moore (New York: Ballinger/Harper & Row, 1988), 293–309; M. B. Brewer, "Ingroup Bias in the Minimal Intergroup Situation: A Cognitive Motivational Analysis," *Psychological Bulletin* 86 (1979): 307–324; and H. Tajfel and J. C. Turner, "The Social Identity Theory of Intergroup Behavior," in *Psychology of Intergroup Relations,* 2nd ed., edited by S. Worchel and W. G. Austin (Chicago: Nelson Hall, 1986), 7–24.

20. I conducted this study in 1995 in the electronic instruments sector of Hewlett-Packard (now part of Agilent). This study consisted of a large network survey among 41 business units, another network survey among the engineers of 120 product-development projects, and a detailed data collection of the characteristics and performance of those projects. The data allowed for hard statistical regression analysis, revealing the effects that I refer to throughout this chapter. See the appendix for a detailed research overview.

21. This result is reported in Morten T. Hansen, Louise Mors, and Bjorn Lovas, "Knowledge Sharing in Organizations: Multiple Networks, Multiple Phases," *Academy of Management Journal* (2005).

The analysis of 120 teams measured the established network of relations among team members and then used that measure to predict whether a team would reach out to other divisions, controlling for their need to do so. The regression analysis revealed that the probability of reaching out decreased with an increasing number of preexisting relations among team members.

22. See Patricia Beard, *Blue Blood and Mutiny: The Fight for the Soul of Morgan Stanley* (New York: HarperCollins, 2007).

23. Carol J. Loomis, "Morgan Stanley Dean Witter: The Oddball Marriage Works Yes, the Morgans and the Witters have their little differences. But that didn't keep them from lapping the competition in profits last year." *Fortune,* April 26, 1999.

24. Robert H. Frank, *Choosing the Right Pond: Human Behavior and the Quest for Status* (Oxford: Oxford University Press, 1985).

25. In the Hewlett-Packard study mentioned earlier in the chapter, we found support for this hypothesis: product developers did not contact expert units for the technologies they were seeking but instead contacted units where they knew people; they sought help from people they knew rather than experts they did not know. See Morten T. Hansen and Bjorn Lovas, "How Do Multinational Companies Leverage Technological Competencies? Moving from Single to Interdependent Explanations," *Strategic Management Journal* (2004). Another study confirms these findings: Tiziana Casciaro and Miguel Sousa Lobo, "Competent Jerks, Lovable Fools, and the Formation of Social Networks," *Harvard Business Review* (June 2005).

26. In intelligence matters, this barrier might be called "not-discovered-here," something that happens when agents are not willing to reach out and ask for information from other agencies.

27. *Final Report of the National Commission on Terrorist Attacks Upon the United States,* 417.

28. *9/11 Report: Joint Congressional Inquiry Report,* 16.

29. This evidence is from Morten T. Hansen et al., "Knowledge Sharing in Organizations: Multiple Networks, Multiple Phases."

30. Jeffrey Pfeffer has many times pointed out this problem with most incentive systems. See Jeffrey Pfeffer, "Six Dangerous Myths About Pay," *Harvard Business Review* (May–June 1998); and Jeffrey Pfeffer and Robert Sutton, *Hard Facts, Dangerous Half-Truths and Total Nonsense: Profiting from Evidence-based Management* (Boston: Harvard Business School Press, 2006), chapter 5.

31. Leslie Perlow, "The Time Famine: Towards a Sociology of Work Time," *Administrative Science Quarterly* 44, no. 1 (March 1999): 57–81.

32. Morten T. Hansen, Joel Podolny, and Jeffrey Pfeffer, "So Many Ties, So Little Time: A Task Contingency Perspective on the Value of Corporate Social Capital in Organizations," *Research in the Sociology of Organizations* (2001).

33. *Final Report of the National Commission on Terrorist Attacks Upon the United States,* 417.

34. Hoarding was so pervasive at the FBI that Deputy Director Bryant informed agents that "too much information sharing could be a career stopper." Talk about narrow incentives! Part of this came from procedures put in place in 1995 to restrict information sharing between the FBI and criminal prosecutors in the Justice Department. But as the 9/11 Commission stated, "These procedures were almost immediately misunderstood and misapplied." FBI agents started to believe that the rule applied to sharing information between *agents,* when in fact the rule concerned sharing between agents and *prosecutors.* The misinterpretation became the rule, which over time became known as "the wall." The 9/11 Commission concluded that "the information flow withered" as a result of the wrong interpretations of the original procedure.

35. This was measured as the percentage of all budgeted engineering-months spent on search; we asked the project managers to estimate this (they kept a detailed log of how project engineers spent their time). See Hansen et al., "Knowledge Sharing in Organizations: Multiple Networks, Multiple Phases."

36. Some commentators claim that distance no longer matters. The title of Frances Cairncross's book *The Death of Distance: How the Communications Revolution Is Changing Our Lives* (Boston: Harvard Business School Press, 1997) says it all. Thomas Friedman's *The World Is Flat: A Brief History of the Twenty-First Century* (New York: Farrar, Straus and Giroux, 2005) also makes the point that physical distance has almost become unimportant. These are exaggerated claims. Larry Prusak provided a rebuttal to this argument in an opinion piece aptly titled "The World Is Round" (*Harvard Business Review,* April 2006). Academic research shows that distance still matters. See Hansen and Lovas, "How Do Multinational Companies Leverage Technological Competencies?"; and Pamela Hinds and Mark Mortensen, "Understanding Conflict in Geographically Distributed Teams: The Moderating Effects of Shared Identity, Shared Context, and Spontaneous Communication," *Organization Science* (2005): 290–307. See also Pamela Hinds and Sara Kiesler (eds), *Distributed Work* (Cambridge, MA: MIT Press, 2002), which focuses on how to manage distributed teams.

37. T. Allen, *Managing the Flow of Technology* (Cambridge: MIT Press, 1977). In Allen's study, the probability of two engineers communicating fell from 0.25 when

they were a couple of meters apart (essentially sitting next to each other) to about 0.05 when they were seated twenty-five meters apart (see figure 8.3, p. 239). One reasonable objection to this is that people who sit farther apart do so because they work in different groups; if so, this finding is only an artifact of the organization structure and has nothing to do with engineers having less communication when physical distance becomes greater. To control for this, Allen divided people into formal work groups and drew a separate line for those who worked within the same group. Here, too, the probability of communicating fell drastically as the physical distance increased (see figure 8.4, p. 241).

38. See Hansen and Lovas, "How do Multinational Companies Leverage Technological Competencies?" The same phenomenon appears between firms. See O. Sorenson and T. Stuart, "Syndication Networks and the Spatial Distribution of Venture Capital Investments," *American Journal of Sociology* 106, no. 6 (2001). Another study of communication in a large organization found that spatial distance is an impediment to communication: Adam M. Kleinbaum, Toby E. Stuart, and Michael L. Tushman, "Communication (and Coordination?) in a Modern, Complex Organization," working paper 09-004, Harvard Business School, Boston, July 2008.

39. Roberta Wohlstetter, *Pearl Harbor: Warning and Decision* (Stanford, CA: Stanford University Press, 1962). The quotation is from page 387. The example of the incoming airplane is also from this book (page 11).

40. Morten T. Hansen and Martine Haas, "Competing for Attention in Knowledge Markets: Electronic Document Dissemination in a Management Consulting Company," *Administrative Science Quarterly* (2001).

41. We found support for this argument in a study of knowledge databases in a large consulting company (ibid.). Consultants more frequently used databases that had fewer documents of high quality on a narrow list of topics (as opposed to databases that had lots of documents that were poorly filtered and that were on lots of topics).

42. Stanley Milgram, "The Small World Problem," *Psychology Today* 2 (1967): 60–67.

43. J. Travers and S. Milgram, "An Experimental Study of the Small World Problem," *Sociometry* 32 (1969): 425–443. A more up-to-date study confirmed this. Duncan Watts of Columbia University, along with fellow researchers Peter Dodds and Roby Muhamad, found that when twenty-four thousand people from around the world sent e-mails to acquaintances to reach one of eighteen target people, the typical number of steps in these search chains was between five and seven (as with Milgram's result). Peter Sheridan Dodds, Roby Muhamad, and Duncan J. Watts, "An Experimental Study of Search in Global Social Networks," *Science,* August 8, 2003.

44. Jasjit Singh, Morten T. Hansen, and Joel Podolny. "The World is Not Small for Everyone: Pathways of Discrimination in Searching for Information in Organizations." INSEAD working paper (Fontainebleau, France: INSEAD, 2009).

45. *Final Report of the National Commission on Terrorist Attacks Upon the United States,* 77.

46. *9/11 Report: Joint Congressional Inquiry Report,* pages 55–56.

47. See Hansen et al., "Knowledge Sharing in Organizations: Multiple Networks, Multiple Phases."

48. The original, authoritative study on tacit knowledge is M. Polanyi, *The Tacit Dimension* (New York: Anchor Day Books, 1966).

49. The equation was obtained from Sergey Brin and Lawrence Page, "The Anatomy of a Large-Scale Hypertextual Web Search Engine," Stanford University (1996), http://infolab.stanford.edu/~backrub/google.html. A good explanation can be found at www.ianrogers.net/google-page-rank. It isn't necessary for my purpose to define the elements of the equation here (see this site for explanations). The key point is that it is a precise formula for determining the rank of a Web site; the higher the rank, the more relevant it is deemed for search on a particular topic. See also http://en.wikipedia.org/wiki/PageRank#_note-0.

50. There is an interesting debate among strategy experts that tacit—versus explicit—knowledge is the more valuable because it is much harder for competitors to copy. It protects a company's source of competitive advantage. If so, it is puzzling why companies were slow to copy Google's search formula. The formula for search was known as early as 1996, when Brin and Page published their paper.

51. The quote is from Fernand Point, *Ma Gastronomie* (English translation, 20080, 61. The book first came out in 1969 (Paris, France). This is a very interesting quote. It suggests that the great chef thinks that his real skills are tacit knowledge and that the skills cannot be captured in a recipe. People sometimes think that great chefs do not really give out their recipes—"the secret sauce"—because others would simply copy them and become equally good. But that is far from the truth, because the real secret sauce lies in the practice of the recipe and not the recipe itself.

52. The following studies have shown how difficult it is to transfer tacit knowledge: Morten T. Hansen, "The Search-Transfer Problem: The Role of Weak Ties in Sharing Knowledge Across Organization Subunits," *Administrative Science Quarterly* (1999); U. Zander and B. Kogut, "Knowledge and the Speed of Transfer and Imitation of Organizational Capabilities: An Empirical Test," *Organization Science* 6 (1995): 76–92; and G. Szulanski, "Exploring Internal Stickiness: Impediments to the Transfer of Best Practice Within the Firm," *Strategic Management Journal* 17, Special Issue: Knowledge and the Firm (Winter 1996): 27–43.

53. Kieran Mulvaney, "Trainer to the Champions Had Unique View of Ali and Other Fighters," Special to ESPN.com, December 18, 2007, http://sports.espn.go.com/sports/boxing/news/story?id=3158201.

54. See Morten T. Hansen, 1999. "The Search-Transfer Problem: The Role of Weak Ties in Sharing Knowledge across Organization Subunits," *Administrative Science Quarterly* 44, 82–11.

55. The evidence for table 3-1 is as follows. Using the survey sample of 107 companies, I ran a regression analysis predicting the effects of each management solution on each of the barriers. The regression coefficients revealed the following results. They show how much return each lever produces in lowering a barrier, as shown in the figure below. For example, the coefficient for the effects of unification on lowering the not-invented-here barrier is 35 percent. This means that a 10-point increase in the scale on unification (on a survey scale from 0 to 100) lowers the barrier by 3.5 points (a survey scale from 0 to 100). Thus, going from 0 to 100 on the unification scale lowers this barrier by 35 points. That's substantial.

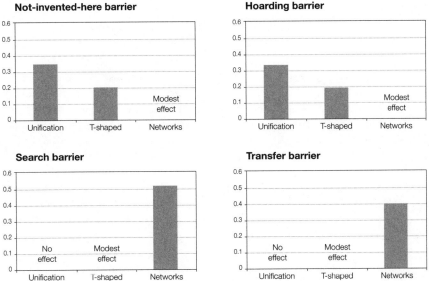

56. Information systems also help search and constitute a fourth solution that could be put on this map; I have not done so because this book is not about information technology.

Chapter 4

1. This account is based primarily on the detailed report provided in Muzafer Sherif, O. J. Harvey, B. Jack White, William R. Hood, and Carolyn W. Sherif, *The Robbers Cave Experiment: Intergroup Conflict and Cooperation* (Middletown, CT: Wesleyan University Press, 1988; first printed in 1961). This is an extraordinary experiment in scope, ambition, and rigor. The 1954 study was the third "summer camp" study in the series. The first (in 1949) was similar to the first two weeks of the 1954 study, whereas the second (in 1953) had to be aborted because the boys attributed the causes of conflict and frustration to camp administrators. The 1954 study is exceptional, because it blends various methods: the field experiment, surveys of the boys, participant observations, and mini-experiments disguised as games. It is sad to see that contemporary academic research rarely does this kind of study. Having said that, the particular method of the 1954 study would surely not pass today's human subject standards, which state that subjects should not be subjected to harm and should give full consent. For this reason the 1954 study has never been repeated.

2. The researchers went to great lengths to carefully select the boys. They first approached principals at various schools and then identified a number of boys (two hundred in total). They interviewed parents and then selected twenty-two boys. They took great care in selecting well-adjusted boys; boys with troubled backgrounds or social problems could act out and ruin the study. Sherif and his colleagues

wanted to rule out the possibility that individual troublemakers would shape the outcomes.

3. Sherif et al., *The Robbers Cave Experiment,* pages 101 and 109.

4. Ibid., 113.

5. Ibid., 171.

6. Ibid., 171. By this time two boys had gone home because of homesickness.

7. Memorandum for the Vice President, 20 April 1961, Presidential Files, John F. Kennedy Presidential Library, Boston, http://history.nasa.gov/Apollomon/apollo1.pdf.

8. Memorandum for the President, Subject: Evaluation of Space Program, Office of the Vice President, April 28, 1961, NASA historical reference collection, NASA Headquarters, Washington, D.C., http://history.nasa.gov/Apollomon/apollo2.pdf.

9. "Transcript of presidential meeting in the cabinet room of the White House; Topic: supplemental appropriations for the National Aeronautics and Space Administration (NASA), 21 November 1962," http://history.nasa.gov/JFK-Webbconv/pages/transcript.pdf. The transcripts were first released in 2001. Andrew Chaikin, "White House Tapes Shed Light on JFK Space Race Legend," *Space & Science,* August 22, 2001.

10. These deliberations are well described in the following NASA document: "Proposals: Before and After May 1961," http://history.nasa.gov/SP-4205/ch3-2.html (accessed January 13, 2008).

11. "Concluding Remarks by Dr. Wernher von Braun About Mode Selection for Lunar Landing Program," 7 June 1962, Lunar-Orbit Rendezvous file, NASA Historical Reference Collection, NASA Headquarters, Washington D.C., http://history.nasa.gov/Apollomon/apollo6.pdf. All quotations from von Braun on mode decisions are taken from this source.

12. There is a confusing range of terms to describe goals: *superordinate goals, vision, mission, overarching goals,* and so on. I simply use *unifying goals,* which may or may not overlap with these other terms, depending on the definitions used. The term *unifying goal* is simple and does not confuse.

The book *Built to Last* outlined big goals as a compelling driver of progress in enduringly great companies; James Collins and Jerry Porras, *Built to Last: Successful Habits of Visionary Companies* (New York: HarperCollins, 1994). The authors use the term *Big Hairy Audacious Goals*—BHAG for short—to describe these compelling goals. Although unifying goals share some characteristics with BHAGs (e.g., being simple and concrete), the key trait of unifying goals—that they must create a common fate—is not a requirement in a BHAG. Jack Welch's "number 1 or number 2" goal (discussed later in this chapter) is a BHAG but not a unifying goal.

13. Catherine Thimmesh, *Team Moon: How 400,000 People Landed Apollo 11 on the Moon* (New York: Houghton Mifflin Company, 2006).

14. Noel Tichy and Ram Charan, "Speed, Simplicity, Self-Confidence: An Interview with Jack Welch," *Harvard Business Review* (September–October 1989).

15. Airbus didn't declare this goal officially. But given the information I obtained by talking to a number of engineers and managers at Airbus, many employees, and especially the engineers, had worked hard to meet the one unifying goal of beating Boeing.

16. Information on orders received was obtained from http://en.wikipedia.org/wiki/Airbus#Orders_and_deliveries(accessed January 8, 2008). Other metrics include orders delivered and value of orders.

17. In mid-2000, Airbus ran into big problems in producing the massive double-decker A380. One significant problem had been to unify the various factions of Airbus, notably the country operations in Germany, France, the United Kingdom, and Spain. In many ways those have been antagonistic relations from the get-go—subject to the "poison of national rivalries," as *Financial Times* wrote in 2007 (Kevin Done, "Airbus Seeks to End 'Poison' of Rivalries," *Financial Times,* February 28, 2007). Given these national rivalries, it is amazing that Airbus was able to perform as well as it did in the 1990s and early 2000, and I think a lot of that had to do with a single dedicated focus on overtaking Boeing. In many ways, that unifying goal kept a lid on boiling rivalries, something that needs to be addressed at a fundamental level of ownership and corporate governance. Airbus is owned by a parent company, EADS, which was set up in 1999 to provide one corporate entity to streamline operations, but the streamlining did not happen. See Peggy Hollinger and Gerrit Wiesmann, "Rivalries Have Disrupted Steep Climb of Airbus," *Financial Times,* November 13, 2006; and "Time for a New, Improved Model," *Economist,* July 22, 2006.

18. "Transcript of presidential meeting in the cabinet room of the White House; Topic: supplemental appropriations for the National Aeronautics and Space Administration (NASA), 21 November 1962."

19. Thimmesh, *Team Moon: How 400,000 People Landed Apollo 11 on the Moon,* 9.

20. Poll conducted by Beta Research Corp. (Syoset, NY) for *BusinessWeek.* Reported in *BusinessWeek,* August 21/28, 2006, 44–48. The result was 44 percent and 47 percent for men and women, respectively.

21. Quoted in *BusinessWeek,* August 21/28 2006, 54.

22. Muzafer Sherif also showed the power of having a common enemy in his summer camp experiments. In an experiment he did a few years before the Robbers Cave experiment, his team created competition and rivalry between two groups of boys (this time they were called the "Red Devils" and the "Bull Dogs"). To bring them back together, Sherif introduced a common enemy—a third group of campers from a neighboring town. The Red Devils and the Bull Dogs formed a common team consisting of their best players to play a softball game against this new group. This proved to be the most effective way to reduce competition and hostility between the two groups (although now there was hostility toward a third group). See Muzafer Sherif and Carolyn W. Sherif, *Groups in Harmony and Tension* (New York: Harper Brothers, 1953), 286.

23. Quoted in *BusinessWeek,* August 21/28, 2006, 55.

24. Ibid., 52.

25. Ibid., 97.

26. See Ruth Wageman, Debra A. Nunes, James A. Burruss, and Richard Hackman, *Senior Leadership Teams: What It Takes to Make Them Great* (Boston: Harvard Business School Press, 2008).

27. Personal interview Tom DeLong, January 2008.

28. This story is told in William A. Sahlman and Alison Berkley Wagonfeld, "Intuit's New CEO: Steve Bennett," Case 9-803-044 (Boston: Harvard Business School, 2003), 11.

29. Varda Liberman, Steven M. Samuels, and Lee Ross, "The Name of the Game: Predictive Power of Reputations Versus Situational Labels in Determining Prisoner's Dilemma Game Moves," *Personality and Social Psychology Bulletin* (2004): 1175–1185.

30. In the study, the authors also found that these results held after seven rounds. In a count of number of "cooperate" decisions after 7 rounds, players in the community game had a mean of 4.63 cooperative decisions (of a maximum of 7), whereas this number was a 2.21 in the Wall Street game. This means that players are about twice as likely to choose a cooperative response. In addition, the authors conducted a similar study among Israeli fighter pilot trainees and obtained similar results.

31. Fabrizio Ferraro, Jeffrey Pfeffer, and Robert Sutton, "Economics Language and Assumptions: How Theories Can Become Self-Fulfilling," *Academy of Management Review* (2005): 9–24.

32. R. H. Frank, T. Gilovich, and D. T. Regan, "Does Studying Economics Inhibit Cooperation?" *Journal of Economic Perspectives* 7 (1993): 159–171. See also D. T. Miller, "The Norm of Self-Interest," *American Psychologist* 54 (1999): 1053–1060.

33. Quoted in Morten Hansen, "Transforming DNV: From Silos to Disciplined Collaboration Across Business Units—Changes at the Top," Case 08/2007-5458 (Fontainebleau, France: INSEAD, 2007).

Chapter 5

1. M. Diane Burton, "Rob Parson at Morgan Stanley (A)," Case 9-498-054 (Boston: Harvard Business School, 1998). The names used are not the persons' real names.

2. Ibid., 7.

3. Ibid., 7.

4. Ibid., 9.

5. Ibid., 5.

6. Ibid., pages 5, 12, and 13.

7. Diane Burton, personal communication, September 9, 2008.

8. Information on this change effort is obtained from the following two sources: M. Diane Burton, Thomas DeLong, and Katherine Lawrence, "Morgan Stanley: Becoming a One-Firm Firm," Teaching Case 9-400-043 (Boston: Harvard Business School, 2000); and M. Diane Burton, "The Firmwide 360-Degree Performance Evaluation Process at Morgan Stanley," Teaching Case 9-498-053 (Boston: Harvard Business School, 1998).

9. The concept of lone stars was introduced in Morten T. Hansen, "Turning the Lone Star into a Real Team Player," *Financial Times,* August 7, 2002.

10. The T-shaped concept was introduced in Morten T. Hansen and Bolko von Oetinger, "Introducing T-Shaped Managers: Knowledge Management's Next Generation," *Harvard Business Review* (March–April 2001).

11. This change program is detailed in Morten T. Hansen and Christina Darwall, "Intuit, Inc.: Transforming an Entrepreneurial Company into a Collaborative Organization (A)," Case 9-403-064 (Boston: Harvard Business School, May 8, 2003).

12. Ibid.

13. In recent years, the concept of "the war for talent" has taken center stage (see Ed Michaels, Helen Handfield-Jones, and Beth Axelrod, *The War for Talent* (Boston: Harvard Business School Press, 2001). The argument is that to get and keep the best people, companies must win the battle to recruit, develop, and retain great talent. This has been disputed. Jeffrey Pfeffer and Robert Sutton, in their superb book *Hard Facts, Dangerous Half-Truths and Total Nonsense: Profiting From Evidence-based Management* (Boston: Harvard Business School Press, 2006), argue that "great systems are often more important than great people" (96). Professor Boris Groysberg at Harvard Business Review has written some of the most nuanced and sensible articles on the subject and shows how stars are dependent on the environment in which they operate (see for example: Groysberg, Boris, Linda-Eling Lee, and Ashish Nanda. "Can They Take It with Them? The Portability of Star Knowledge Workers' Performance: Myth or Reality." *Management Science* 54, 2008). This chapter in my book is based on these more nuanced views. I argue that a system set up to select and foster T-shaped management trumps an approach that strives to recruit and retain great talent of all sorts, including lone stars.

14. This section is taken from Hansen and von Oetinger, "Introducing T-Shaped Managers: Knowledge Management's Next Generation."

15. Steven Kerr, "On the Folly of Rewarding A, While Hoping for B," *Academy of Management Journal* 18, no. 4 (December 1975): 769–783.

16. Hansen and Darwall, "Intuit, Inc.: Transforming an Entrepreneurial Company into a Collaborative Organization (A)."

17. Ibid. Here is another example from Intuit. Carol Novello, who used to be vice president of marketing in the small business and personal finance unit at Intuit, used cross-selling metrics to gauge collaboration: "We started measuring revenues per customer and the average number of products purchased per customer [across all products], and I've found that it's definitely easier to be collaborative when you use the right metrics. For example, we did a pilot with one of our phone channels. Before the experiment, we sold additional products or services on only 5 percent of the calls. We increased the skills level of our reps so that they could sell multiple products in a single call, and we began allocating the revenues, along with the proportional costs, back to the BUs [business units] whose products we sold. We now sell on approximately 25 percent of the calls, and our revenues jumped almost fivefold with only a minimal increase in costs."

18. The 360-degree feedback approach has become very popular in recent years, but it also has come under criticism. Although it can deliver valuable feedback, it can also be misused and hurt feelings, violate privacy, and cause people to leave. Watson Wyatt released a 2001 study that showed that companies using 360-degree feedback had a 4.9 percent lower market value than similar companies that didn't use it (see Bruce Pfau and Ira Kay, "Does 360-Degree Feedback Negatively Affect Company

Performance? Studies Show That 360-Degree Feedback May Do More Harm than Good," *HR Magazine*, 2002). This argument obviously does not hold up, because there is no evidence that using the 360-degree tool *caused* the decline; lower-performing companies may simply be more diligent in using the tool to try to improve performance. Nevertheless, the tool can be misused, and caution is needed, as suggested in Mary Carson, "Saying It Like It Isn't: The Pros and Cons of 360-Degree Feedback," *Business Horizons* 49 (2006): 395–402.

19. This information is obtained from Martin Gargiulo, Gokhan Ertug, and Charles Galunic, "The Two Faces of Control: Network Closure and Individual Performance Among Knowledge Workers," *Administrative Science Quarterly*, forthcoming.

20. Hansen and von Oetinger, "Introducing T-Shaped Managers: Knowledge Management's Next Generation."

21. Jeff Pfeffer has outlined some of these problems in "Six Dangerous Myths About Pay," *Harvard Business Review* (May–June 1998), where he argues, among other things, that pay systems can backfire and undermine teamwork. One of my favorite stories, as told by Pfeffer in *What Were They Thinking? Unconventional Wisdom About Management* (Boston: Harvard Business School Press, 2007, chapter 11), is the pay-for-performance plan launched in the city of Albuquerque, New Mexico, where officials hit upon the idea of paying garbage collectors for eight hours no matter how long it took them to cover their routes. If they worked hard, they might finish earlier, so there was a great deal of incentive in place to promote efficiency, or so the managers thought. You can imagine how it went. Drivers found they could finish faster if they didn't pick up all the garbage, if they sped, and if they didn't go to the dump as frequently but drove around with overloaded trucks. And the system turned out to be more expensive than before, because the city had to make up for these shortcomings, such as sending out extra trucks to pick up the garbage left behind. The upshot of the story: be careful what you pay for!

22. The same fragile assumptions also underlie the argument for stock options: "Our people think about the company first because they are owners," some leaders might say. It may be the case that in small companies, stock options encourage collaboration, but in large companies, and for managers below the top rank, such incentives are hollow.

23. The information on Bain comes from Morten T. Hansen, Nitin Nohria, and Thomas Tierney, "What's Your Strategy for Managing Knowledge?" *Harvard Business Review* (1999).

24. There is one caveat here: the take-home cash must be significant enough for this logic to matter. I often see bonus schemes wherein the collaboration component becomes too small. In a typical bonus scheme, the bonus can be up to 20 percent of base salary (higher in sales jobs). Managers then use a bucket full of items to determine the bonus, one of which is collaboration, which may receive a 20 percent weight. How much does this yield? Well, 20 percent of 20 percent is 4 percent—not much. For a manager earning a base salary of $200,000, his bonus for the collaboration part—if he gets high scores on it—will amount to $8,000 pretax (or about $5,000 after tax). How many managers will keep hopping on a plane throughout a year to go collaborate with colleagues, knowing that if they do it well, there will be a

$5,000 check waiting for them at the end of the year? Not many, I think. It's not enough. Make it count. Make it big.

25. Interviews at Roy's restaurant, San Francisco, 2001.

26. This approach was described in Matthew Brelis, "Unconventional Business Strategy Makes Southwest Airlines a Model for Success," Knight Ridder/Tribune Business News, November 6, 2000.

27. Quoted in Jeff Pfeffer and Charles O'Reilly, "Southwest Airlines (A)," Teaching Case HR-1A (Stanford, CA: Stanford University, 1995).

28. Howard Leventhal, Robert Singer, and Susan Jones, "Effects of Fear and Specificity of Recommendation upon Attitudes and Behavior," *Journal of Personality and Social Psychology* 2, no.1 (1965): 20–29.

29. The original article that laid out this argument for job attitudes is Gerald R. Salancik and Jeffrey Pfeffer, "A Social Information Processing Approach to Job Attitudes and Task Design," *Administrative Science Quarterly* 23 (1978): 224–253. Since then, research has generally confirmed that it runs both ways: attitudes predict behaviors, and behaviors predict attitudes, with the latter having more robust impact (Jeffrey Pfeffer, personal communication, February 2008).

30. See David Garvin and Artemis March, "Harvey Golub: Recharging American Express" Case 9-396-212 (Boston: Harvard Business School, 1996).

31. This scenario is based on the assumptions laid out in the following table.

Simulation: Changing the number of T-shaped managers in a top 100 group

		Year 1	Year 2	Year 3
Mix	**Start**			**End**
Lone stars	30			18
T-shaped	20			65
Butterflies	30			12
Laggards	20			5
Total	*100*			*100*
People leaving top 100 group				
Natural turnover: 10% per year		10	20	30
Laggards: 10% fired per year		2	4	6
= sum of vacancies in top 100		*12*	*24*	*36*
New people selected to vacancies				
Promoted from below: Half of new slots		6	12	18
Recruited from outside: Half of new slots		6	12	18
Of new people, 80% are T		10	20	30
Of new people, 20% are lone stars (mistakes)		2	4	6

People changing to T-shaped behaviors

From lone stars to T: 10% converted per year	3	6	9
From butterfly to T: 10% converted per year	3	6	9
From laggard to T: 5% converted to T per year	1	2	3

Sum of T-shaped

Original 20 less 10% natural turnover	18	16	14
Sum new T-shaped promoted and recruited	10	20	30
Sum changing to T-Shaped behaviors	7	14	21
Sum	*35*	*50*	*65*

Sum of laggards

Original 20 less natural turnover	18	16	14
Less fired	−2	−4	−6
Less converted to T	−1	−2	−3
Sum	*15*	*10*	*5*

Sum of butterflies

Original 30 less natural turnover	**27**	**24**	**21**
Less converted to T	−3	−6	−9
Sum	*24*	*18*	*12*

Sum lone stars

Original 30 less natural turnover	27	24	21
Less converted to T	−3	−6	−9
Plus newly picked	2	4	6
Sum	*26*	*22*	*18*

Grand sum | **100** | **100** | **100**

Chapter 6

1. This example comes from Morten T. Hansen and Bolko von Oetinger, "Introducing T-Shaped Managers: Knowledge Management's Next Generation," *Harvard Business Review* (March–April 2001). Name, locations, and commercially sensitive information have been changed in the example, although Les Owen is a real name.

2. This event took place in 1994 at Corpus Christi, Texas, when a lightning strike caused a malfunction at Koch Industries' Three Rivers pumping station. The lightning shut a valve while the oil was flowing, causing the corroded pipe to explode. Koch eventually agreed to pay more than $45 million in damages to settle two lawsuits. Reported in Ralph K. M. Haurwitz and Jeff Nesmith, "Polluters Punished Through 'the Back Door,'" *American Statesman,* July 23, 2001.

3. Martine R. Haas and Morten T. Hansen, "When Using Knowledge Can Hurt Performance: The Value of Organizational Capabilities in a Management Consulting Company," *Strategic Management Journal* (2005).

4. For example, Philip Evans and Bob Wolf of the Boston Consulting Group argue that "cheap, plentiful transactions" improve collaboration; see Philip Evans and Bob Wolf, "Collaboration Rules," *Harvard Business Review* (July–August 2005). This is essentially a version of "the more, the better." But research linking network size to performance suggests otherwise. For another critique of "the more, the merrier" myth, see Rob Cross, Nitin Nohria and Andrew Parker, "Six Myths About Informal Networks—and How to Overcome Them," *Sloan Management Review,* Spring 2002.

5. Malcolm Gladwell, *The Tipping Point: How Little Things Can Make a Big Difference* (New York: Little, Brown and Company, 2000), 45.

6. Ibid., 38.

7. Morten T. Hansen. "Knowledge Networks: Explaining Effective Knowledge Sharing in Multiunit Companies." *Organization Science* (2002).

8. All information and quotes about Vivi Nevo are from, Tim Arango, "A Media Powerhouse Everyone and Nobody Knows," *New York Times*, July 28, 2008.

9. Some research has tried to analyze the effects of personality traits on people's network positions. In one study—Katherine Klein, Beng-Chong Lim, Jessica Saltz, and David Mayer, "How Do They Get There? An Examination of the Antecedents of Centrality in Team Networks," *Academy of Management Journal* (2004): 952–963—the authors looked at personality traits, including extroversion, the one most closely related to social giftedness. But the study found that this factor was not related to a person's centrality in a network; extroverts did not have larger networks than introverts. I should note that this area is not widely researched; there is an enormous body of research on networks, but very few studies analyze the effects of personality traits on network factors. Also, this doesn't mean that no personality traits affect a person's network. For example, one study found that a person's self-monitoring trait affected how central he or she became in a network; see Ajay Mehra, Martin Kilduff, and Daniel Brass, "The Social Networks of High and Low Self-Monitors: Implications for Workplace Performance," *Administrative Science Quarterly* 46 (2001): 121–146.

10. There has been a substantial body of academic network research in companies over the past decade, and scholars have increasingly translated findings into managerial advice. See for example: Herminia Ibarra and Mark Hunter, "How Leaders Create and Use Networks," *Harvard Business Review,* January 2007; and Robert Cross and Robert Thomas, *Driving Results Through Social Networks: How Top Organizations Leverage Networks for Performance and Growth,* San Francisco, CA: Jossey-Bass. 2009.

11. A study of e-mails, calendars, and teleconferences in a very large organization confirmed that most communication occurs within formal boundaries. Of course, this is to be expected if work is formally divided into chunks that need the most interactions. Nevertheless, this division of work can impede working across an organization. See Adam M. Kleinbaum, Toby E. Stuart, and Michael L. Tushman, "Communication (and Coordination?) in a Modern, Complex Organization," Working Paper 09-004 (Boston: Harvard Business School, July 2008).

12. Some locations and information have been modified to protect the identity of the company.

13. I use *diversity* as shorthand for the idea that it is the diversity of network contacts that counts. Diversity can be measured, crudely, as a count of different types of network contacts (known as range in the network literature). A more sophisticated measure is structural holes, a measure of the absence of links between a person's contacts (the fewer such ties, the more diverse the contacts, because they are likely to possess different kinds of information if they do not talk to each other). See Ronald Burt, "Structural Holes and Good Ideas," *American Journal of Sociology* (2004).

14. Morten T. Hansen, "Knowledge Networks: Explaining Effective Knowledge Sharing in Multi-unit Companies," *Organization Science* (May–June 2002).

15. A business unit's network diversity led teams to be more innovative, as measured by patent count. This result—analyzing the effect of network diversity on patent count—has not been published in an academic article. Here are the results from the logistic regression analysis. It predicts the probability that a business unit will file for patents in a given year, as a function of the range of technologies accessed through its network. Range is measured here in the crude fashion of counting the number of different technologies that a unit can access through its relationships (ranging from four to seventeen out of a maximum of twenty-two). The results also hold with a more nuanced entropy measure.

	Estimated regression coefficients (dependent variable = probability of patenting in a year)
Range	0.55*
Number of projects in unit	−0.78
Experience	0.11
Year	0.42
Unit size (log sale)	−0.09
Age of unit	2.1
Proportion of links between contacts	5.5
9 dummy variables for technologies	Not significant

* Significant at 0.05 level.
Pseudo R-squared: 0.51.

This analysis controls for some obvious alternative explanations, including that bigger and older business units have a wider range, that units with more projects in the hopper patent more frequently, and that different types of technologies in a unit (versus the contacts themselves) drive the diversity.

16. There is an enormous amount of research on this particular point of diversity. The best-known work is Ronald Burt, *Structural Holes: The Social Structure of Competition* (Cambridge, MA: Harvard University Press, 1992).

17. The original work on weak ties was Mark Granovetter, "The Strength of Weak Ties," *American Journal of Sociology* 6 (1973): 1360–1380.

18. This result is obtained by running a regression analysis in which search months (number of engineering months spent searching) were the dependent variable, and the average strength of the project team's interunit network was one of the independent variables. The coefficient was +1.60 months. That is, for every increment of strength (on a scale of 1 to 7), the team spent an extra 1.6 engineering months searching. Teams had on average a strength score of 4. A very weakly tied team would spend 1.6 × 2 = 3.2 months searching, whereas a very strongly tied team would spend 1.6 × 5 = 8 months searching (which is 12 percent of all engineering months spent on a project, on average, so this is not a trivial amount). For more on these results, see Morten Hansen, Marie Louise Mors, and Bjorn Lovas, "Knowledge Sharing in Organizations: Multiple Networks, Multiple Phases," *Academy of Management Journal* (2005).

19. Sticking with the familiar is such an empirical regularity that sociologists even refer to it as the "law of homophily" (and there aren't many laws in sociology). The evidence is overwhelming. See M. McPherson, L. Smith-Lovin, and J. M. Cook, "Birds of a Feather: Homophily in Social Networks," *Annual Review of Sociology* 27 (2001): 415–444.

20. Singh, Jasjit, Morten T. Hansen, and Joel Podolny. "The World is Not Small for Everyone: Pathways of Discrimination in Searching for Information in Organizations." INSEAD working paper (Fontainebleau, France: INSEAD, 2009).

21. Quoted in Morten T. Hansen and Bolko von Oetinger, "Introducing T-Shaped Managers: Knowledge Management's Next Generation."

22. The importance of job rotation is discussed in Nitin Nohria and Sumantra Ghoshal, *The Differentiated Network: Organizing Multinational Corporations for Value Creation* (San Francisco: Jossey-Bass, 1997).

23. This tactic is similar to the idea of having closure in networks. *Closure* means that people are more likely to cooperate if there are plenty of common third-party ties: if John wants something from Jim, then the more common ties that exist between them (e.g., Mary is a friend of both John's and Jim's), the less likely it is that Jim will mess with John and hoard. In the network research literature, scholars debate which is best: such closures or *holes* (lack of common ties). The debate has moved beyond this dichotomy to consider the mix of the two. See R. S. Burt, "Structural Holes and Good Ideas," *American Journal of Sociology* (2004), for a discussion. See also Martin Gargiulo, "Network Closure and Third Party Cooperation" INSEAD Working Paper (Fontainebleau, France: INSEAD, 2003).

24. Gladwell, *The Tipping Point,* 45.

25. This assumes that there *are* common contacts—people who are linked to you and to the target you are trying to influence. A paradox of networks is that people who have good search networks—those with wide range and weak ties—often have fewer common contacts and find it difficult to swarm targets.

26. A great reference for this is Robert B. Cialdini, *Influence: The Psychology of Persuasion* (New York: Collins Business Essentials, 2007). An easier read is provided in Noah J. Goldstein, Steve J. Martin, and Robert B. Cialdini, *Yes! 50 Scientifically Proven Ways to Be Persuasive* (New York: Free Press, 2008).

27. The Shield case and the quotations are taken from Anca Metiu and Lynn Selhat, "Shield: Product Development in a Distributed Team," Case 06/2005-5285 (Fontainebleau, France: INSEAD, 2005).

28. Virtual teams present communication challenges. See the following article for an exposition: Pamela Hinds and Mark Mortensen, "Understanding Conflict in Geographically Distributed Teams: The Moderating Effects of Shared Identity, Shared Context, and Spontaneous Communication," *Organization Science* (2005): 290–307.

29. Notice that the combination of weak ties and explicit knowledge does not pose many difficulties: although people hardly know each other, they collaborate on routine and easy-to-understand topics, so the communication is much easier.

30. See Morten T. Hansen, "The Search-Transfer Problem: The Role of Weak Ties in Sharing Knowledge Across Organization Subunits," *Administrative Science Quarterly* (1999).

31. Research suggests the importance of early mobilization to ensure team success. See Jeff Ericksen and Lee Dyer, "Right from the Start: Exploring the Effects of Early Team Events on Subsequent Project Team Development and Performance," *Administrative Science Quarterly* 49 (2004): 438–471.

32. Several comprehensive network-mapping tools and methods exist and are available from a number of consulting companies. Using them correctly requires quite a bit of effort.

Chapter 7

1. Quotes from video footage from the convention, http://www.youtube.com/watch?v=SUzUbtIptqQ (accessed on November 21, 2008).

2. Peter Nicholas, "Schwarzenegger Deems Opponents 'Girlie Men'—Twice," *San Francisco Chronicle,* July 18, 2004.

3. Ibid.

4. John Wildermuth, "Schwarzenegger Hits the Road: Governor Barnstorms for Budget," *San Francisco Chronicle,* July 22, 2004.

5. Ibid.

6. Lynda Gledhill, "Governor's Gibes Stall Budget, Dems Say," *San Francisco Chronicle,* July 20, 2004.

7. John M. Broder, "Not on Ballot, Schwarzenegger Is Still Rebuked," *New York Times,* November 10, 2005. The proposals were on state spending caps, political redistricting, teacher tenure, and union spending.

8. Ibid.

9. "Governor Schwarzenegger's 2006 State of the State Address, Office of the Governor, January 5, 2006 (as delivered), www.http/gov.ca.gov.

10. "Sadly, Arnold Schwarzenegger Is Likely to Prove a One-Off," *Economist,* November 3, 2007.

11. Jim Carlton, "Buddy Movie: Over Cigars, Schwarzenegger, Speaker Build Unlikely Bond—How Núñez Helped Drive Governor's Left Turn; 'You're Danny DeVito,'" *Wall Street Journal,* May 31, 2007.

12. Ibid.

13. Both the greenhouse gas and infrastructure bills were contentious. For the greenhouse gas emission bill (AB 32), the governor wanted his own advisory group

(the Climate Action Council) to have oversight. The Democrats resisted that and argued that the California Air Resources Board should have the authority to work out the details, including the implementation of a cap-and-trade system. The main sticking point in the trading system was that the Democrats wanted mandatory cuts (requiring companies to reduce their emissions by a certain amount as of a certain date), whereas the governor wanted the option for companies to buy and sell credits from a trading system (allowing noncompliant companies to buy units from complying companies, instead of cutting gases, to meet the standard). Schwarzenegger gave in on the oversight issue, and the Democrats relented on the mandatory requirement. The solution was a 25 percent cap by 2020, a trading system, a provision that the requirements could be lifted in an emergency, and oversight by ARB.

The infrastructure bill was also difficult to pass. In January 2006, Schwarzenegger proposed a ten-year, $222 billion spending plan that would be financed in part by issuing $68 billion in new bonds. Thorny problems popped up. The governor wanted to issue bonds worth $68 billion, but the lawmakers wanted something smaller. The Democrats wanted to include money for parks and affordable housing. The governor wanted money for building new prisons. By March, no deal was struck. But they were making headway. Republican Kevin McCarthy said at that time that the talks had been "closer and less partisan than I've ever seen Sacramento to date" (Josh Richman, "Lawmakers Close In on Bond Deal," *Oakland Tribune,* April 19, 2006). Collaborating and reaching compromises, Schwarzenegger gave up $31 billion and the prison expansion project, and the Democrats gave up money for parks, housing, and the fees. They ended up with a $37 billion bond for roads, schools, and levees. Voters approved it in November 2006.

14. Tom Chorneau and Mark Martin, "Even Top Dems Help Governor with Turnaround: Assembly Speaker Especially Works Well with Schwarzenegger," *San Francisco Chronicle,* August 31, 2006.

15. Data sources for these scales: each scale (e.g., redefining success) consists of survey questions that ask similar questions. This is more robust than asking only one question. The statistical measures for whether these are picking up the same underlying dimension is called Cronbach Alpha (CA), a measure of covariance among the questions. CAs for the various scales are redefining success (CA = 0.72); being inclusive (CA = 0.83); and being accountable (CA = 0.60). The last number is quite low (it is low because being accountable is really two subscales: accountable for oneself, and holding others accountable).

16. This principle is similar to the level five leadership principle articulated by Jim Collins, *Good to Great: Why Some Companies Make the Leap . . . and Others Don't* (New York: HarperCollins Business, 2001). The highest form of leadership behavior, in Collins' framework, occurs when leaders subordinate their own egos in pursuit of company goals. This behavior is clearly important for collaboration: instilling collaboration in a company, and getting people to help each other, is easier if people are working for goals bigger than their own narrow interests and for CEOs who put the company, and not themselves, first.

17. Revenues climbed from $21,311 million in 1994 to $63,367 million in 2007; Target annual reports (fiscal year ends January 2008). Stock price calculated on

a daily basis (adjusted for stock splits) for Ulrich's CEO tenure from April 14, 1994, to April 30, 2008. The S&P 500 index went up 271 percent during his tenure, so the Target increase of 750 percent handily beat the index. Source: Datastream via Thomson One Banker, retrieved September 7, 2008.

18. This biographical sketch is taken from Neal St. Anthony, "Behind the Bull's-Eye: Bob Ulrich Transformed Target, but the Chain Still Faces Tough Competition," *Star-Tribune* (Minneapolis), November 30, 2003.

19. Ibid.

20. Jennifer Reingold, "Target's Inner Circle," *Fortune,* March 31, 2008.

21. "Target's Ulrich: Quiet Coach for a Winner," *Discount Store News,* September 20, 1993.

22. Reingold, "Target's Inner Circle."

23. There is some academic research that links a CEO's narcissistic tendency to a tendency to engage in bold actions that attract attention to themselves. See Arijit Chatterjee and Donald Hambrick, "It's All About Me: Narcissistic Chief Executive Officers and Their Effects on Company Strategy and Performance," *Administrative Science Quarterly* (2007): 351–386. See also Rakesh Khurana, *Searching for a Corporate Savior: The Irrational Quest for Charismatic CEOs* (Princeton, N.J.: Princeton University Press, 2002); Manfred Kets de Vries and Katharina Balazs, "Greed, Vanity, and the Grandiosity of the CEO Character," in *Leadership and Governance From the Inside Out,* edited by R. Gandossy and J. Sonnenfeld (New York: Wiley, 2004), 51–61; and Michael Maccoby, *Narcissistic Leaders: Who Succeeds and Who Fails* (Boston: Harvard Business School Press, 2007).

24. Robert F. Kennedy, *Thirteen Days: A Memoir of the Cuban Missile Crisis* (Boston: W.W. Norton & Company, 1971), 34.

25. Ibid., 28.

26. Ibid.

27. Ernest R. May and Philip D. Zelikow, eds., *The Kennedy Tapes: Inside the White House During the Cuban Missile Crisis* (New York: W.W. Norton & Company, 2002), 113.

28. Arthur M. Schlesinger Jr., *A Thousand Days: John F. Kennedy in the White House* (Boston: Houghton Mifflin Company, 1965). The Bay of Pigs fiasco was one of the policy-making mistakes that gave rise to the term *groupthink,* which refers to "a mode of thinking that people engage in when they are deeply involved in a cohesive in-group, when the members' striving for unanimity overrides their motivation to realistically appraise alternative courses of action"; Irving L. Janis, *Victims of Groupthink: A Psychological Study of Foreign-Policy Decisions and Fiascoes* (New York: Houghton Mifflin Company, 1972), 9.

29. This is detailed in Janis, *Victims of Groupthink,* 147–148. See also Richard Hackman and Richard Walton, "Leading Groups in Organizations," in *Designing Effective Work Groups,* edited by Paul S. Goodman (San Francisco: Jossey-Bass, 1986), 93–103.

30. Robert F. Kennedy, *Thirteen Days,* 36.

31. From Irving Janis, *Victims of Groupthink,* 149.

32. Robert F. Kennedy, *Thirteen Days,* 34.

33. Quoted in Bill George and Andrew N. McLean, "Kevin Sharer at Amgen: Sustaining the High-Growth Company," Case 9-406-020 (Boston: Harvard Business School, October 5, 2005).

34. David Brooks, "The Obama-Clinton Issue," *New York Times*, December 18, 2007.

35. Information in this section comes from Robert Berner, "P&G: New and Improved," *BusinessWeek*, July 7, 2003.

36. Ingrid Marie Nembhard and Amy Edmondson, "Making It Safe: The Effects of Leader Inclusiveness and Professional Status on Psychological Safety and Improvement Efforts in Health Care Teams," Special Issue on Healthcare, *Journal of Organizational Behavior* 27, no. 7 (November 2006): 941–966. See also Amy Edmondson, "Psychological Safety and Learning Behavior in Work Teams," *Administrative Science Quarterly* 44, no. 4 (December 1999): 350–383.

37. See David Garvin and Michael Roberto, "What You Don't Know About Making Decisions," *Harvard Business Review* (September 2001).

38. The argument that managers achieve greater buy-in by using a collaborative decision-making process has been well supported by research (ibid.). For a discussion of much of this research, see Michael Roberto, *Why Great Leaders Don't Take Yes for an Answer: Managing for Conflict and Consensus* (Upper Saddle River, NJ: Wharton School Publishing, 2005).

39. I have used the excellent summary provided in www.wikipedia.org under the entry "Kitty Genovese." Much has been written about this story. See, for example, A. M. Rosenthal, *Thirty-Eight Witnesses: The Kitty Genovese Case* (Berkeley: University of California Press, 1964). The events have been revisited several times, and *American Psychologist* has published a revisionist account that disputes that so many—thirty-eight—were essentially standing by observing the murder. See R. Manning, M. Levine, and A. Collins, "The Kitty Genovese Murder and the Social Psychology of Helping: The Parable of the 38 Witnesses," *American Psychologist* 62 (September 2007): 555–562.

40. Darley, J. M. & Latané, B., "Bystander intervention in emergencies: Diffusion of responsibility." *Journal of Personality and Social Psychology* (1968).

41. I am describing this experiment from the point of view of "Carl," a made-up character. The data is from A. G. Ingham, G. Levinger, J. Graves, and V. Peckham, "The Ringelmann Effect: Studies of Group Size and Group Performance," *Journal of Experimental Social Psychology* (1974). The original study was done by a French engineer named Max Ringelmann, who reportedly did the rope-pulling experiment in the late 1880s. Hence, it has been called "The Ringelmann effect." See David A. Kravitz and Barbara Martin, "Ringelmann Rediscovered: The Original Article," *Journal of Personality and Social Psychology* (1986).

42. The researchers controlled for the plausible explanation that team effort decreased because people couldn't coordinate so easily with all those hands on the rope. They reran the experiment, this time blindfolding the participants and letting them believe that they were pulling together with others (when in fact they were not), and the conclusion was the same; one part of the decline of performance was due to a coordination loss, and another part was due to lowered effort.

43. The researchers who labeled this *social loafing* also replicated Ringelmann's original findings; see Bibb Latane, Kipling Williams, and Stephen Harkins, "Many

Hands Make Light the Work: The Causes and Consequences of Social Loafing," *Journal of Personality and Social Psychology* (1979).

44. Carlos Ghosn, "Saving the Business Without Losing the Company," *Harvard Business Review* (January 2002).

45. Mark Magnier, "Nissan Unveils Plan for Sweeping Restructuring," *Los Angeles Times,* October 19, 1999.

46. Carlos Ghosn, "Saving the Business Without Losing the Company," *Harvard Business Review* (January 2002).

47. Quoted in Michael Y. Yoshino and Masako Egawa, "Implementing the Nissan Renewal Plan," Case 9-303-111 (Boston: Harvard Business School, 2006). See also A. Gold, M. Hirano, and Y. Yokoyama, "An Outsider Takes On Japan: An Interview with Nissan's Carlos Ghosn," *McKinsey Quarterly* (2001): 95–105.

48. Michael Yoshino and Masako Egawa, "Nissan Motor Co., Ltd., 2002," Case 9-303-042 (Boston: Harvard Business School, 2006).

49. Ghosn, "Saving the Business Without Losing the Company."

50. Quoted in Michael Yoshino and Masako Egawa, "Nissan Motor Co., Ltd., 2002," Case 9-303-042 (Boston: Harvard Business School, 2006).

51. The following table shows the results from the statistical analysis (the first number in box is the correlation coefficient; the second number is the regression coefficient):

	Redefine success	Inclusiveness	Accountability
Power	- 0.62 (-0.32, sign.)	-0.54 (not sign.)	-0.25 (not sign.)
Arrogance	- 0.45 (not sign.)	-0.69 (-0.40, sign.)	-0.13 (not sign.)
Defensiveness	- 0.55 (-0.13, sign.)	-0.60 (-0.20, sign.)	-0.33 (-0.26, sign.)
Fear	-0.39 (not sign.)	-0.38 (not sign.)	-0.10 (sign.)
Ego	-0.35 (not sign.)	-0.31 (not sign.)	-0.08 (sign.)
Control variables (for regression analysis)	Age Tenure Sr. executive Business unit head Exed program** Job performance***	Age Tenure Sr. executive Business unit head Exed program** Job Performance***	Age Tenure Sr. executive Business unit head Exed program** Job Performance***
	N=170* R-squared = 0.55	N=170* R-squared = 0.58	N=170* R-squared = 0.39

* Original sample of 185 was reduced to 170 due to missing data.
** A dummy variable was entered for 5 out of the 6 executive courses that the responded participated in. This controls for any variance across these courses.
*** Question: "Your assessment of the person's overall performance?" (top 10 percent, top 11-25 percent, top 26-50 percent, 51-75 percent, lower 76 to 100 percent).

The first number in each cell is the correlation between the two factors (e.g., –0.62 between "power" and "redefine success" means that they are negatively correlated by 0.62, a very high negative relationship).

The second number is the coefficient from a regression analysis, where the dependent variable (e.g., "redefine success") is a function of the five personality factors and a set of control variables (age, tenure, type of job, and job performance). "Sign." means that the variable was statistically significant in predicting the dependent variable, and "not sign." means that it was not. For example, "power" had an estimated coefficient of –0.32 in explaining "redefine success"; if a person moves from 4 to 5 on the power scale, the person's ability to redefine success goes down by 0.32 (on the scale of 1 to 7).

Two notes of caution about inferring too much from the data. First, it is difficult to infer causality because the data is cross-sectional. We don't know that a thirst for power determines the inability to redefine success, for instance. Rather, it offers only a correlation: that high levels of power hunger are negatively associated with redefining success as bigger goals.

Second, the data is gathered from one source, which gives rise to what is called a "common methods" problem. It could be that the rater simply thought the person was a great performer (or a bad one) and then proceeded to answer the questions on that basis, giving high scores to things that sound good (being inclusive) and low scores to what sounds bad (power hunger). For this reason, I entered the respondent's rating of the person's job performance as a *control* variable in the regression analysis: this control should remove some of the variance due to such potential perceptual issues.

Our survey of 185 managers must be seen as preliminary and tentative. More research is needed to uncover these correlations between the personal blockers and collaborative leadership behaviors.

52. The definition of power comes from Jeffrey Pfeffer of Stanford Business School, who has written the two authoritative books on power in business: *Managing with Power* (Harvard Business School Press, 1994) and *Power in Organizations* (Prentice Hall, 1981).

53. Kevin Allison and Chrystia Freeland, "View from the top: John Chambers, chief executive of Cisco Systems," *Financial Times* (April 25, 2008), http://www.un.org/Pubs/chronicle/2006/issue2/0206p24.htm.

BIBLIOGRAPHY

Allen, Thomas J. *Managing the Flow of Technology*. Cambridge, MA: MIT Press, 1977.

Ancona, Deborah, and Henrik Bresman. *X-teams: How to Build Teams That Lead, Innovate, and Succeed*. Boston: Harvard Business School Press, 2007.

Barnett, William P., and Morten T. Hansen. "The Red Queen in Organizational Evolution." *Strategic Management Journal* 17 (1996): 139–157.

Barsoux, Jean-Louis. "Bertelsmann: Corporate Structure *and* the Internet Age." Teaching Note 06/2007-4907, INSEAD, Fontainebleau, France, 2000.

Barsoux, Jean-Louis, and Charles D. Galunic. "Bertelsmann (A) Corporate Structures and the Internet Age." Case 06/2007-4907. Fontainebleau, France: INSEAD, 2000.

Bartlett, Christopher A., Kenton Elderkin, and Barbara Feinberg. "Jan Carlzon: CEO at SAS (A)." Case 9-392-149. Boston: Harvard Business School, 1992.

Beard, Patricia. *Blue Blood and Mutiny: The Fight for the Soul of Morgan Stanley*. New York: HarperCollins, 2007.

Brandenburger, Adam, and Barry Nalebuff. *Co-opetition: A Revolutionary Mindset That Combines Competition and Cooperation*. New York: Doubleday, 1996.

Brewer, Marilynn B. "Ingroup Bias in the Minimal Intergroup Situation: A Cognitive Motivational Analysis." *Psychological Bulletin* 86 (1979): 307–324.

Brin, Sergey, and Lawrence Page. "The Anatomy of a Large-Scale Hypertextual Web Search Engine." Working Paper, Stanford University, Stanford, 1996.

Bruner, Robert F. *Deals from Hell: M&A Lessons That Rise Above the Ashes*. Hoboken, NJ: John Wiley & Sons, 2005.

Burt, Ronald S. *Structural Holes: The Social Structure of Competition*. Cambridge: Harvard University Press, 1992.

Burt, Ronald S. "Structural Holes and Good Ideas." *The American Journal of Sociology* 110, no. 2 (2004): 349–399.

Burton, Diane M. "Rob Parson at Morgan Stanley (A)." Case 9-498-054. Boston: Harvard Business School, 1998.

Burton, Diane M. "The Firmwide 360-degree Performance Evaluation Process at Morgan Stanley." Case 9-498-053. Boston: Harvard Business School, 1998.

Burton, Diane M., Thomas J. DeLong, and Katherine Lawrence. "Morgan Stanley: Becoming a One-Firm Firm." Case 9-400-043. Boston: Harvard Business School, 1999.

Cairncross, Frances. *The Death of Distance: How the Communications Revolution Is Changing Our Lives.* Boston: Harvard Business School Press, 1997.

Carlton, Jim. *Apple: The Inside Story of Intrigue, Egomania, and Business Blunders.* New York: Collins, 1998.

Carson, Mary. "Saying It Like It Isn't: The Pros and Cons of 360-degree Feedback." *Business Horizons* 49 (2006): 395–402.

Casciaro, Tiziana, and Miguel S. Lobo. "Competent Jerks, Lovable Fools, and the Formation of Social Networks." *Harvard Business Review* 83, no. 6 (2005): 92–99.

Chakrabarti, Abhirup, Kulwant Singh, and Ishtiaq Mahmood. "Diversification and Performance: Evidence from East Asian Firms." *Strategic Management Journal* 28, no. 2 (2007): 101–120.

Chatterjee, Arijit, and Donald Hambrick. "It's All About Me: Narcissistic Chief Executive Officers and Their Effects on Company Strategy and Performance." *Administrative Science Quarterly* 52, no. 3 (2007): 351–386.

Cialdini, Robert B. *Influence: The Psychology of Persuasion.* New York: Collins Business Essentials, 2007.

Collins, James C., and Jerry I. Porras. *Built to Last: Successful Habits of Visionary Companies.* New York: HarperBusiness, 1994.

Collins, James C. *Good to Great: Why Some Companies Make the Leap . . . and Others Don't.* New York: HarperBusiness, 2001.

Cross, Rob, Nitin Nohria, and Andrew Parker. "Six Myths About Informal Networks— and How to Overcome Them." *Sloan Management Review* 43, no. 3 (2002): 67–75.

Cross, Rob and Robert Thomas, *Driving Results Through Social Networks: How Top Organizations Leverage Networks for Performance and Growth,* San Francisco, CA: Jossey-Bass. 2009.

Darley, J. M. & B. Latané, "Bystander intervention in emergencies: Diffusion of responsibility." *Journal of Personality and Social Psychology* (1968).

Davenport, Thomas H., and Morten T. Hansen. "Knowledge Management at Andersen Consulting." Case 9-499-032. Boston: Harvard Business School, 1998.

Day, Dwayne A. *Transcript of Presidential Meeting in the Cabinet Room of the White House: Supplemental Appropriations for the National Aeronautics and Space Administration (NASA),* NASA, 1962.

Dodds, Peter S., Roby Muhamad, and Duncan J. Watts. "An Experimental Study of Search in Global Social Networks." *Science* 301, no. 5634 (2003): 827–829.

Donini-Lenhoff, Fred G., and Hannah L. Hedrick. "Growth of Specialization in Graduate Medical Education." *Journal of the American Medical Association* 284, no. 10 (2000): 1284–1289.

Edmondson, A. "Psychological Safety and Learning Behavior in Work Teams," *Administrative Science Quarterly* 44, no. 4 (December 1999): 350–383.

Ericksen, Jeff, and Lee Dyer. "Right from the Start: Exploring the Effects of Early Team Events on Subsequent Project Team Development and Performance." *Administrative Science Quarterly* 49, no. 3 (2004): 438–471.

Evans, Philip, and Bob Wolf. "Collaboration Rules." *Harvard Business Review* (July 2005): 96–103.

Ferraro, Fabrizio, Jeffrey Pfeffer, and Robert I. Sutton. "Economics Language and Assumptions: How Theories Can Become Self-Fulfilling." *Academy of Management Review* 30, no. 1 (2005): 8–24.

Fleming, Lee, Santiago Mingo, and David Chen. "Collaborative Brokerage, Generative Creativity, and Creative Success." *Administrative Science Quarterly* 52 (2007): 443–475.

Frank, Robert H. *Choosing the Right Pond: Human Behavior and the Quest for Status.* Oxford: Oxford University Press, 1985.

Frank, Robert H., Thomas Gilovich, and Dennis T. Regan. "Does Studying Economics Inhibit Cooperation?" *Journal of Economic Perspectives* 7, no. 2 (1993): 159–171.

Friedman, Thomas L. *The World Is Flat: A Brief History of the Twenty-First Century.* New York: Farrar, Straus and Giroux, 2005.

Gandossy, Robert, and Jeffrey Sonnenfeld. *Leadership and Governance from the Inside Out.* New York: John Wiley & Sons, 2004.

Gargiulo, Martin. "Network Closure and Third Party Cooperation" INSEAD Working Paper. Fontainebleau, France: INSEAD, 2003.

Gargiulo, Martin, Gokhan Ertug, and Charles Galunic. "The Two Faces of Control: Network Closure and Individual Performance Among Knowledge Workers." *Administrative Science Quarterly* (forthcoming, 2009).

Garvin, David A., and Artemis March. "Harvey Golub: Recharging American Express." Case 9-396-212. Boston: Harvard Business School, 1996.

Garvin, David A., and Michael A. Roberto. "What You Don't Know About Making Decisions." *Harvard Business Review* 79, no. 8 (2001): 108–116.

George, Bill, and Andrew N. McLean. "Kevin Sharer at Amgen: Sustaining the High-Growth Company." Case 9-406-020. Boston: Harvard Business School, 2005.

Ghosn, Carlos. "Saving the Business Without Losing the Company." *Harvard Business Review* 80, no. 1 (2002): 37–45.

Gladwell, Malcolm. *The Tipping Point: How Little Things Can Make a Big Difference.* New York: Little, Brown & Company, 2000.

Goldstein, Noah J., Steve J. Martin, and Robert B. Cialdini. *Yes! 50 Scientifically Proven Ways to Be Persuasive.* New York: Free Press, 2008.

Goshal, Sumantra. "Scandinavian Airlines System (SAS) in 1988." Case 3041. Fontainebleau, France: INSEAD, CEDEP, 1988.

Granovetter, Mark. "The Strength of Weak Ties." *American Journal of Sociology* 78, no. 6 (1973): 1360–1380.

Groysberg, Boris, Linda-Eling Lee, and Ashish Nanda "Can They Take It with Them? The Portability of Star Knowledge Workers' Performance: Myth or Reality." *Management Science* 54, 2008.

Haas, Martine R., and Morten T. Hansen. "When Using Knowledge Can Hurt Performance: The Value of Organizational Capabilities in a Management Consulting Company." *Strategic Management Journal* 26, no. 1 (2005): 1–24.

Haas, Martine R., and Morten T. Hansen. "Different Knowledge, Different Benefits: Toward a Productivity Perspective on Knowledge Sharing in Organizations." *Strategic Management Journal* 28, no. 11 (2007): 1133–1153.

Haas, Martine R. "Cosmopolitans and locals: Status rivalries, deference, and knowledge in international teams." Research on Managing Groups and Teams (2005): 203-230.

Hackman, J. Richard and Richard Walton, "Leading Groups in Organizations," in *Designing Effective Work Groups,* edited by Paul S. Goodman (San Francisco: Jossey-Bass, 1986), 93–103.

Hackman, J. Richard. *Leading Teams: Setting the Stage for Great Performance.* Boston: Harvard Business School Press, 2002.

Hansen, Morten T. "Knowledge Integration in Organizations." Unpublished PhD diss., Graduate School of Business, Stanford University, 1996.

Hansen, Morten T. "The Search-Transfer Problem: The Role of Weak Ties in Sharing Knowledge Across Organization Subunits." *Administrative Science Quarterly* 44, no. 1 (1999): 82–111.

Hansen, Morten T., Nitin Nohria, and Thomas Tierney. "What's Your Strategy for Managing Knowledge?" *Harvard Business Review* 77, no. 2 (1999): 106–116.

Hansen, Morten T., Henry W. Chesbrough, Nitin Nohria, and Donald Sull. "Networked Incubators: Hothouses of the New Economy." *Harvard Business Review* 78, no. 5 (2000): 74–83.

Hansen, Morten T., and Martine R. Haas. "Competing for Attention in Knowledge Markets: Electronic Document Dissemination in a Management Consulting Company." *Administrative Science Quarterly* 46, no. 1 (2001): 1–28.

Hansen, Morten T., and Bolko von Oetinger. "Introducing T-Shaped Managers: Knowledge Management's Next Generation." *Harvard Business Review* 79, no. 3 (2001): 106–116.

Hansen, Morten T., Joel Podolny, and Jeffrey Pfeffer. "So Many Ties, So Little Time: A Task Contingency Perspective on the Value of Corporate Social Capital in Organizations." *Research in the Sociology of Organizations* 18 (2001): 21–57.

Hansen, Morten T. "Knowledge Networks: Explaining Effective Knowledge Sharing in Multiunit Companies." *Organization Science* 13, no. 3 (2002): 232–248.

Hansen, Morten T. "Turning the Lone Star into a Real Team Player." *Financial Times,* August 7, 2002.

Hansen, Morten T., and Christina Darwall. "Intuit, Inc.: Transforming an Entrepreneurial Company into a Collaborative Organization (A)." Case 9-403-064. Boston: Harvard Business School, 2003.

Hansen, Morten T., and Bjorn Lovas. "How Do Multinational Companies Leverage Technological Competencies? Moving from Single to Interdependent Explanations." *Strategic Management Journal* 25, no. 8 (2004): 801–822.

Hansen, Morten T., and Nitin Nohria. "How to Build Collaborative Advantage." *MIT Sloan Management Review* 46, no. 1 (2004): 4–12.

Hansen, Morten T., Louise Mors, and Bjorn Lovas. "Knowledge Sharing in Organizations: Multiple Networks, Multiple Phases." *Academy of Management Journal* 48, no. 5 (2005): 776–793.

Hansen, Morten T. "Collaborate for Value." *Financial Times,* July 13, 2007.

Hansen, Morten T. "Transforming DNV: From Silos to Disciplined Collaboration Across Business Units—the Food Business." Case 08/2007-5458. Fontainebleau, France: INSEAD, 2007.

Hansen, Morten T. "Transforming DNV: From Silos to Disciplined Collaboration across Business Units—Changes at the Top." Case 08/2007-5458. Fontainebleau, France: INSEAD, 2007.

Hansen, Morten T., and Julian Birkinshaw. "The Innovation Value Chain." *Harvard Business Review* 85, no. 6 (2007): 121–130.

Hargadon, Andrew. *How Breakthrough Happens: The Surprising Truth About How Companies Innovate.* Boston: Harvard Business School Press, 2003.

Hayek, Friedrich A. "The Use of Knowledge in Society." *American Economic Review* 35 (1945): 519–530.

Hinds, Pamela J., and Mark Mortensen. "Understanding Conflict in Geographically Distributed Teams: The Moderating Effects of Shared Identity, Shared Context, and Spontaneous Communication." *Organization Science* 16, no. 3 (2005): 290–307.

Hinds, Pamela J., and Sara Kiesler. *Distributed Work.* Cambridge, MA: MIT Press, 2002.

Huston, Larry, and Nabil Sakkab. "Connect and Develop: Inside Procter & Gamble's New Model for Innovation." *Harvard Business Review* (March 2006): 58–68.

Ibarra, Herminia, and Mark Hunter. "How Leaders Create and Use Networks." *Harvard Business Review* (January 2007): 40–47.

Ingham, Alan G., G. Levinger, J. Graver and V. Peckham, "The Ringelmann Effect: Studies of Group Size and Group Performance." *Journal of Experimental Social Psychology* 10, no. 4 (1974): 371–384.

Janis, Irving L. *Victims of Groupthink: A Psychological Study of Foreign-policy Decisions and Fiascoes.* Boston, MA: Houghton, Mifflin Company, 1972.

Kao, John J. "Scandinavian Airlines System." Case 9-487-041. Boston: Harvard Business School, 1996.

Kennedy, Robert F. *Thirteen Days: A Memoir of the Cuban Missile Crisis.* New York: W.W. Norton & Company, 1971.

Kets de Vries, Manfred and Katharina Balazs. "Greed, Vanity, and the Grandiosity of the CEO Character," in *Leadership and Governance From the Inside Out,* edited by R. Gandossy and J. Sonnenfeld. New York: Wiley, 2004.

Kerr, Steven. "On the Folly of Rewarding A, While Hoping for B." *Academy of Management Journal* 18, no. 4 (1975): 769–783.

Khanna, Tarun, and Krishna Palepu. "Why Focused Strategies May Be Wrong for Emerging Markets." *Harvard Business Review* 75, no. 4 (1997): 41–51.

Khurana, Rakesh. *Searching for a Corporate Savior: The Irrational Quest for Charismatic CEOs.* Princeton, N.J.: Princeton University Press, 2002.

Klein, Katherine J., Beng Chong Lim, Jessica Saltz and David Mayer. "How Do They Get There? An Examination of the Antecedents of Centrality in Team Networks." *Academy of Management Journal* 47, no. 6 (2004): 952–963.

Kleinbaum, Adam M., Toby E. Stuart, and Michael L. Tushman. "Communication (and Coordination?) in a Modern, Complex Organization." Working Paper 09-004, Harvard Business School, Boston, 2008.

Kravitz, D. A., and B. Martin. "Ringelmann Rediscovered: The Original Article." *Journal of Personality and Social Psychology* 50 (1986): 936–941.

Lafley, A. G. and Ram Charan, *The Game Changer: How You Can Drive Revenue and Profit Growth With Innovation,* New York: Crown Business (2008).

Lal, Rajiv, Nitin Nohria, and Carin-Isabel Knoop. "UBS: Towards the Integrated Firm." Case 9-506-026. Boston: Harvard Business School, 2006.

Latané, Bibb, Kipling Williams, and Stephen Harkings. "Many Hands Make Light the Work: The Causes and Consequences of Social Loafing." *Journal of Personality and Social Psychology* 37, no. 6 (1979): 822–832.

Leventhal, Howard, Robert Singer, and Susan Jones. "Effects of Fear and Specificity of Recommendation upon Attitudes and Behavior." *Journal of Personality and Social Psychology* 2 (1965): 20–29.

Levy, Steven. *The Perfect Thing: How the iPod Shuffles Commerce, Culture, and Coolness.* New York: Simon & Schuster, 2006.

Liberman, Varda, Steven M. Samuels, and Lee Ross. "The Name of the Game: Predictive Power of Reputations Versus Situational Labels in Determining Prisoner's Dilemma Game Moves." *Personality and Social Psychology Bulletin* 30, no. 9 (2004): 1175–1185.

Maccoby, Michael. "Narcissistic Leaders: Who Succeeds and Who Fails." Boston: Harvard Business School Press, 2007.

Magee, David. *Turnaround: How Carlos Ghosn Rescued Nissan.* New York: Collins Business Essentials, 2003.

Manning, Rachel, Mark Levine, and Alan Collins. "The Kitty Genovese Murder and the Social Psychology of Helping: The Parable of the 38 Witnesses." *American Psychologist* 62, no. 6 (2007): 555–562.

Markides, Constantinos C. "Consequences of Corporate Refocusing: Ex ante Evidence." *Academy of Management Journal* 35, no. 2 (1992): 398–412.

Martin, Jeffrey, and Kathleen Eisenhardt. "Creating Cross-business Collaboration: A Recombinative View of Organizational Form." Working Paper, University of Texas at Austin, 2005.

May, Ernest R., and Philip D. Zelikow (eds). *The Kennedy Tapes: Inside the White House During the Cuban Missile Crisis.* New York: W.W. Norton & Company, 2002.

McPherson, Miller, Lynn Smith-Lovin, and James M. Cook. "Birds of a Feather: Homophily in Social Networks." *Annual Review of Sociology* 27 (2001): 415–444.

Mehra, Ajay, Martin Kilduff, and Daniel J. Brass. "The Social Networks of High and Low Self-Monitors: Implications for Workplace Performance." *Administrative Science Quarterly* 46, no. 2 (2001): 121–146.

Metiu, Anca, and Lynn Selhat. "Shield: Product Development in a Distributed Team." Case 06/2005-5285. Fontainebleau, France: INSEAD, 2005.

Michaels, Ed, Helen Handfield-Jones, and Beth Axelrod. *The War for Talent.* Boston: Harvard Business School Press, 2001.

Milgram, Stanley. "The Small-World Problem." *Psychology Today* 2 (1967): 60–67.

Miller, Dale T. "The Norm of Self-Interest." *American Psychologist* 54, no. 12 (1999): 1053–1060.

Moran, Steven, Immanuel Hermreck, and Charles D. Galunic. "Bertelsmann (B): Corporate Structures for Value Creation." Case 06/2007-4907. Fontainebleau, France: INSEAD, 2004.

Nembhard, Ingrid Marie, and A. Edmondson. "Making It Safe: The Effects of Leader Inclusiveness and Professional Status on Psychological Safety and Improvement

Efforts in Health Care Teams." Special Issue on Healthcare. *Journal of Organizational Behavior* 27, no. 7 (November 2006): 941–966.

Nohria, Nitin, and Sumantra Ghoshal. *The Differentiated Network: Organizing Multinational Corporations for Value Creation.* San Francisco: Jossey-Bass, 1997.

Perlow, Leslie A. "The Time Famine: Towards a Sociology of Work Time." *Administrative Science Quarterly* 44, no. 1 (March 1999): 57–81.

Pfau, Bruce, and Ira Kay. "Does 360-Degree Feedback Negatively Affect Company Performance?" *HR Magazine* 47, no. 6 (2002): 54–59.

Pfeffer, Jeffrey. *Power in Organizations.* New York: Financial Times Prentice Hall, 1981.

Pfeffer, Jeffrey. *Managing with Power: Politics and Influence in Organizations.* Boston: Harvard Business School Press, 1994.

Pfeffer, Jeffrey, and Charles O'Reilly. "Southwest Airlines (A)." Case HR1A. Stanford, CA: Stanford University Press, 1995.

Pfeffer, Jeffrey. "Six Dangerous Myths About Pay." *Harvard Business Review* 76, no. 3 (1998): 109–119.

Pfeffer, Jeffrey, and Robert I. Sutton. *Hard Facts, Dangerous Half-Truths, and Total Nonsense: Profiting from Evidence-Based Management.* Boston: Harvard Business School Press, 2006.

Pfeffer, Jeffrey. *What Were They Thinking? Unconventional Wisdom About Management.* Boston: Harvard Business School Press, 2007.

Piskorski, Mikolaj Jan, and Alessandro L. Spadini. "Procter & Gamble: Organization 2005." Case 9-707-519. Boston: Harvard Business School, 2007.

Point, Fernand. *Ma Gastronomie.* Paris: Flammarion, 1969.

Point, Fernand. *Ma Gastronomie* (English translation). New York: Overlook/Rookery, 2008.

Polanyi, Michael. *The Tacit Dimension.* New York: Anchor Day Books, 1966.

Prusak, Laurence. "The World Is Round." *Harvard Business Review* 84, no. 4 (2006): 18–20.

Quelch, John A., and Rohit Deshpande. *The Global Market: Developing a Strategy to Manage Across Borders.* San Francisco: Jossey-Bass, 2004.

Ramanujam, Vasudevan, and P. "Rajan" Varadarajan. "Research on Corporate Diversification: A Synthesis." *Strategic Management Journal* 10, no. 6 (1989): 523–551.

Rivkin, Jan W. , Michael A. Roberto, and Erika M. Ferlins. "Managing National Intelligence (A): Before 9/11." Case 9-706-463. Boston: Harvard Business School, 2006.

Roberto, Michael A. *Why Great Leaders Don't Take Yes for an Answer: Managing for Conflict and Consensus.* Upper Saddle River, NJ: Wharton School Publishing, 2005.

Rosenthal, Abraham M., ed. *Thirty-Eight Witnesses: The Kitty Genovese Case.* Berkeley: University of California Press, 1964.

Rumelt, Richard P. *Strategy, Structure, and Economic Performance.* Boston: Harvard University Press, 1974.

Sahlman, William A., and Alison B. Wagonfeld. "Intuit's New CEO: Steve Bennett." Case 9-803-044. Boston: Harvard Business School, 2003.

Salancik, Gerald R., and Jeffrey Pfeffer. "A Social Information Processing Approach to Job Attitudes and Task Design." *Administrative Science Quarterly* 23, no. 2 (1978): 224–253.

Schlesinger, Arthur M. *A Thousand Days: John F. Kennedy in the White House.* Boston, MA: Houghton Mifflin, 1965.

Sherif, Muzafer, and Carolyn W. Sherif. *Groups in Harmony and Tension.* New York: Harper and Brothers, 1953.

Sherif, Muzafer, O. J. Harvey, B. Jack White, William R. Hood and Carolyn W. Sherif. *The Robbers Cave Experiment: Intergroup Conflict and Cooperation.* Middletown, CT: Wesleyan University Press, 1988.

Singh, Jasjit, Morten T. Hansen, and Joel Podolny. "The World is Not Small for Everyone: Pathways of Discrimination in Searching for Information in Organizations." INSEAD working paper (Fontainebleau, France: INSEAD, 2009).

Sirower, Mark L. *The Synergy Trap: How Companies Lose the Acquisition Game.* New York: Free Press, 2007.

Sobel, Robert. *I.T.T.: The Management of Opportunity.* New York: Times Books, 1982.

Sobel, Robert. *The Rise and Fall of the Conglomerate Kings.* New York: Beard Books, 1999.

Sorenson, Olav, and Toby Stuart. "Syndication Networks and the Spatial Distribution of Venture Capital Investments." *American Journal of Sociology* 106, no. 6 (2001): 1546–1588.

Szulanski, Gabriel. "Exploring Internal Stickiness: Impediments to the Transfer of Best Practice Within the Firm." *Strategic Management Journal* 17 (1996): 27–43.

Tajfel, H. and J. C. Turner, "The Social Identity Theory of Intergroup Behavior," in *Psychology of Intergroup Relations,* 2nd ed., edited by S. Worchel and W. G. Austin, Chicago: Nelson Hall, 1986, 7–24.

The House Permanent Select Committee On Intelligence And The Senate Select Committee On Intelligence. *The 9/11 Report: Joint Congressional Inquiry. Report of the Joint Inquiry into the Terrorist Attacks of September 11, 2001.* 2003.

The National Commission on Terrorist Attacks Upon the United States. *Final Report of the National Commission on Terrorist Attacks Upon the United States.* New York: W.W. Norton & Company, 2004.

Thimmesh, Catherine. *Team Moon: How 400,000 People Landed Apollo 11 on the Moon.* New York: Houghton Mifflin Company, 2006.

Tichy, Noel M. and Ram Charan. "Speed, Simplicity, Self-Confidence: An Interview with Jack Welch." *Harvard Business Review* (September–October 1989): 112–120.

Travers, Jeffrey, and Stanley Milgram. "An Experimental Study of the Small World Problem." *Sociometry* 32 (1969): 425–443.

Tushman, Michael L., and William L. Moore, eds. *Readings in the Management of Innovation.* 2nd ed. New York: Ballinger/Harper & Row, 1988.

Villalonga, Belen. *Research Roundtable Discussion: The Diversification Discount.* Boston: Harvard Business School, 2003.

Wagemann, Ruth, Debra A. Nunes, James A. Burruss, and Richard Hackman. *Senior Leadership Teams: What It Takes to Make Them Great.* Boston: Harvard Business School Press, 2008.

Wohlstetter, Roberta. *Pearl Harbor: Warning and Decision.* Stanford, CA: Stanford University Press, 1962.

Yoshino, Michael, and Masako Egawa. "Nissan Motor Co. Ltd." Case 9-303-042. Boston: Harvard Business School, 2006.

Yoshino, Michael, and Masako Egawa. "Implementing the Nissan Renewal Plan." Case 9-303-111. Boston: Harvard Business School, 2003.

Young, Jeffrey S., and William L. Simon. *Icon Steve Jobs: The Greatest Second Act in the History of Business.* New York: John Wiley & Sons, 2005.

Zander, Udo, and Bruce Kogut. "Knowledge and the Speed of Transfer and Imitation of Organizational Capabilities: An Empirical Test." *Organization Science* 6, no. 1 (1995): 76–92.

ACKNOWLEDGMENTS

I have been fortunate to have received so much help from many people for the research behind this book and for the task of writing it. I would like to thank my coauthors who have worked with me over the years to produce academic and managerial articles that have provided the foundation for this book: Julian Birkinshaw, Martine Haas, Roger Lehman Bjorn Lovas, Louise Mors, Nitin Nohria, Joel Podolny, Jeffrey Pfeffer, Jasjit Singh, Thomas Tierney, and Bolko von Oetinger.

I have also been blessed with having had outstanding mentors in my career. Professor Jeffrey Pfeffer at Stanford Business School was the chair of my PhD committee at Stanford and has always provided great guidance in my research. Professor Nitin Nohria at Harvard Business School has been a mentor, a coauthor, and a continuous source of support over the past decade. Professor Kim Clark, former dean of Harvard Business School, provided the early impetus for this project when he suggested I focus on the topic of collaboration. My colleague over the past fifteen years, Jim Collins, has been a guiding light, an inspiration, a tough critic, and, above all, a great friend.

A number of other people gave of their time to read early versions of the book manuscript and provide invaluable comments: Ron Adner, Eric Benhamou, Nana Von Bernuth, Harald Boerner, Peter Boback, Jeff Bradach, Bertil Chappuis, Jim Collins, Patrick Forth, Marianne Gillam, Egill Hansen, André Hoffmann, Cecilie Heucht, Martine Haas, Herminia Ibarra, Wistar H. MacLaren, Birger Magnus, Bjørn Matre, Louise Mors, Bolko von Oetinger, Jeffrey Pfeffer, Geoff Ralston, Mika Salmi, Einar Venold, Ludo Van Der Heyden, Jan Weetjens, and four anonymous reviewers.

Don Sull and Herminia Ibarra helped me in thinking through titles, and my assistant Jayne Brocklehurst helped with a number of inquiries and other administrative work behind the book.

Along the way, my research assistant, Nana von Bernuth, deserves special mention. She has diligently conducted numerous background queries into all kinds of material for this book and analyzed company financials. She has done a wonderful job.

This book would not be close to what it has become without the support of my editors. Melinda Merino at Harvard Business School early on urged me to write this book, and I thank her for her encouragement and guidance. She has been a terrific editor. Connie Hale provided superb guidance on the writing. Alev Croutier offered great help on language and the art of storytelling. I thank Betsy Hardinger for her excellent help with the final copy edit. Stephani Finks did a great job with the jacket design. Paul Hemp did a wonderful job with our original Harvard Business Review article on T-shaped management. Sarah Cliff, Nick Carr, Alden Hayashi, and David Light were excellent editors on prior Harvard Business Review and Sloan Management Review articles on which this book builds. Jennifer Waring at Harvard Publishing did a great job seeing through the manuscript to a finished book. Laurie Anderson helped with the charts, while Hailey Reeser helped with photo editing.

My family has been a great support during the two years of writing this book. My two daughters, Julia and Alexandra, put up with me and also got involved in thinking about titles. My wife, Hélène, not only read more drafts than anyone else and provided insightful comments but also supported me throughout the whole process. I am a lucky person to have such a wonderful family.

I thank everyone for all the help I have been so fortunate to have received.

—Morten T. Hansen
Sausalito, California,
January 2009

INDEX

ABOUT THE AUTHOR

MORTEN T. HANSEN is a management professor at the School of Information, University of California, Berkeley, and at INSEAD. He was previously a professor at Harvard Business School for a number of years. Prior to joining Harvard University, professor Hansen obtained his PhD from the Graduate School of Business at Stanford University.

Hansen's research on collaboration has won several prestigious awards, including the best article award from the *Sloan Management Review* and the award for having made exceptional contributions to the field of organization studies from *Administrative Science Quarterly*, the leading academic journal in the field. Several of his *Harvard Business Review* articles on collaboration have been bestsellers for a number of years.

Having studied collaboration for more than a decade, Hansen combines academic rigor with practical applications. His research is published in leading academic and management journals including *Strategic Management Journal*, *Academy of Management Journal*, *Organization Science*, *Administrative Science Quarterly*, *Harvard Business Review*, and *Sloan Management Review*. He has also written opinion pieces for *Financial Times*.

Professor Hansen's expertise extends beyond collaboration and also includes research on corporate transformation, family business, leadership, profitable growth, and innovation. Together with Jim Collins (author of *Good to Great*), he is conducting new research on how organizations can become great in turbulent worlds.

In addition to his academic career, Morten Hansen has been a senior management consultant in the London, Stockholm, and San Francisco offices of the Boston Consulting Group, where he was a member of the BCG Strategy Institute. He continues his own consulting practice for large companies, facilitates top team seminars, and is regularly a speaker at top leadership gatherings at companies.